Asian Competitors

**Marketing for Competitiveness in the
Age of Digital Consumers**

AMF
Asia Marketing Federation

Asian Competitors

Marketing for Competitiveness in the Age of Digital Consumers

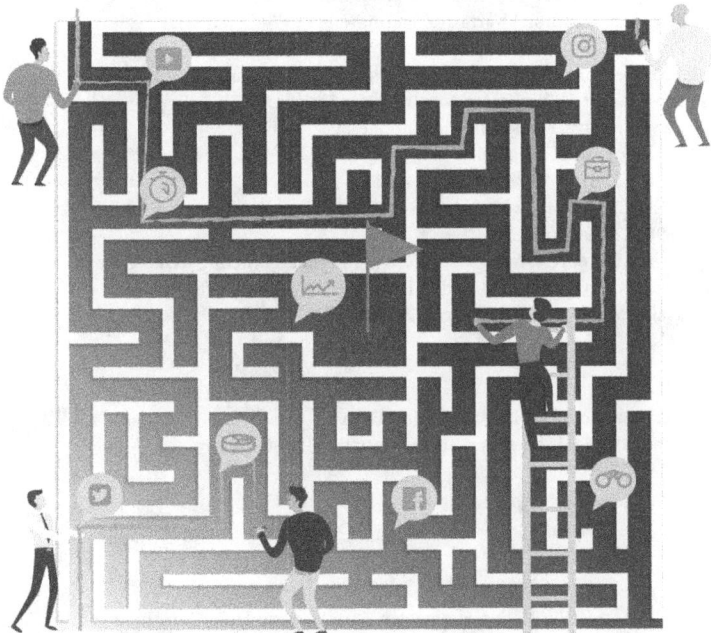

HERMAWAN KARTAJAYA
MarkPlus, Inc.
Indonesia

PHILIP KOTLER
Northwestern University
USA

HOOI DEN HUAN
Associate Professor, Nanyang
Business School, Nanyang
Technological University
Singapore

World Scientific

NEW JERSEY · LONDON · SINGAPORE · BEIJING · SHANGHAI · HONG KONG · TAIPEI · CHENNAI · TOKYO

Published by

World Scientific Publishing Co. Pte. Ltd.

5 Toh Tuck Link, Singapore 596224

USA office: 27 Warren Street, Suite 401-402, Hackensack, NJ 07601

UK office: 57 Shelton Street, Covent Garden, London WC2H 9HE

Library of Congress Cataloging-in-Publication Data
Names: Kotler, Philip, author. | Kartajaya, Hermawan, 1947–   author. |
    Hooi, Den Huan, author.
Title: Asian competitors: marketing for competitiveness in the age of
    digital consumers / Philip Kotler, Northwestern University, USA;
    Hermawan Kartajaya, MarkPlus, Inc., Indonesia;
    Den Huan Hooi, NTU, Singapore.
Description: New Jersey: World Scientific, [2018]
Identifiers: LCCN 2018054782 | ISBN 9789813275461 (hardback) |
    ISBN 9789813275997 (pbk.)
Subjects: LCSH: Marketing–Asia–Case studies. | Internet marketing–Asia–Case studies.
Classification: LCC HF5415.12.A8 K68 2018 | DDC 658.8/72095–dc23
LC record available at https://lccn.loc.gov/2018054782

British Library Cataloguing-in-Publication Data
A catalogue record for this book is available from the British Library.

For any available supplementary material, please visit
https://www.worldscientific.com/worldscibooks/10.1142/11135#t=suppl

Desk Editor: Daniele Lee

ACKNOWLEDGEMENTS

We deeply appreciate the invaluable help given by all staff of MarkPlus including Michael Hermawan, Chief Executive Officer; Dr Jacky Mussry, Deputy Chairman; Iwan Setiawan, Deputy Chief Executive Officer; Hendra Warsita, Chief Corporate Officer; Stephanie Hermawan, Council At-Large; and, in particular, Ardhi Ridwansyah and Priyanka Shekhawat who were deeply involved in this project.

We specially acknowledge Ardhi for his immense efforts for this book.

We are also grateful for the support from Rohan, Goto-san and Gwen, the president and immediate past presidents of the Asia Marketing Federation; Pak Junardy, Chairman of the Asia Marketing Federation Foundation; and our colleagues from all the sixteen national marketing associations who are members of the Asia Marketing Federation. These include the following:

- CCPIT Commercial Sub-Council

- Hong Kong Institute of Marketing

- Indonesia Marketing Association

- Institute of Marketing Malaysia

- Japan Marketing Association

- Marketing Association of Cambodia

- Marketing Association of Thailand

- Marketing Institute of Singapore

- Marketing Society of Bangladesh

- Marketing Society of Korea

- Mongolian Marketing Association

- Myanmar Marketing Society

- Philippine Marketing Association

- Sri Lanka Institute of Marketing

- Taiwan Institute of Marketing Science

- Vietnam Marketing Association

Last but not least, we are ever grateful for the support and encouragement from all our loved ones.

DEDICATION

To my lovely wife, Nancy Kotler
Philip Kotler

To Darren Dominique Hermawan, the next Great Marketeer
Hermawan Kartajaya

To my lovely wife, Wan Fei, and wonderful daughters,
Ren Yi and Ren Syn
Hooi Den Huan

ABOUT THE AUTHORS

Philip Kotler

Dr Philip Kotler is the S.C. Johnson Distinguished Professor of International Marketing at the Kellogg School of Management. He has been honored as one of the world's leading marketing thinkers. He earned his MA degree in economics (1953) from the University of Chicago and his PhD degree in economics (1956) from the Massachusetts Institute of Technology (MIT), and has received honorary degrees from 22 foreign universities. He is the author of over 70 books and over 150 articles. He has been a consultant to IBM, General Electric, Sony, AT&T, Bank of America, Merck, Motorola, Ford, and others. *The Financial Times* included him in its list of the top 10 business thinkers. They cited his *Marketing Management* as one of the 50 best business books of all times.

Hermawan Kartajaya

Hermawan Kartajaya is the founder of the Asia Marketing Federation and the chairman of the Asia Council for Small Business. In 2003, he was named as one of the "50 Gurus Who Have Shaped the Future of Marketing" by CIM UK. In 2009, he received the Distinguished

Global Leadership Award from the Pan-Pacific Business Association. He is both a strategic business thinker and a marketing practitioner. He has written five international books with Philip Kotler — the father of modern marketing. His books, *Marketing 3.0* is widely acknowledged globally and is published in 27 languages, while *Marketing 4.0* is already published in 23 languages. Hermawan is the founder and executive chairman of Mark-Plus Inc., a leading integrated marketing solution provider that provides comprehensive consulting, research, training, and media services with branches in 12 cities in Indonesia. He received an honorary doctorate degree from ITS Surabaya.

Hooi Den Huan
Hooi Den Huan is an associate professor at the Nanyang Business School, Nanyang Technological University. He is a supervisor of the Asia Marketing Federation Foundation, an advisor of the Asian Council for Small Business, an honorary consultant for the CCPIT Commercial Sub-Council, and an advisory board member of the Times Higher Education, *Times of India* and the School of Business Management, ITB. Den schooled at St. Michael's Institution in Ipoh, received his bachelor's degree from the University of Bradford, and his PhD from the University of Manchester, and was a visiting scholar at the Sloan School of Management, MIT. He is a chartered marketer (CIM UK), a chartered accountant (ICAEW), and a Babson TETA Fellow. Den was conferred the Distinguished Global Leadership Award by the Pan-Pacific Business Association in 2011, the ICSB President's Award in 2014, and a fellowship by the Marketing Institute of Malaysia in 2016 and the Marketing Institute of Singapore in 2018.

LIST OF ORGANISATIONS

CONTENTS

PREFACE

Asia is a fast-growing market, both in size and in value. Its overall high population growth, accompanied by strong rising purchasing powers, has made this region a lucrative target market for companies from all over the world. However, the business dynamics in Asia cannot be fully understood without also understanding the struggles and successes of Asian enterprises. Their creativity and effectiveness in utilizing digital technology to gain customers and defeat competitors, offers invaluable lessons for all marketers.

In this book, we have put together success stories from eighteen Asian countries that operate in local, regional, and global markets. Through these stories, one can discern how the various marketing strategies and tactics in the digital era, that are discussed in the sister book, *Marketing for Competitiveness: Asia to the World!* are applied in the real world. We have set out to offer a comprehensive new wave marketing approach in presenting these business stories so that readers have a clear picture of how to win over competition in this digital era.

There are some important points to highlight regarding the selection and placement of the companies in each chapter in this book. There are far too many successful Asian companies to be able to include all of them in one book and for any that is not included, it does not imply at all, that it is not successful.

The placement of companies in particular chapters does not indicate any particular ranking. For example, the order in which companies appear in the book, such as those discussed in the chapters about the product-centric perspective does not represent any hierarchy by itself or vis-à-vis the companies featured in the chapters about the customer-centric perspective.

It does not also mean that companies placed in a particular category, such as being product-centric are not customer nor human-centric. For instance, when we discuss company A in the chapter about product-centric perspectives, it does not mean that the company does not also utilize strategies in the customer-centric and human-centric perspectives. Indeed, many of the companies practice the various perspectives, which enabled them to be strong companies.

We wish to also emphasize that whichever perspective is discussed, is meant to demonstrate how well the company has adapted to technology in this new digital era. The discussions of a successful aspect about a company, does not mean that the company is successful only in that particular aspect.

In addition, when we place a company in a chapter about local champions, it does not mean that the company is not also a champion at other levels — regional and global. Placement of a company in certain chapters is done with the aim to make it easier for readers to understand the particular perspective.

To facilitate relating the core concepts to the real world practices, introductions of the core concepts are provided in this book. Further details of these core concepts can be found in the sister book, *Marketing for Competitiveness: Asia to the World!*.

We hope that through the lessons from these Asian Competitors, any marketer will be better prepared to effectively deal with competition in this increasingly connected era.

Part I

Marketing Is Transforming?

Over the past decades, marketing has transformed through several stages. Long ago, during the industrial age — when industrial machinery was the core technology — marketing was about selling the factory's products to all who would buy them. The products were fairly basic and were designed to serve a mass market. This was Marketing 1.0 or the product-centric era.

Marketing 2.0 evolved as a result of today's information age, with information technology at the core of the digital revolution. Consumers are now well informed and can easily compare several similar product offerings. They can choose from a wide range of functional characteristics and alternatives. Marketers try to win the consumer's mind and heart. This forms the basis of Marketing 2.0 or the customer-centric era. Unfortunately, the consumer-centric approach implicitly assumes that consumers are passive targets of marketing campaigns.

After that, we witnessed the rise of Marketing 3.0 or the human-centric era. Instead of treating people simply as consumers, marketers are beginning to approach them as human beings with minds, hearts, and spirits. Increasingly, consumers are not only more aware of social and environmental concerns but also look for solutions to their anxieties about making the globalized world a better place. They seek not only functional and emotional fulfillment but also human spiritual fulfillment in the products and services they choose.

Today, although technology continues to play an important role, customers are also becoming more human. Machine-to-machine (M2M) marketing tools are becoming more powerful if a company can utilize them to deliver human-to-human (H2H) interactions. In this transition and adaptation period in the digital economy, a new marketing approach is required to guide marketers in anticipating and leveraging on the disruptive technologies while maintaining the human-centric approach of Marketing 3.0. We call this approach Marketing 4.0.

Hence, we can say that some approaches in marketing are product-centric, customer-centric, and human-centric. Despite the trend toward Marketing 3.0, some business players continue to adopt product- and customer-centric perspectives. That is something normal. However, to win the new digital consumers, the old perspective should take into account new technology. Chapters 1–4 show how Asian companies can use different approaches by adopting new technology and the New Wave paradigm to win in the digital era.

CHAPTER 1

PRODUCT-CENTRIC PERSPECTIVE: CONNECTIVITY IN PRODUCT DEVELOPMENT

In today's era of hyperconnectivity, a product-centric company in Asia cannot solely rely on its internal structure and resources to generate new ideas and innovate. In order for the new product development (NPD) process to run with as much accuracy and speed, the involvement of external parties such as customers, suppliers, and regulators is absolutely necessary. The contribution of external parties in each stage and gate of the NPD process becomes increasingly important. For example, in the discovery stage, companies cannot just rely on the marketing research team to look for new ideas out in the market; at this stage, customers should be actively engaged to provide inputs. Technological advancements have greatly improved companies' abilities to establish greater connectivity with customers, thus aiding the process of collaboration on the development of new products.

Open innovation is an expression that was promoted by Chesbrough in 2003. It is defined as the purposive use of knowledge that exists in inputs and outputs of organizations to increase the speed of internal innovations and expansion of markets through the external use of innovations. Thus, open innovation is a paradigm that promotes the use of both external and internal ideas by organizations. In contrast, closed innovation is a traditional paradigm wherein an innovating organization generates its own ideas and then develops them.

The ability to perform open innovation, supported by internal and external connectivity, will make a product-centric organization develop competitive advantages over other industry players. The organization will be better prepared at capturing ideas from outside and swifter at executing them into a product or service, compared with its competitors.

New Wave technology has also enabled organizations not only in getting smarter at developing new products through open innovation but also in creating smarter and connected products. Connectivity in the product itself is becoming important. According to Porter and Heppelmann (2014), smart-connected products have three core elements: physical components, "smart" components, and connectivity components. Smart components amplify the capabilities and value of physical components, whereas connectivity components amplify the capabilities and value of smart components and enable some of them to exist outside the physical product itself.

A physical product is typically made of mechanical and electrical components. These components constitute the tangible part of the product — the part responsible for providing a benefit to the customer. However, if the other two components — smart and connectivity — weren't there, a product consisting of only a physical component will be of limited use. For instance, consider a vehicle consisting of an engine, a powertrain, tires, and batteries. All these physical components form a very basic product primarily functioning as a means of transport, but as we add smart components in the product, such as think sensors, microprocessors, data storage, controls, software, as well as an embedded operating system and enhanced user interface, it serves to improve the functionality and user experience. In a vehicle, this will amount to adding smart components such as engine control unit, antilock braking system, rain-sensing windshields with automated wipers, and touch-screen displays.

In this chapter, we will learn how Hyundai Motor (Korea), Millennium (Bangladesh), FPT Corporation (Vietnam), and KYMCO

(Taiwan) apply product-centric approaches by adopting open innovation and developing smart-connected products.

Hyundai Motor Company

The South Korea-based automotive manufacturer Hyundai Motor Company successfully became a global company, competing with five other biggest global automotive companies, including Toyota Motor Corporation and Mercedes-Benz. By integrating the open innovation center and R&D program and manufacturing innovative products to satisfy customers' needs, Hyundai Motor Company can sustain its existence in the automotive field even though the technology has shifted significantly.

A Brief Company History

Hyundai Motor Company is an automotive manufacturer and a part of the Hyundai Group from Seoul, South Korea. Hyundai was established as a construction company by its founder, Chung Ju-Yung, in 1967 (Hyundai Motor Company, 2018a). It has achieved sustainable growth by taking part in product competitions and delivering an interactive brand experience, which allows direct communication with customers about innovation and future technologies. Hyundai Motor Group has become the world's fifth largest motor group in less than 50 years. Its vision is to be a "lifetime partner in automobiles and beyond" and work "together for a better future".

Hyundai produces many more goods than automobiles, including electronics, ships, steel, and energy products, but its best-known division is automotive. Over the years, Hyundai Motor Group designs, manufactures, and sells cars, commercial vehicles, buses, and many others. Its current product range includes cars, trucks, buses, vans, Special-CVs, and engines (industrial engine and generator engine). It sold 4.86 million vehicles globally in 2015 (Hyundai Motor Company, 2018b).

Today, Hyundai Motor Company has expanded its branches in countries such as United States, China, India, Czech Republic, Turkey, Brazil, and Russia, with more than 110,000 employees around the world. As of 2015, the company continues to improve its products with localized models and strives to strengthen its excellence in clean technology. It pioneered the ix35 Fuel Cell in 2013, the world's first mass-produced hydrogen-powered vehicle, and IONIQ in 2016, the world's first model with three electrified powertrains in a single body type (Hyundai Motor Company, 2018b).

By offering a wide range of vehicles with high quality, unique style, exciting performance, impressive efficiency, smart features, comfortable cabins, and awesome warranties at a competitive price, Hyundai has competed successfully with other companies and become a global brand (Table 1.1). In 2017, Hyundai Motor became the sixth most reputable automotive brand in the world, after Toyota, Mercedes-Benz, BMW, Honda, Ford, and Volkswagen (Interbrand, 2018).

Table 1.1:   Hyundai's milestones.

Year	Events
1967	Hyundai Motor Company was incorporated
1968	Began mass production of Cortina
1976	Launched the first Korean passenger car Hyundai Pony
1983	The Canadian subsidiary HMC was incorporated
1985	• Launched Pony Excel and the first-generation Sonata • The US subsidiary HMA was incorporated
1986	Launched the large-sized luxury car Grandeur (Azera)
1988	Launched the mid-sized luxury sedan Sonata
1990	Launched Elantra and Scoupe
1991	• Developed Alpha engine, the first engine created in Korea and Sonata EV • Launched Galloper
1993	Launched Sonata II
1994	• Launched Accent and Avante (Elantra) • Developed solar-powered and fuel-cell electric vehicles
1995	Established Hyundai Motor Europe Technical Center (HMETC)
1996	• Inaugurated the Namyang Technology Research Center • Launched Dynasty and Tiburon

(*Continued*)

Table 1.1: *(Continued)*

Year	Events
1997	• Independently developed the Epsilon engine • Established the Turkey and the Asan plants
1998	• Independently developed the world-class, high-performance V6 Delta engine • Launched Grandeur (Azera) and Sonata • Acquired Kia Motors
1999	• Launched Equus (Centennial: its ultra large-sized sedan), Verna, and Trajet XG • Developed Korea's first automotive fuel-cell battery
2000	• Developed Korea's first passenger diesel engine and large commercial engine • Developed Korea's first fuel-cell electric vehicle Santa Fe
2001	• Established Hyundai European Design Center • Launched Tuscani (Hyundai's sports coupe), Terracan, and Lavita
2002	• Launched Chinese-made Elantra
2003	Established the California Design and Technical Center, Europe Technical Center, and Namyang Design Center
2004	Launched its first compact SUV Tucson (ix35) Developed Theta engine and Lambda engine
2005	• Established the US proving ground, Alabama plant, Environmental Technology Research Center, Hyundai America Technical Center, and Eco-Friendly Vehicle Recycling Center • Developed clean Mu V6 engine
2006	• Developed Gamma engine and V6 diesel S engine • Launched new Avante (Elantra) • Established new Hyundai Motor Europe building
2007	• Launched a European strategic model i30 and the next-generation compact car i10 by HMI • Developed F, G, and H diesel engines for commercial vehicle
2008	• Launched Genesis, a European strategic model i20 and Blue Drive brand for green models • Developed the next-generation clean diesel R-engine and high-performance Theta GDi

(Continued)

Table 1.1: *(Continued)*

Year	Events
2009	Established the Czech plant, Hyundai Motor India Engineering Pvt. Ltd., the Russia plant, eco-friendly electric car BlueOn, and fifth-generation Grandeur (Azera) and Veloster, Sonata Hybrid, i40 wagon
2010	• Launched the eco-friendly electric car BlueOn and ix20 small minivan at the Paris Motor Show • Developed Tucson fuel-cell electric vehicle
2011	Launched the Veloster and the HCD-12 concept car in North America, fifth-generation Grandeur (Azera) and Veloster and EON (India)
2012	• Launched the New Santa Fe, i40 Saloon, Veloster Turbo and Maxcruz, Hyundai Motorsport, All-new Genesis • Established the Brazil plant
2013	• Launched the Grandeur Hybrid, New i20, at the International Automobile Ausstellung • Supplied ix35 (Tucson) fuel-cell electric vehicles to the City of Copenhagen
2014	• Launched the All-new Sonata, new Sonata Hybrid • Established Hyundai Motorstudio Seoul
2015	• Established Hyundai Motorstudio Moscow • Launched the Sonata Turbo, All-new Tucson, mid-duty truck, All-new Mighty, All-new Elantra, global luxury brand "Genesis" and Genesis G90
2016	• Launched the IONIQ eco-friendly hybrid car model, Genesis EQ900 limousine, Genesis G80 sports car • Introduced the Project IONIQ future mobility innovation program and development strategy for connected cars • Opened Hyundai Motorstudio Hanam
2017	• Established the smart safety technology center for the production of autonomous cars • Launched the IONIQ Plug-in and Sonata face-lift model • Unveiled the fuel-cell electric vehicle concept

As a global brand company, Hyundai strives to gain global competitiveness. Competitive advantage is closely related with innovations. Without innovations, a brand loses its market and lags behind its competitors. Research and development (R&D) plays a critical role in the innovation process. It is essentially an investment in technology and future capabilities, which transforms into new products, processes, and services. R&D is a crucial component of innovation and a key factor in developing new competitive advantages (Heneric *et al.*, 2015).

Hyundai's Open Innovation Centers

Hyundai Motor has been focusing on R&D to create engines that can achieve high efficiency in customer mobility and connectivity today. The R&D centers are located in the United States, Germany, Japan, Korea, China, and India. Hyundai Motor continuously invests in R&D, with its focus on three core future technologies — Clean Mobility, Freedom in Mobility, and Connected Mobility — to ensure future growth.

Besides R&D, open innovation is one of the strategies to better understand the customer's needs. From open innovation, the company can easily get some ideas that can contribute to the development of new products. Hyundai Motor Group has started an open innovation center and planned to set up other open innovation centers in Beijing and Berlin within a year. Along with those in Korea, Silicon Valley in the United States, and Tel Aviv in Israel, a total of five advanced bases will be set up to accommodate excellent ideas from start-ups.

Hyundai Motor Group established the Venture Plaza in Korea in 2000 and Hyundai Ventures in Silicon Valley 12 years later to enable business practitioners, start-ups, entrepreneurs, academicians, and researchers to collaborate in technology development. An example of this is the commercialization of a radio audio notification system, which is applied in a new model of the Veloster. This was developed together with Sound Hound of the United States. The Israel-based Open Innovation Center will work on the development of future mobility, including artificial intelligence and sensing, whereas the Open Innovation Center in China will reinforce its collaboration with the players in the ICT industry. The center in Germany will devise start-ups related to smart cities, and the Korean Innovation Center will be responsible for supervising the strategies of each base and will actively control and manage the merger and acquisition processes (Min-Hee, 2018). From these open innovation centers, Hyundai hopes to create breakthrough products that will satisfy the needs of today's dynamic customers.

Product Innovation in the New Era

Technology has evolved, but the main challenge to compete with others remains the same, which is how to conceive and discover customers' hidden needs and convert them into innovative products. Developing products that meet customers' needs is important, but the most important thing is how to do that one step ahead of competitors so as not to become just a me-too player. The developed product should also adopt new technology as optimum as possible. That's called a "smart-connected product".

In the digital age, smart-connected products will become a source of competitive advantage for product-centric companies (Kotler, Kartajaya and Hooi, 2017). According to Porter and Heppelmann (2014), smart-connected products have three core elements: physical components, "smart" components, and connectivity components. Smart components amplify the capabilities and value of physical components, whereas connectivity components amplify the capabilities and value of smart components and enable some of them to exist outside physical products.

Higher mobility and connectivity in this millennial era lead industries to provide a product that can be connected to other products. This enables customers to interact with other devices or other customers anytime and anywhere. By collaborating with other companies, an interconnected product can be developed to enable communications between the product's system and other related systems to build great connectivity.

Aiming to create hyperconnected intelligent cars that boast the safest and the most advanced self-driving systems in the market, Hyundai Motor is working together with Cisco, a world-renowned IT and security technology company. The collaboration will allow an optimal platform for connected cars. This will help enable two-way communications both internally between the car's system and externally with the road infrastructure, other vehicles, mobile devices, and the cloud (Hyundai Motor Company, 2017).

Smart-connected products evolve continuously. One of the developments is the alteration from a restrictive Controller Area Network system to Ethernet communications within vehicles. Using an Ethernet-based software, integrated data control can be supported. As such, flexible expansion of connections to handle large datasets coming from various components can occur in the vehicles simultaneously. With this product, Hyundai hopes that it can fulfill human connectivity today and be a preferred brand around the world.

References

Min-Hee, J (January 2018). Hyundai Motor builds global new venture capital investment system. *Business Korea*. http://www.businesskorea.co.kr/news/articleView.html?idxno=20237 [1 August 2018].

Heneric, O, G Licht and W Sofka (eds.) (2015). *Europe's Automotive Industry on the Move: Competitiveness in a Changing World*. Heidelberg: Physica-Verlag.

Hyundai Motor Company (2017). *Hyundai Motor Reveals Future Vision for Connected Cars*. https://www.hyundai.com/worldwide/en/about-hyundai/news-room/news/hyundai-motor-reveals-future-vision-for-connected-cars-0000006598 [4 August 2018].

Hyundai Motor Company (2018a). *History*. https://www.hyundai.co.uk/about-us/think-you-know-hyundai/history [1 August 2018].

Hyundai Motor Company (2018b). *Hyundai Motor Enters Partnership with Baidu for Connected Car Leadership in China*. https://www.hyundai.com/worldwide/en/about-hyundai/news-room/news/hyundai-motor-enters-partnership-with-baidu-for-connected-car-leadership-in-china-0000015025 [1 August 2018].

Interbrand (1 August 2018). *Best Global Brand* 2017. Retrieved from Interbrand: https://www.interbrand.com/best-brands/best-global-brands/2017/ranking/#?listFormat=ls

Kotler, P, H Kartajaya and DH Hooi (2017). *Marketing for Competitiveness: Asia to the World*. Singapore: World Scientific.

Porter, ME and JE Heppelmann (November 2014). How smart, connected products are transforming competition. *Harvard Business Review*.

Millennium Information Solution Ltd.

The market potential of software products for global Islamic financial institutions is promising in view of the growing Islamic banking and financial service industry. Millennium Information Solution Ltd. — a Bangladesh-based IT firm that started its business as an outsourcing company — recognizes this and is set to tap on this potential. By establishing a strong network of connectivity with its clients, Millennium has succeeded in developing special products for Islamic financial institutions. The next challenge for the company is to market its products in the global market.

The Company at a Glance

Bangladesh is one of the world's most densely populated countries in the world with a population of 162 million people. With an area of 143,998 sq. km., the average density of population in Bangladesh is 1.125 (*BBC News*, 2018), which has created an opportunity for the country in terms of the supply of labor. According to the Bangladesh Association of Software and Information Services (BASIS), the advantages of Bangladesh in the IT sector include low cost of labor, high programmer productivity, and a wide knowledge of English. This has led to a significant growth of IT firms in Bangladesh over the past decades, and their number stands at more than 770, with Millennium Information Solution Ltd. being one of them (Anwar *et al.*, 2014).

Millennium Information Solution Ltd. (hereafter, Millennium) was established through a merger of two companies: ONUS and Horizon. ONUS was established in 1996, and Horizon was established in 1998. In 2001, ONUS took the initiative to merge with Horizon and create Millennium.

Since its inception, Millennium has been working as a reliable software company with commitment and dedication to satisfy its clients through innovations and the quality of its products and services. The company specializes in developing software solutions for companies and organizations. Its products help improve decision-making processes and enhance the performance of the clients, thereby creating a competitive edge in their performance (Anwar *et al.*, 2014).

Company Objectives

The company's ultimate goal is to position itself globally as a reliable software development company. The company focuses on solutions for Islamic banking and finance, with its flagship product "Ababil", specializing in the area of core Islamic banking and complying with Islamic shariah and global rules or regulations. Along with the core Islamic banking solutions, Millennium has also launched a number of sub-modules, such as Islamic trade finance, internet banking, sukuk (Islamic bonds) management, off-shore banking, Islamic treasury management, finance origination system, and mobile banking. The company also owns a flagship product in the form of a comprehensive Human Resource Management Solution (HRMS) called Sylvia (Millennium Information Solution, Ltd., 2016).

The main objective of the company was to establish itself as a successful global software company, using its unique products and leveraging on a highly talented group of programmers in Bangladesh. The company invested heavily in the training of its employees and coaching and mentoring young talented programmers to make them valuable resources for its outsourcing initiatives.

Initially, Millennium was successful as an outsourcing company; it secured the highest number of outsourcing clients in Bangladesh in its early years of operation (2000–2003). It received appreciations and satisfaction certificates from its major clients. However, it also realized that outsourcing would not take the company to a place where it wanted to go. It wanted to build a line of software solutions that could be replicated for many companies with minimum effort. This was absent in project-based outsourcing activities.

The company further realized that there were certain risks in becoming a project-based solution provider through outsourcing, such as

- Many of its trained people went abroad; so sustaining resources for continuous software development was difficult.

- To keep trained people, the company needed a steady flow of projects in the pipeline or investment in overseas markets.

- In the absence of adequate market protection, competitors often underprice their services ito gain contracts.

From an Outsourcing to a Product-Centric Company

Millennium decided to globally market its product Ababil (developed by ONUS), a software solution developed for the Islamic Bank Bangladesh Limited (IBBL) in 1996. A professor of the Indian Institute of Management (IIM), who evaluated several Indian companies that were not doing well in outsourcing, suggested transforming Millennium from an outsourcing company to a product-centric IT company. It agreed and started this transformation.

Millennium faced a lot of challenges to convert itself from an outsourcing company to a product-centric company. The initiative required substantial investments and efforts to steer the company to its new-found direction. Within a few years, Millennium was able to use its software Ababil to enter into a niche market. At present, a number of financial institutions working on Islamic finance — such as Al Arafah Islamic Bank Ltd., The City Bank Ltd., AB Bank Ltd., Hajj Finance Company Ltd., Social Islami Bank Ltd, Agrani Bank Ltd., and Union Bank — are using this product.

One of the keys to Millennium's success in product development is the connectivity it maintains with its clients in outsourcing projects. Such connectivity is particularly important in order for companies to be able to quickly capture innovative product ideas as it is not sufficient to rely solely on the internal research and development team. In doing so, there needs to be more intensive connectivity with external parties, especially customers (Kotler, Kartajaya and Hooi, 2017). This is an important asset that Millennium has been able to develop to trigger its transformation into a product-centric company.

Ababil is an example of a successful product that is created as a result of Millennium's long interactions with its clients. Ababil is a total end-to-end solution, based on Islamic principles, for all activities of financial institutions. With Ababil, the company has been able to maintain a steady growth in its revenue earnings. Despite the prediction that the Islamic finance industry will continue to expand, although with slower growth in 2018 (S&P Global Ratings, 2017), Millennium was still unable to have a major breakthrough into the global market. The potential for Millennium exists, but making an entry into the global market is still a major challenge.

To enhance its credibility, Millennium went through an evaluation by IBM Bangalore Lab and obtained a certificate showing a decent performance of its product compared with other global banking software solutions. Its product is within the top 10 softwares in terms of functionalities as ranked by Gartner Inc. It has also entered into an agreement with the International Islamic University Malaysia (IIUM) to train people on Islamic Finance Automation.

Next Challenge: Penetrating the Global Market

Despite arranging seminars and symposiums globally and attending a lot of global events for IT products, Millennium is not able to penetrate the global market for software products on Islamic finance. The reasons for this failure could be attributed to the image of Bangladesh as a number of global financial institutions do not have trust in the products that require continuous quality control and monitoring in Bangladesh. Many overseas banks with assets ranging between USD5 billion and USD10 billion find it too risky to buy software from Bangladesh.

To establish a credible image globally, Millennium needs to establish its presence in the global media, an endeavor that requires a large investment. The rule of thumb in global software marketing is that the product developer must invest nearly 70% of its development cost in the marketing of its products. This level of investment is hard for Millennium. Moreover, there is a need for foreign exchange to be present in the global media, and Millennium cannot do this with its local earnings due to foreign exchange regulations in Bangladesh.

Millennium is a 100% equity-funded business firm. Its local revenue is not sufficient to finance its global marketing efforts. As a result, its option is to raise funds globally by selling equity share of the company using its current successes and demonstrating its potential in the global market. This is a relatively new concept for the pioneers of the company. It took 3–4 years for the company to find and convince its original owners to agree on such investments.

In an ideal scenario, a company should be able to raise its required funds by selling shares to a foreign investor. However, as there was no such precedence in Bangladesh, Millennium was only able to find a written consent from one buyer who would pay only a couple of million USD for a substantial portion of its stake. In contrast, the company equity was not big enough to raise funds publicly from the global capital markets.

As a product-centric company, Millennium also faces another challenge in the market entry of its products in foreign markets. This relates to its inability to adapt the product it offers to suit the demands of the local market. Companies achieve "product-market fit" in one country at a time. Yet all too often, companies try to come up with identical products for different markets, overlooking the fact that the type of customers in a certain market may be completely dissimilar from that in another market. A software company won't succeed abroad if it sells the same product that it offers at home and if users in the new market aren't as familiar with certain advanced features. Instead, the company could begin the accustomization effort by offering a more basic version of a product to familiarize the new set of customers. In the same way, in an advanced market, it is ideal for a software company to offer more sophisticated solutions with added features (Kelly, 2015).

Note: This case is contributed by Syed Ferhat Anwar, A. K. Enamul Haque, Mahmud Hossain, and Afrida Alim Nisha from Insight Institute of Learning, Bangladesh. Some updates and additions of information have been made to match the topic of the book.

References

Anwar, SF, AKE Haque, M Hossain and AA Nisha (2014). *Millennium Information Solution Ltd: How to Access the Global Market*. Dhaka: Insight Institute of Learning.

BBC News (August 2018). Bangladesh Country Profile. https://www.bbc.co.uk/news/world-south-asia-12650940 [29 July 2018].

Kelly, N (September 2015). The most common mistakes companies make with global marketing. *Harvard Business Review*. https://hbr.org/2015/09/the-most-common-mistakes-companies-make-with-global-marketing [29 July 2018].

Kotler, P, H Kartajaya and DH Hooi (2017). *Marketing for Competitiveness: Asia to the World*. Singapore: World Scientific.

Millennium Information Solution, Ltd. (2016). *Corporate Profile*. http://www.mislbd.com/page/corporate-profile [29 July 2018].

S&P Global Ratings (2017). *Islamic Finance Outlook: 2018 Edition*. https://www.spratings.com/documents/20184/4521646/Islamic+Finance+2018+Digital-1.pdf/cf025a76-0a23-46d6-9528-cecde80e84c8 [29 July 2018].

FPT Corporation

Product innovation is key to the growth and success of every organization, especially those engaged in the information and communications technology (ICT) business. As a pioneer and market leader in Vietnam, FPT

Corporation has consistently and routinely affirmed that commitment in its organizational vision. Entering the new era of interconnectedness, FPT has embarked upon a more open system of innovation, involving parties outside the organization. That apart, FPT has also spawned a variety of smart-connected products, giving it a novel competitive advantage.

FPT Corporation: Milestone and Business Transformation

FPT, founded on 13 September 1988 by the name The Food Processing Technology Company, began its journey in food technologies. Later, the company pivoted into ICT business as a result of entering into a contract with the Soviet Union Academy of Sciences for supplying computers. This important move led to the establishment of an information technology (IT) department in FPT. FPT signed its first commercial software contract Vietnam Airlines to manage its reservation and booking process, which paved the way for FPT's foray into software development for other sectors such as banking and telecommunications. Eventually, FPT became a technology distribution partner for companies such as Compaq, HP, and IBM. On 27 October 1990, the company was renamed as The Corporation for Financing and Promoting Technology, focusing on the informatics business.

Barely 8 years into operations, FPT established itself as a market leader and became a household name in Vietnam's IT market. In 2008, the corporation was once again renamed as FPT Corporation and its core businesses were reaffirmed, that is, telecommunications, digital content, and information technology services (FPT Corporation, 2012). Table 1.2 provides details on the various milestones achieved by FPT from the time it was founded to its emergence as a leading IT and telecommunications company in Vietnam. FPT currently has operations in 21 countries across the world. This expansive global presence helps the company leverage resources, both from the home country and from abroad, to better serve its clients and customers. FPT counts over 450 biggest technology giants from all over the world as its customers, out of which 50 are Fortune 500 companies. FPT is also an esteemed and reputed partner of technology firms such as GE, Microsoft, Amazon Web Services, IBM, and SAP.

Table 1.2:   FPT's milestones.

Year	Events
1988	The Food Processing Technology Company (original name of FPT) was established in Hanoi, Vietnam, with 13 employees
1990	FPT renamed as The Corporation for Financing and Promoting Technology, establishing its core business in the IT sector
1994	Entered the distribution sector focussing on bringing new technology products to Vietnam
1997	Ventured into the Internet segment and made a breakthrough
1998	Became one of the four leading Internet service providers in Vietnam
1999	Penetrated foreign markets with a strategic direction toward software exports
2001	Launched VnExpress.net, one of the first online newspapers in Vietnam
2002	• Equitized and became a joint stock company • Produced FPT-branded products
2006	• Listed on the local stock market • Established FPT University
2012	• Expanded the technology product retailing chain (FPT Shop) • Invested in e-commerce
2014	• Executed the first cross-border M&A by acquiring a Vietnamese IT firm • Provided Pay TV services • Became the first IT company in Vietnam to acquire a foreign IT company, RWE IT Slovakia (a member of RWE, a leading European energy corporation)
2015	• Became the first foreign enterprise licensed to provide fixed line telecommunications services in Myanmar • Signed a contract in Bangladesh to open a new development direction in the South Asian market
2016	• Partnered with leading global firms in the digital economy such as GE, AWS, and Microsoft • Opened offices in Korea and China

Source: FPT Corporation (2017a) and Wikipedia (2017).

Regarded as Vietnam's leading IT services company, FPT Corporation is engaged in the key fields of IT and telecommunications: from software development, systems integration, IT services, telecommunications, technology product distribution, and retail to high-quality IT human resource training. The company classifies its business under four main sectors: technology, telecommunications, technology product distribution and retail, as well as education. A more detailed explanation of the business sectors that FPT operates in can be found in Table 1.3. FPT's vision is to become a leader in the market by continuous innovation in technological development. This vision is realized by providing great attention to its research and development (R&D), especially in new product development.

Table 1.3: FPT's business sectors.

Sectors	Products and Services	Description
Technology Sector	Software Development	• Customized software solutions for various industry players • Specialized enterprise resource planning (ERP), human capital management (HCM), business intelligence (BI), and data warehousing (DWH) • Consultancy, R&D, provision and deployment of IoT-based technology services • Others
	IT Infrastructure Services	• Database design and construction for enterprises • Network systems and security • Payment, surveillance systems, and specialized equipment for the banking sector; specialized products for telecommunications, transportation, and customs
		• Implementation of banking, securities, and telecommunications solutions • Server hosting and database management
	IT Services	• FPT e-services: certificate of authorization service, customs filing service, and online tax filing service • Authorized warranty and maintenance of IT products for hardware vendors • Provision and repair of IT equipment and components

(Continued)

Table 1.3: *(Continued)*

Sectors	Products and Services	Description
Telecom	Telecom Services	• Broadband internet (xDSL, FTTH) • Television services: FPT Television, FPT Play • Leased lines • Data centers • Landline telephones • Interprovincial and international connection services • Online and OTT services • Video conferencing
	Digital Content	• Online newspapers • Online advertising • Smart advertisement system
Distribution and Retail	Technology Product Distribution	• Distribution of IT products and solutions, mobile devices from Apple, IBM, Lenovo, Microsoft, HP, Nokia, and Toshiba • Production of FPT-branded products, including desktops, smart phones, and tablets
	Technology Product Retail	• Computers, tablets, smartphones, accessories • Apple products sold via a chain of retail stores
Education and Others	Education and Training	• Higher secondary education, vocational education, graduate and postgraduate education • International associated programs, international student development programs • Corporate training programs

Source: FPT Corporation (2017a).

FPT's Product Development: Toward a More Open Innovation

In today's competitive environment, FPT understands that companies which can constantly churn out innovative products can instantly meet the evolving needs of their customers and also beat the rivals. As one of the pioneering technology companies in Vietnam, consistent product innovation is the key to FPT's success. For example, FPT, which started out as a distributor of devices from Apple, IBM, Lenovo, Microsoft, HP,

Nokia, and Toshiba, now has its own brands of desktops, smartphones, and tablets — wholly produced by FPT.

Innovation is also at the heart of FPT's rigorous drive to provide the most relevant solutions to its enterprise clients (business-to-business customers). Aiming to help its clients develop products with greater added value and benefit from improved efficiency in operations, FPT has also come up with newer solutions in the field of e-governance, smart healthcare, intelligent transportation, automotive technologies, and energy. In 2016, FPT deployed some typical technologies to serve its customers (FPT Corporation, 2017a), which are as follows:

- **Comprehensive e-government solutions:**
  FPT provides tools that are totally based on a digital platform with 100% digitalized and reliable data, resulting in improvements made to administrative processes and procedures that are typical for public sector organizations. This in turn offers more convenience to users.

- **Solutions for the healthcare sector:**
  FPT has devised hospital management solutions, which support a fully functional cloud version. Such solutions have been converted into a fully functioning cloud-based version that meets the needs of hospital management in 40 functional areas.

- **Solutions in the transportation sector:**
  Developing and deploying the "Free-flow electronic toll collection and vehicle load controlling systems" solution across the country.

- **Solutions for the energy sector:**
  Researching smart metering solutions for electricity suppliers with added advantages.

- **Solutions for the automotive industry:**
  Researching and developing the driverless auto concept.

In contrast to the pre-connectivity era, innovations for a company today does not necessarily have to revolve around its own resources and capabilities. Technological advancement has dramatically improved a company's ability to establish greater connectivity with external parties, thus aiding in development of new products through collaborative means. This is called "open innovation" (Kotler, Kartajaya and Hooi, 2017). This is defined as the purposive use of knowledge that exists in inputs and outputs of organizations for improving innovation. Thus, open innovation is a paradigm that promotes using both external and internal concepts (Chesbrough, 2003).

FPT has also adopted the principles of open innovation in the development of new products. One example is the collaboration between FPT Corporation and Siemens AG in utilizing and implementing MindSphere, the cloud-based open IoT operating system from Siemens, for global customers . FPT's deep knowledge in analytics, Internet of Things (IoT), cloud technologies, engineering services, and application development makes it a valuable partner for Siemens and its customers. As for FPT, the company benefits from collaborating with Siemens, which has vast experience in designing open operating systems for industrial companies.

Commenting on the collaboration, Mr. Hoang Viet Anh, CEO of FPT Software said, "*As we are in the era of the 4th Industrial Revolution, companies must transform themselves into more digital-centric entities. Our partnership with Siemens, a global market leader in Industrial and Manufacturing, in MindSphere is a testament to FPT's commitment to help businesses drive digital transformation. By combining FPT's expertise in IoT enablement for various industries, with MindSphere's vision to simplify IoT interaction and experience, we can open doors to limitless inspiring digital innovations.*" (FPT Software, 2017).

A similar collaboration has been conceived between FPT and Airbus in developing solutions to improve business efficiency in the aviation industry (FPT Corporation, December 2017b).

In the implementation of open innovation, customers can also be involved as potential partners in the development of new products. FPT has explored such potential collaborations earlier with customers through various initiatives. One such initiative is through the "Customer Voice" program. The program, a part of FPT's Telecom Services segment, is conceptualized with the objective to improvise products and services by listening to customers' views and their feedback. To evaluate customer satisfaction, their feedback is recorded at various critical touch points, including call centers, Live Chat, Facebook, and mobile apps such as

Hi FPT (FPT Corporations, 2017a). With flourishing interactive digital technology, FPT is confident to expand further through the periodical feedback of customers.

FPT's Smart-Connected Products

New Wave technologies have enabled companies not only to get smarter in developing new products through open innovation but also in creating smarter and connected products. Connectivity within the product itself is becoming key. Such connected products will lend a stronger competitive advantage to companies in the digital age, especially for product-centric companies. Dealing with connected products opens up a door of opportunities for companies who collaborate with external parties — this could be conducive to players in today's time and age by bringing in more diverse inputs, enabling better cost control, and improving efficiency. The greater the number of users, the higher the ways in which connectivity can be harnessed in product development. This results in a continuous cycle of value improvement. (Kotler, Kartajaya and Hooi, 2017).

According to Porter and Heppelmann (2014), smart-connected products have three core elements: physical components, smart components, and connectivity components. Smart components help improve the capabilities and values of the physical components, whereas connectivity components help augment the capabilities of the smart components, thus allowing the product to exist outside its physical form as well. The connectivity offered by a smart-connected product can be of three types: one to one, one to many, and many to many. Following are a few examples of smart-connected solutions developed by FPT.

One-to-One Connectivity: Mobile Devices

This is the simplest form of connectivity; two devices can connect with each other to share data. The mobile devices developed by FPT generally possess this function. A smartphone can connect with other mobile devices through various features and applications. In fact, it is common these days to find mobile devices that can be connected to other smart electronic devices at home.

One such solution is in the form of FPT TV remote: an entertainment app that can help users control the FPT Television through their smartphones, while also enabling users to watch the television on their mobile devices, thus avoiding the need of a traditional hand-held remote.

One-to-Many Connectivity: Toll and Traffic Monitoring System.

FPT has deployed intelligent transportation systems, including an application system at toll booths and a Traffic Violations, Monitoring, and Management system to improve traffic flow on the highways. The solutions make use of video image processing through traffic cameras and GPS systems to provide on-the-spot as well as offline ticketing. The applications are also used in the monitoring of traffic flows, measuring, and counting of vehicles as well as in better traffic administration (FPT Corporation, 2017a).

In this one-to-many connectivity solution, data from various products or devices are processed through a central system. The resulting system will help improve flow of traffic, making it convenient for the users, in this case, highway commuters.

Many-to-Many Connectivity: FPT eGOV

An example of this type of connectivity is the eGOV project initiated by FPT in Quang Ninh province. The project was commissioned in late 2013 — the largest e-governance project bagged by FPT to date. This marked a holistic e-government solution being deployed for the first time at a provincial administration unit in Vietnam, opening up opportunities in other provinces nationwide.

The e-governance system allowed government agencies to provide easier, faster, transparent, and user-friendly services to the public with the help of IT solutions and more efficient leadership tools at all levels, thus improving the general functioning of the administration (FPT Information System, 2014). The scheme also includes developing an integrated data center, building a database, and upgrading LAN and WAN infrastructure as well as data lines. Moreover, it was reported that Quang Ninh province had planned to develop public service centers in 14 of its districts and a province-level center (Oanh, 2013).

With the help of such an eGOV initiative, people can connect online and access the various services offered by the provincial government, thus saving their time and energy. In contrast, fellow government employees can also connect with each other easily and reduce the chances of miscommunication. This is a type of many-to-many connectivity solution that FPT aims to deploy across provinces and regions in Vietnam.

References

Chesbrough, H (2003). The logic of open innovation: Managing intellectual property. *California Management Review*, 45(3), 33–58.

FPT Corporation (2012). *2011 Annual Report*. https://fpt.com.vn//Images/files/bao-cao-thuong-nien/2011_annual.pdf [17 January 2018].

FPT Corporation (2017a). *2016 Annual Report*. https://fpt.com.vn//Images/files/bao-cao-thuong-nien/2016-Annual-report_EN_web.pdf [15 January 2018].

FPT Corporation (December 2017b). *FPT Software and Airbus to Cooperate in Aviation Technology*. https://fpt.com.vn/en/newsroom/detail/fpt-software-and-airbus-to-cooperate-in-aviation-technology [16 January 2018].

FPT Information System (2014). *Launch of Largest FPT.eGOV Project in Quang Ninh*. http://fptis.vn/en/news/launch-largest-fptegov-project-quang-ninh [16 January 2018].

FPT Software (2017). *FPT and Siemens Partners in MindSphere IoT Operating System*. https://www.fpt-software.com/fpt-siemens-partners-in-mindsphere-iot-operating-system [16 January 2018].

Kotler, P, H Kartajaya and DH Hooi (2017). *Marketing for Competitiveness: Asia to the World*. Singapore: World Scientific.

Oanh, V (January 2013). Quang Ninh to spend VND600 billion on e-government. *The Saigon Times*. http://english.thesaigontimes.vn/27371/Quang-Ninh-to-spend-VND600-billion-on-e-government.html [16 January 2018].

Porter, ME and JE Heppelmann (November 2014). How smart, connected products are transforming competition. *Harvard Business Review*.

Wikipedia (2017). *FPT Group*. https://en.wikipedia.org/wiki/FPT_Group [15 January 2018].

KYMCO

With technology from Japan, Kwang Yang Motor Company (KYMCO) is slowly transforming itself from a component manufacturer into a global brand owner. Through product innovation, KYMCO has not only strengthened its position in the domestic market but also became a preferred brand in the global market, especially in Europe.

KYMCO: Corporate Transformation and Market Expansion

Kwang Yang Motor Company (KYMCO), a leading global power sports brand, is headquartered in Taiwan's second largest city Kaohsiung. Its office buildings, manufacturing plants, and testing and research and development (R&D) facilities are located in the over five-decade-old KYMCO corporate campus, which is spread across 188,300 sq. m. The mission of KYMCO is to be recognized as a manufacturer whose personal vehicles win the hearts of consumers all over the world. Its current product range includes scooters, motorcycles, mobility scooters, all-terrain vehicles (ATVs), and utility vehicles (KYMCO, 2018).

Established in 1964, KYMCO started its journey with the help of technology obtained from a Japan-based automotive company, Honda. Between the 1960s and the 1980s, foreign technology, especially from Japan, made further inroads in the Taiwanese local market (*Taiwan Today*, 2006). The technical expertise built as a result eventually led domestic companies to start manufacturing components. This made KYMCO one of Honda's first high-quality overseas manufacturing facility. KYMCO built its first model, the C200, in 1964 (KYMCO, 2018).

As the relationship developed over the next two decades, Honda increased its business interest in KYMCO and became a significant shareholder of the company. Eventually, in 1992, KYMCO began marketing products that it developed independently from Honda and sold them under its own brand. Starting 2003, following a successful 28-year collaboration with Honda, KYMCO went on to reacquire the business interest in the company from Honda and began building the KYMCO brand globally. Today, KYMCO is Taiwan's largest scooter manufacturer (*Taiwan Today*, 2006; see Table 1.4 for KYMCO's detailed milestones).

Besides strengthening its dominant position in the local market, KYMCO is also aggressively expanding globally. The KYMCO Group now comprises manufacturing facilities and marketing or sales companies in 102 countries worldwide. Through such expansive marketing efforts, KYMCO has earned a strong position in the European market. Revenues generated in Europe contribute more than 50% to the entire overseas

Table 1.4: KYMCO's milestones.

Year	Events
1963	Was founded, with NT10,000,000 in capital
1964	Was officially inaugurated
1970	Opened its first factory
1977	Opened its second factory
1983	Rolled off the 1,000,000th unit from the production line
1992	Began selling products developed independently from Honda and marketed them under its own brand
1995	Established a joint venture with Kwang Yang Li-Bo Motor (Indonesia)
1999	Opened its R&D building
2003	• Acquired back Honda's business interest in the company and started focusing on developing and marketing its own brand globally • Launched its first heavy motorcycle, the XCITING 500 • Became the exclusive agent of Kawasaki in Taiwan • Entered into a joint venture with SPMC, Iran, for the manufacture and sale of KYMCO products
2004	Received the "Industrial Technology Advancement Award"
2006	Was awarded "TPM Award-Special Honor" by the Japan JIPM association
2007	Received the "eAsia Award" from the Ministry of Economic Affairs in Taiwan
2011	Founded Klever Mobility Europe in Germany to offer the best e-bike rear motor
2016	• Became the market leader in Taiwan for 17 consecutive years, with a 36.9% market share • Led the scooter market in Spain • Earned the top spot as a brand in Germany's and France's ATV markets • Its mobility scooters were Motability's most prescribed scooters for four consecutive years
2017	Was ranked third for the "Best Brands" in the scooter category in a nationwide survey conducted in Germany
2018	Launched "Ionex" in Tokyo, Japan, as its flagship product in the electric vehicle industry

Source: KYMCO (2018), KYMCO Healthcare (2017), and Smart Motor Indonesia (2018).

sales of the KYMCO Group. In the scooter market, the company is the market leader in Spain. In the ATV market, it is the number one brand in Germany and France (KYMCO, 2018).

Product Innovation at KYMCO

To achieve success as a technology firm, the company has leveraged its ability to develop products that satisfy customers' needs better than the products of its competitors. As such, it is necessary that product-centric companies like KYMCO conduct thorough research on such needs and generate ideas and solutions that can best satisfy them. KYMCO, therefore, puts great attention on its R&D efforts. The company is committed to creating technologically advanced products, which are developed especially to meet the specific demands of its customers. KYMCO established its R&D center in 1978 and employs over 500 engineers dedicated to R&D, as of 2017. The total R&D investment has accounted for an average of 7% of the total sales revenue (KYMCO, 2018).

KYMCO's research capabilities especially lie in the design and development of automotive components, including advanced chassis structure, efficient gasoline engines, electric motor controls, and power transmission systems. These products act as the company's core competencies, laying the foundation of R&D work of its entire product range, including street and sports bikes, scooters, electric scooters, ATVs, utility vehicles, generators, and mobility scooters. The company has also ventured into the medical device industry to diversify its product portfolio. It now offers electric vehicles such as mobility scooters and power wheelchairs under a different brand name called KYMCO Healthcare. Its KforU brand is leading the mobility scooter market in the United Kingdom and is even becoming popular in other European markets outside the United Kingdom. The company has also established KYMCO HealthCare USA in Beverly Hills, California, to repeat the success in the US market. It sells its freshly designed products under the brand "Stars N Stripes".

KYMCO has also forayed into e-mobility to promote its efforts towards a greener environment. The electric bikes manufactured by Klever Mobility, KYMCO's subsidiary in Europe, have earned great popularity and are considered big winners among European industry observers in terms of design and usability.

However, KYMCO has not stopped at all these achievements. Product innovation undertaken by KYMCO has entered the next stage with the development of products that offer more connectivity to customers. One such product is a new e-bike developed by Klever Mobility.

KYMCO's Smart-Connected Products

Since its establishment in 2011, Klever Mobility has targeted the European urban customers looking at cooler and more ecofriendly ways for the daily commute. The e-bike market in Europe is quite promising, and people are widely embracing these alternative means of transportation. For example, e-bike sales in Germany, Europe's biggest e-bike market, were expected to grow around 12% in 2017 (*Bike Europe*, August 2017).

Belgium is another European market with a huge potential for e-bikes. Belgians have developed a great fascination for e-bikes like no other Europeans. According to a recent market study conducted by Belgium's biggest bicycle show Velofollies, in 2017, e-bikes represent the largest bicycle category in Belgium, with a market share of over 45% (based on units). They are followed by city bikes, with a market share of up to 23%, and road race bikes at 10.7% (*Bike Europe*, January 2018).

This huge potential has certainly attracted the attention of other industry players, especially those from China. According to the European Bicycle Manufacturers Association, imports of Chinese e-bikes to Europe have increased from almost zero in 2010 to an estimated 800,000 in 2017. E-bikes equipped with batteries are not that abundantly available in Europe although they are extremely popular in China where sales have exploded from around 1 million annually back in the 2000s to about 30 million in 2016. In recent times, however, bike-sharing schemes have also taken off in some cities, which has made some dent to the sales. The imported e-bikes from China might pose a threat due to their low price.

Despite the increasingly fierce competition, product innovation has become one of the keys to building a strong competitive advantage. Without it, the company will only be stuck in a price war, which may hurt it in the end, both financially and in terms of brand image. The resulting product must also be able to adopt new technologies as optimally as possible. That is what is called a "smart-connected product".

In the digital age, smart-connected products will become a source of competitive advantage for product-centric companies (Kotler, Kartajaya and Hooi, 2017). According to Porter and Heppelmann (2014), smart-connected products have three core elements: physical components, "smart" components, and connectivity components. Smart components help elevate the capabilities and the value of physical components and allow some of the functions to exist regardless of the limitations of the physical products. How is KYMCO shaping its innovation efforts on smart connectivity to create new products?

In 2017, Klever Mobility came out with a new product series at its headquarters in Cologne, Germany. The newly launched product would target the high-end segment. The company is optimistic that there is a huge market potential in this category, especially in Central Europe. However, there is a special feature in the new product. As of 2018, Klever Mobility will offer a new Connect + module as an upgrade for the X-series — an e-bike product that has won various designs and technical awards. This feature allows the bike to be controlled via a smartphone and also has the option of GSM tracking and an electronic antitheft ability (*Bike Europe*, July 2017).

The physical components of Klever's e-bike, including bicycle frames, engines, and batteries, tend to perform better with in-house software "smart" component produced by KYMCO.

KYMCO also adds another "smart" component in the form of Connect + module, which enables wireless connection with other products — at this early stage, a smartphone.

This new module is the "connectivity component" of Klever's X-series e-bike. In subsequent developments, this kind of connectivity would allow users to record their activities related to cycling on a smartphone. This data recording can certainly be used by various parties, including companies, to create customized offerings and experiences. With this kind of product innovation, KYMCO's e-bike is expected to remain a preferred brand in Europe.

References

Bike Europe (July 2017). Klever adds power, range & connectivity to 2018 e-bikes. http://www.bike-eu.com/sales-trends/nieuws/2017/7/klever-adds-power-range-connectivity-to-2018-e-bikes-10130588 [10 March 2018].

Bike Europe (August 2017). Once again e-bikes prove to be industry's trump card. http://www.bike-eu.com/sales-trends/nieuws/2017/8/once-again-e-bikes-prove-to-be-industrys-trump-card-10131142 [10 March 2018].

Bike Europe (January 2018). E-bikes take lead in Belgian market. http://www.bike-eu.com/sales-trends/nieuws/2018/1/e-bikes-take-lead-in-belgian-market-10132617 [10 March 2018].

Kotler, P, H Kartajaya and DH Hooi (2017). *Marketing for Competitiveness: Asia to the World.* Singapore: World Scientific.

KYMCO (2018). *About Us.* http://www.kymco.com/about-us/ [10 March 2018].

KYMCO Healthcare (2017). *KYMCO Healthcare UK Are Motability's No1 Scooter Supplier again for 2016,* http://www.kymcohealthcare.com/?q=news/show/25[10 March 2018].

Porter, ME, and JE Heppelmann (2014). How smart, connected products are transforming competition. *Harvard Business Review.*

Smart Motor Indonesia (2018). *KYMCO Will Unveil Ionex.* https://www.kymco.co.id/kymco-will-unveil-ionex/ [10 March 2018].

Taiwan Today (November 2006). Taipei World Trade Center hosts first international scooter show. *Taiwan Today.* https://taiwantoday.tw/print.php?unit=6&post=8125 [10 March 2018].

CHAPTER 2

CUSTOMER-CENTRIC PERSPECTIVE: CONNECTING WITH DIGITAL CONSUMERS

Companies need not always be competing for product leadership. They may choose a different marketing strategy by putting customers at the center of gravity. This is the main idea of the customer-centric perspective. Firms must create value for customers and see the business from the customers' point of view. The strategic question that drives the customer-centric perspective is not "what else can we make?" but "what else can we do for our customers?" Customers and the market — not the factory or the product — stand at the core of the business.

As a practical framework for customer management, we have categorized the following four core activities:

- Get: Gain prospects and acquire new customers.

- Keep: Focus on loyalty building to keep valuable customers.

- Grow: Add values for both customers and the company.

- Win Back: Seek opportunities to get back lost customers.

These core activities in the customer-centric perspective cover the full spectrum of interactions with current and future customers. Some variations may exist across different firms.

The business landscape is moving at a fast rate due to growing technological connectivity in Asia. It has created a whole new set of opportunities and threats. Today, consumers are becoming increasingly connected. Digitalization is transforming them from mere consumers into smarter value demanders. Now that company-to-consumer dynamic digital interaction is given, companies without an engaging online presence or an effective mobile strategy or app will suffer in comparison with those who do have them. Therefore, customer management should apply the same logic. The following cases discuss how the Asian competitors can get, keep, grow, and win back their digital consumers.

AirAsia

The AirAsia Group is the second largest airline in Asia in terms of passenger numbers, after Air China. Today, the low-cost, no-frills airline serves 222 routes and flies to 110 destinations from 20 hubs. AirAsia has also been named the World's Best Low-Cost Airline in the annual World Airline Survey by Skytrax for eight consecutive years from 2009 to 2016. However, in a service industry like aviation, customer loyalty is highly coveted. AirAsia cannot rely on the low-cost strategy to build a long-term relationship with its customers. This case discusses AirAsia's other initiatives in customer management, especially how the airline utilizes digital technology to keep flyers loyal.

Country and Industry Profile

Malaysia is one of the most competitive economies in Asia, supported by massive industrialization in the last decade with an open investment climate. Malaysia — the third-largest economy in Southeast Asia, after Indonesia and Thailand — is an upper middle-income economy, with the third highest GDP per capita in the region, after the city states of Singapore and Brunei. The World Economic Forum's (WEF) Global Competitiveness Index 2016–2017 ranks Malaysia 25th out of 138 countries and one among the five Asian countries in the top 25, with others being Singapore, Japan, Hong Kong, and Taiwan in that order. Malaysia is also ranked 23rd in the World Bank Doing Business Survey 2017 — and second in ASEAN.

Efforts to successfully diversify into a multisector economy have borne fruit as the country has been able to reduce its dependence on oil and gas revenues to 14% in 2017 from 41% in 2009. The administration has been making a great concerted effort to advance value-added production in the country, especially by expanding investments in high-technology and knowledge-based services. Accordingly, domestic and foreign investments in ICT are on the rise. Chinese telecom giant Huawei has announced its plans to make Malaysia its global operation headquarters, as well as data hosting center and global training center, with a total project cost of USD510 million (RM2.2 billion).

Internet use in the country is also growing. According to Malaysia's Department of Statistics' "ICT Use and Access by Individuals and Households Survey Report", the percentage of individuals aged 15 years and above accessing the Internet was 71.1% in 2015, up 14.1 percentage points in 2013. Furthermore, up to 97.5% individuals used mobile phones in 2015 compared to 94.2% in 2013 (Figure 2.1).

The report further states that over 70% of individuals use the Internet the most at their homes and while commuting. Social networking is the primary Internet activity, followed by searching for information on goods and services (e-commerce) and downloading contents such as images, videos, and music.

Impact on Politics

Digitalization has a strong influence on political processes across the world and Malaysia is no exception. It is being embraced in various political spheres of governance for purposes such as bridging the digital divide and developing the communications infrastructure. In the field of e-governance, ICT development has also cast a significant impact on the field of e-governance. One of the foremost initiatives taken by the government has been the MSC, formerly called the Multimedia Super Corridor. The national ICT development initiative, which was launched

ICT Services and Equipment	2013 (Per cent)	2015 (Per cent)	Percentage Points Change
Internet	57.0%	71.1%	+14.1
Computer	56.0%	68.7%	+12.7
Mobile phone	94.2%	97.5%	+3.3

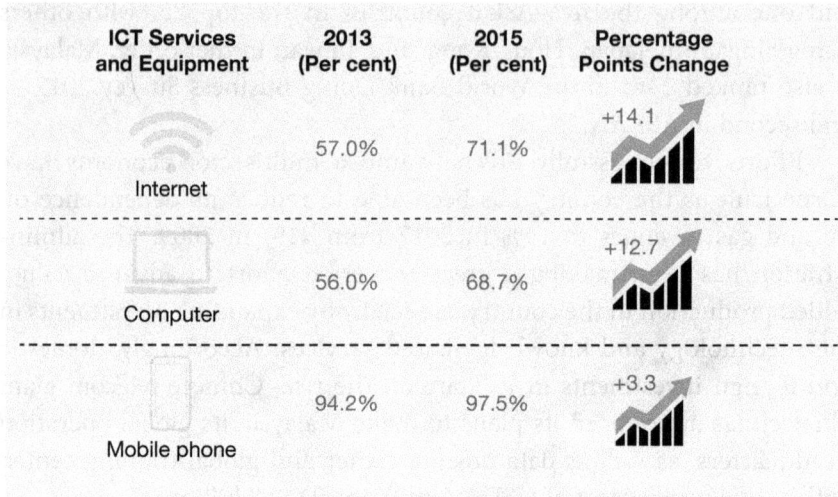

Figure 2.1: ICT services and equipment use by individuals in Malaysia, 2013 and 2015.
Source: Department of Statistics, Malaysia.

in 1996, is managed by Malaysia Digital Economy Corporation (MDEC). In 2005, MDEC launched Malaysia Government Portals and Websites Assessment (MGPWA) to maintain and evaluate around 1,000 government websites. In their journal, *E-government Success in Malaysia Through Government Portal and Website Assessment* (2012), authors Haidar and Bakar described Malaysia's stellar performance in international rankings. In global E-Government ranking conducted by Brown University (BU) and Brookings Institution (BI), Malaysia managed to reach 11th position in 2008, from 153rd among 198 countries in 2005. MSC has also been successful to some extent in advancing smart schooling.

The government has aimed to integrate digitalization as a key component for the development of the Malaysian economy. For instance, the Development Bank of Sarawak, a proposed new state bank, has been established to finance four strategic projects: ICT infrastructure (digital economy), energy, public transport, and healthcare.

Malaysia introduced the Goods and Services Tax in 2016. One of the more recent initiatives undertaken by the Malaysian government is the introduction of an online system for filing and paying GST. This is also supported by another system to provide consumer credit scores, thus strengthening the credit reporting process.

Digitalization—Impact on the Economy

Malaysia harbors a strong ambition of becoming a high-income, developed country by 2020, which requires its Gross National Income per capita to rise to USD15,000, up from USD9,096 in 2016. In recognition of the changing and advancing technologies, especially in the digital space, the Digital Malaysia initiative was announced in 2012 to transform the country into a fully developed digital economy.

The program acted upon three thrusts: to move Malaysia from being a *supply- to a demand-focused economy*, to shift behavior from being *consumption to production centric,* and to evolve from *low knowledge add to high knowledge add.*

In global ICT evaluation reports, having capitalized on its early-mover advantage, Malaysia has earned considerable praise for its proactive approach in spearheading digitalization and ICT development. The WEF's Global Economic Competitiveness Report 2017 argues that becoming "more innovative is a pressing imperative", especially if countries such as Malaysia, China, and Thailand are to avoid the middle-income trap.

Malaysian Prime Minister Najib Razak, in office since 2009, is reckoned to have taken a personal interest in pushing the digital economy forward. In 2016, Jack Ma, the cofounder of Alibaba Group and Asia's richest man, was appointed the digital economy advisor of the Malaysian government. The move was followed by the launch of supposedly the world's first Digital Free Trade Zone (DFTZ) to provide a conducive environment to digital entrepreneurs. The initiative is a part of the National E-Commerce Strategic Roadmap launched in 2016, which aims to double the e-commerce growth in Malaysia from a CAGR of 10.8% in 2015 to 20.8% in 2020. Clearly, special emphasis is laid on e-commerce, which contributed about USD15 billion (RM68 billion), 5.9% of the GDP, in 2015.

The country is also marching ahead with designated efforts in preparing for the next industrial age, termed as the Industrial Revolution 4.0, spearheaded by Malaysia's Human Resources Development Fund (HRDF). It envisions the creation of "smart factories", which include digitalisation of the production process. This initiative – while some may argue could remove some manual labor jobs — ultimately aims to "upskill and reskill" the Malaysian workforce and improve productivity, ultimately benefitting sluggish economies. The Centres of Excellence in Technology (CoETs) will form an integral component of this master plan to facilitate training programs in ICT adoption and Big Data.

AirAsia: Company History

The AirAsia Group is the second largest airline in Asia in terms of passenger traffic, after Air China. The low-cost, no-frills airline, which was originally established by a government-owned Malaysian conglomerate in 1993 started its operations in 1996. The original airline entity soon ran into trouble and became heavily indebted. In December 2001, Tony Fernandes, a Malaysian entrepreneur and the founder of Tune Air Sdn. Bhd., purchased this airline at a price of USD0.23 (RM1) and also inherited its USD9.3 million (RM40 million) debt.

Tony Fernandes harbored a childhood dream of running an airline, and acquiring an airline business helped him envision another dream of making air travel more affordable. The rationale for launching a budget airline offering discounted fares was questioned at the time when peers focused on right sizing and cost reduction. Tony's bids to arrange funds were unheeded by most international banks until he received USD30 million from Credit Suisse. Within a year of purchase, AirAsia recorded a profit in 2002. This was made possible by making flying affordable to the emerging middle-class consumer and, thus, tapping a large unmet demand. The airline operated from its hub in Kuala Lumpur and offered domestic fares for as low as RM1, ultimately breaking into Malaysia Airline's monopoly.

A Robust Plan of Rapid Expansion

AirAsia aimed to be a truly ASEAN airline by introducing international flights in the region. The effort began with the launch of the second hub in Johor Baru in Malaysia, situated near Singapore, and its first international flight to Bangkok (Thailand) in 2003. It was followed by the establishment of regional affiliates in 2004, starting with Thai AirAsia and Indonesia AirAsia.

In 2006, AirAsia announced intentions to further its expansion in Asia by introducing additional routes to Vietnam, Indonesia, Southern China, and India. By 2007, AirAsia was flying almost 14 million passengers annually. The following several years witnessed consistent expansion and the establishment of new hubs in Jakarta and Bangkok (CAPA Centre for Aviation, 2018).

It was also in 2007 that AirAsia launched its long-haul budget airline called AirAsia X. The sister company experienced early turbulence, which was partly attributed to high oil prices and the choice of aircrafts, Airbus A330-200 and A340-300, which were not considered particularly thrifty to operate for long-haul journeys. Eventually, AirAsia X not only switched to the more economical A330-300, but also downsized operations by cutting long-range loss-making routes including London, Paris, and Abu Dhabi. The focus was shifted to routes witnessing higher demand, especially in Southeast Asia. The sister company finally managed to report a profit in 2016. Despite talks of plans being underway to reintroduce flights to some of the cutback destinations, including London, AirAsia Founder Tony Fernandes, an active social media user, tweeted in 2017 about AirAsia X not resuming ultra long-haul flights.

In 2013, AirAsia sought permission to begin operations in India by making a foreign direct investment through its investment arm. With the launch of AirAsia India in 2014, the company became the first foreign airline to set up a subsidiary in India.

Today, AirAsia serves 222 routes and flies to 110 destinations from 20 hubs in Malaysia, Thailand, Indonesia, Philippines, and India. It operates four affiliates: Thai AirAsia, Indonesia AirAsia, Philippines AirAsia, and AirAsia India. The "Now Everyone Can Fly" philosophy of the company, due to low fares, has been aptly complemented with service quality. The airline has been named the World's Best Low-Cost Airline in the annual World Airline Survey by Skytrax for 8 consecutive years from 2009 to 2016. It has won similar accolades at the annual World Travel Awards by emerging as the World's Leading Low-Cost Airline for 4 consecutive years from 2013 to 2016.

In line with its route expansion, the company has been strategically extending its fleet. The AirAsia Group expanded its fleet by 28 aircrafts in 2017, increasing its fleet size to over 400 (Sidhu, BK, 9 January 2017). The company is also eyeing the consolidation of all its Southeast Asian units into a single holding company, which would be publically listed if things go as per the plan.

Customers and Marketing Strategy

In a service sector like aviation, customer loyalty is highly coveted. The lowest price may be an attractive factor for first-time flyers; but if the service quality is not up to the mark, loyalty would be hard to come by. A loyal customer will not only fly frequently but also act as a brand advocate and build a long-term relationship with the airline.

In the case of AirAsia, the five factors instrumental in determining customer satisfaction include purchasing flight ticket, check-in counter service, flight attendant, aircraft condition and food service.

Even though the online air-ticket purchase is a standard industry service today, not all airline websites have the same standards. The speed, simplicity, and security of a transaction are highly important. The self-service facilities available to AirAsia customers not only improve efficiency but are also economical for the airline. From March 2012, AirAsia has begun to use full automation and self-service procedures, starting from Malaysia and Singapore. Along with the provision of online portals for tickets purchasing and other flight-related activities, AirAsia also provides automated check-in machines at airports that enable customers to skip the queue and check-in directly by themselves. Moreover, to adapt to the current trend of using smartphones, AirAsia has developed mobile apps for iPhone devices and Android-based smartphones. Providing some similar features as in the portal online version, the mobile apps enable the users to check out flight schedules, purchase tickets, and check-in, using their smartphones.

In terms of flight attendants, AirAsia has maintained a simple approach of keeping employees happy. In the words of CEO Tony Fernandes, employees come before customers, as a happy workforce will take care of its customers.

Customer loyalty programs are offered by many airlines, and AirAsia has launched a loyalty program fairly recently. In keeping up with its digitalization endeavor, the AirAsia BIG is a joint venture between the airline and Tune Money, a "no-frills" financial services company from

Malaysia. The loyalty program, which is enabled through a prepaid Visa card system, is meant for AirAsia customers who can earn and spend points with their BIG card or use the BIG ID linked to that card.

A Fully Digital Airline

AirAsia's digitalization endeavor is in line with its ambition to boost ancillary revenues, as well as in cognizance with customers' emerging preferences for personalized and seamless flying and travel experiences. Cofounder and CEO Tony Fernandes announced plans for 2017, with it being the landmark year for AirAsia to begin its journey to become a fully digital airline. Digitalization, according to the CEO, is projected to boost per-passenger-ancillary-revenue income from USD10.75 (RM48) to USD13.50 (RM60). The digitalization dream also envisions the company going cashless, making 100% of its transactions electronic. In-flight transactions, the majority of which are by cash as of now, would also be digitalized. The personalization of AirAsia's website is also meant to provide a more customized experience for its passengers.

The company provides a host of digital services, including BIG Duty Free, AirAsia's online travel retail portal where passengers can buy duty-free and duty-paid products online; BIG Pay, a quick one-click payment facility using BIG Member account; roKKi on-board Wi-Fi service; and Xcite in-flight entertainment. The idea is to provide mechanisms for customers, so that they can use their mobile phones to pay for flights, food, Wi-Fi, and duty-free goods.

AirAsia has also launched MyCorporate, which provides a range of products for corporate business travelers. These are specialized sets of corporate travel products and services for large corporations and small and medium enterprises. Companies making use of MyCorporate will be able to access an online booking system, as well as keep track of their corporate traveling expenses.

An interesting acquisition of a travel planning start-up, Touristly, was finalized by AirAsia in 2017. The USD2.6 million convertible loan will allow Touristly to tap into AirAsia's customer base of over 60 million passengers through website promotions, in-flight magazine placements, in-flight advertising, and social media activity. Touristly mainly focuses on Asia-Pacific, especially Southeast Asia, a region which has the majority of AirAsia's routes. With this alliance, AirAsia is aiming at a whole new set of potential ancillary revenues related to flyers' trips, by connecting with flyers beyond their flights and exploring new touch points during their journeys.

Another tie-up has been with Tune Protect, in which AirAsia is the largest shareholder, with 13.65% stake (April 2017). The company provides digital insurance to travelers. In a bid to further its digitalization initiatives, AirAsia is now targeting dynamic pricing for baggage allowance, in-flight meal enhancement options, extra seat-booking, along with Tune Protect Insurance.

At the back end, digitalization of data at AirAsia would be aimed at automating more operations and integrating operational data into useful insights for enhanced customer experience. According to Nikunj Shanti, Chief Data Officer, Group Digital, AirAsia, as quoted in the *The Hindu Business Line* (Kuala Lumpur, 19 March 2017), "Transacting in different currencies on international flights can get cumbersome, making it harder for the customer. What we are trying to do is make it faster and easier. This could also give us better information in terms of stock control, etc., so that we are stocking the right goods on the plane. Right now, it is all manual. If we get this information digitally, we can apply learning algorithms and classification algorithms and put better products on the plane". Even the cabin crew will be handed a mobile phone with the profiles of passengers on board in order to be able to serve them better.

These initiatives have helped the airline march forward on the digitalization road, though an idea that warrants more attention is how to integrate all these offerings in order to provide a more seamless experience to the user (Balqis Lim, 2017). Airlines need to utilize digitalization in terms of different aspects of flyers' experience, which airlines end up making more convenient for flyers, such as an easier and secure online booking, a more personalized in-cabin service, digital assistance with baggage, and the provision of information about any changes in flight schedule (gate changes, for instance), through their smartphones.

Making the Digital Customer Happy

AirAsia could be considered one of the early movers when it comes to identifying the power of digital marketing platforms, including social media. Today, AirAsia not only has a highly interactive presence on social media platforms but also sells its air tickets through Facebook, which accounts for 3% of its total sales, Line and WeChat.

The AirAsia digital team recognizes customers' evolving needs to be cared for, across all touch points. During the process, customers get what they look for, seamlessly and across channels, be it booking a ticket through the website or raising a query through Twitter or getting updated with useful travel information, without actively searching for it.

In an event organized this year, AirAsia's first-ever Hackathon event, the airline put forward a customer's profile, and computer programmers who participated in the event had to enrich the customer's experience based on his digital profile. The winning idea from Singapore was considered for AirAsia's incubator program for further enrichment.

Intensifying Competition

The trend of budget airlines, which was started by AirAsia, has caught on big time in ASEAN. There are over 50 low-cost carriers (LCCs) operating in Asia today, including notable carriers such as Lion Air (Indonesia), Malindo Air (Malaysia), Scoot (Singapore), JetStar Asia (Singapore), Cebu Pacific (The Philippines), Indigo (India), Spice Jet (India), Air Busan (South Korea), Air Seoul (South Korea), and Batik Air (Indonesia).

In 2016, an FT Confidential Research of 3,000 consumers in Indonesia, Malaysia, the Philippines, Thailand, and Vietnam — top aviation markets — suggested a considerable increase in the number of flyers in countries such as the Philippines and Vietnam, even though Indonesia, Malaysia, and Thailand witnessed flat growth. The research also indicated that AirAsia was termed the most popular airline by survey respondents in Indonesia, Malaysia, and Thailand. However, several new competitors are eating into the pie, and this could cause a legitimate concern for AirAsia.

The major competitors of AirAsia at local and regional markets include Malaysian Airlines' independent subsidiary, Firefly; Indonesia's largest low-cost carrier, Lion Air; Malaysia–Indonesia joint venture airline, Malindo Air; Singapore's growing low-cost airline, Scoot; and Australia's low-cost carrier, JetStar. Each of these players claims to have built a strong position in their respective home countries and are now looking to expand regionally.

On home turf, Malaysia Airlines, following recent restructuring, is also giving a tough competition by introducing an aggressive pricing strategy and improving load factor. The airline is also eyeing expansion in China and India, which are critical growth markets for AirAsia as well. With its digitalization efforts, the airline was able to catch attention, mainly through its MABHackathon challenge, a much more elaborate event than AirAsia's Hackathon, that lasted 4 months, with the airline facilitating a host of hacking labs and activities. The initiative was aimed at improving customer experience and operational efficiency at the airline via innovative solutions. The digital team at Malaysia Airlines, which has expanded over the course of a year, includes 30 specialists as of 2017 against only 5 earlier. The focus of the airline is on building in-house expertise on database marketing, rather than relying on outsourcing, and furnishing a more agile customer experience, from booking tickets to prepurchasing excess baggage and meals, and managing loyalty points and bundled offers to fulfil unique needs.

Lion Group's Malindo is also expanding in the region and pursuing several of AirAsia's attractive routes. Nevertheless, despite the intensifying competition, AirAsia is generally considered the "older brother" among its rivals as some of the business models they have adopted are inspired from AirAsia, and therefore, AirAsia management does not seem too worked up about the competition. In fact, Tony Fernandes has gone as far as to say that AirAsia thrives on competition. Discounted fares will force the rivals to function at relatively higher operating costs, and also put pressure on revenues. AirAsia, in contrast, maintains that it has hedged the bulk of its operating cost and is targeting greater ancillary revenues to deal with higher costs.

Ultimately, the action plan thrives on an incessant focus on four foundations — low cost, efficiency, stimulation of new markets, and strong cash-flow — supporting four pillars of strategy — safety, low fare, service, and simplicity — all of which aimed to achieve acceptable margins and sustainable growth that enable AirAsia to continue to be the lowest cost airline in the market.

Customer Management

AirAsia's success story includes a mix of factors, some strategic and some serendipitous. The company's CEO's foresight of an untapped demand, which could be leveraged through low-fare proposition, not only worked in its favor but also lent it a strong early mover advantage in Asia, as the airline has become a pioneer of the low-cost low-frill airline model in the region. AirAsia's strategic location in ASEAN is also a factor behind its success, allowing the company to cater to over 600 million customers. The no-frills low-fare model complemented the airline's high aircraft productivity goals due to a rapid turnaround of the aircraft, as well as systems placed on the ground. Consequently, AirAsia became the most cost-efficient low-cost airline in the world.

Going forward, AirAsia will continue to exploit digital channels to get new customers, through active social media marketing and sales promotion. The company seems to be well-acquainted with the tactics. Having started early, back in 2010, AirAsia marketed its newly launched campaign "Mind Blowing Fare" on Facebook and Twitter. In one day, the airline sold over 500,000 seats. That said, the rules of the game have changed considerably, with consumers' shortening attention span and explosive competition on digital platforms. The proverbial task of catching consumer attention in the "first few seconds" is getting harder to accomplish as consumers have begun to block marketers or they simply look away to get a breather from information overload. Content marketing armed with creativity and relevance will help marketers like AirAsia engage customers and contribute to building brand image.

The ambition to provide seamless personalized experience, facilitated through digitalization and database marketing, is intended to help retain customers, while the BIG loyalty programs are aimed at earning loyalty and potentially winning back lost customers. That said, in this era of artificial intelligence and M2M learning, Human-to-Human (H2H) inter-action is even more important. In a service–business like airlines, it is a huge advantage that all employees are marketers, especially those who interact with customers, such as flight attendants and guest services staff.

In addition to a sharp focus on digitalization to improve operational efficiency and customer satisfaction, AirAsia has also laid out an expan-sion plan in ASEAN, with a joint venture (JV) impending in Vietnam and further plans to begin operations in Cambodia. A JV in China is also in the pipeline and operations in Japan are expected to be reintroduced in the second half of 2017, after the first JV was dissolved due to delays in regulatory approvals.

In line with the regional route expansion, the fleet is also going to witness robust additions, with a fleet delivery plan chalked up to 2028. In 2017, the group fleet size is expected to increase by 29 aircrafts, which will bring the total to 203 A320s by end of this year.

Tony Fernandes, who has helmed the company for almost two decades, has one more gigantic task up his sleeves before he considers retirement. His vision is to consolidate AirAsia Southeast Asia operations into one umbrella company based in Malaysia — a daunting task in view of regulatory hurdles, the biggest being negotiations with governments in various countries to allow full ownership of each of the subsidiaries there. The company's boss meanwhile believes in taking one step at a time and focusing on consolidation first which, when (and if) done well, would pave the way for an IPO.

References

Balqis Lim (14 August 2017). Malaysia airlines moves a step ahead in digital aviation. *New Strait Times.* https://www.nst.com.my/lifestyle/bots/2017/08/267642/malaysia-airlines-moves-step-ahead-digital-aviation [28 August 2017].

CAPA Centre for Aviation (2018). Profile on AirAsia Berhad. https://centreforaviation.com/data/profiles/airlines/airasia-ak [29 November 2018].

Department of Statistics Malaysia (29 July 2016). *ICT Use and Access by Individuals and Households Survey Report.* https://www.dosm.gov.my/v1/index.php?r=column/pdfPrev&id=Q3l3WXJFbG1PNjRwcHZQTVlSR1UrQT09 [20 February 2019].

Haidar, GG and AZ Abu Bakar (11 August 2018). *E-Government Success in Malaysia through Government Portal and Website Assessment.* https://www.ijcsi.org/papers/IJCSI-9-5-1-401-409.pdf [11 August 2018].

Sidhu, BK (9 January 2017). Fernandes: AirAsia thrives on competition. *The Star Online.* http://www.thestar.com.my/business/business-news/2017/01/09/fernandes-airasia-thrives-on-competition [11 August 2017].

PTT Public Company Limited

PTT Public Limited Company (PTT), Thailand's state-owned, fully integrated petroleum and petrochemical company, is one of the strongest players in the country's oil and gas sector. Since its inception in the late 1970s, the company has envisioned to become Thailand's premier multinational energy company. This case highlights the customer management practices the company's oil marketing unit—one of PTT's main business units—employed to face intense competition and win the Thai consumers' heart. The reader will also learn how PTT maintains brand loyalty through integrated online-to-offline (O2O) customer experiences.

Energy Sector: Global and Thailand Perspective

In recent years, the global price of crude oil has dipped, partly due to its abundant supply. The Organization of the Petroleum Exporting Countries' (OPEC's) attempts to maintain prices by cutting back on oil production could not stop the low prices. Even the ongoing crisis in Iraq and Libya — two large producers who could contribute 4 million barrels of crude oil per day — failed to have any significant impact on prices. This came as a surprise to many.

The use of new fracking and drilling technologies has allowed US oil companies to produce shale oil in large volumes and at cheaper production costs. Shale oil is basically the oil produced from kerogen-rich rock sediments. The discovery of the technology in the late 1960s and its eventual massive adoption in the 2000s has helped the United States become the world's largest oil producer, ahead of Saudi Arabia, in 2016, for the fifth consecutive year. The country has become an exporter, as well of crude oil, meaning its production reserves have exceeded domestic consumption.

Despite a recovery in oil prices starting in 2017 due to restrained production and call for stability ahead of a planned IPO by Saudi Arabia's national petroleum company, the reduction in crude oil prices since 2014 has sent a number of oil and gas companies out of operations. According to law firm Haynes & Boone, in North America, where the crude oil boom began, at least 42 oil and gas companies announced bankruptcy in 2015, and their number may grow in future (Thomas, 2016).

The good news is that the global demand for commodities, including crude oil, is on its way to recovery. According to the US Energy Information Administration report (EIA, 2017), world energy consumption will increase to 663 quadrillion British thermal units (Btu) by 2030 and 736 quadrillion Btu by 2040, from 575 quadrillion Btu in 2015. The report also states that most of the increase in energy demand is expected to come from non-OECD countries due to strong economic growth, increased access to energy, and rapidly growing populations. This growth in the global demand for crude oil will continue to drive the prices of crude oil up. EIA's Annual Energy Outlook report expects oil prices to hit USD117 billion by 2050, from about USD63 billion in November 2017.

But what about the situation in Thailand? In 2016 and 2017, the domestic economy expanded, supported by public spending and government investments on megaprojects and economic stimulus measures, along with the booming tourism sector that offset weak exports and private investments.

In 2016, Thailand's primary commercial energy consumption (excluding renewables) reached 2.09 million barrels per day equivalent, up 1.2% over the previous year. The consumption of oil increased by 4.0% due to depressed prices, thus improving demand, whereas the consumption of natural gas fell by 1.9% due to low demand for power generation, gas separation plants, and natural gas vehicles (NGVs) (PTT Public Company Limited, 2016).

In 2016, Thailand's petroleum product consumption increased 4.0% from 2015. Diesel continued to be the most consumed product in the petroleum product group, with 3.3% growth in consumption due to an increase in demand by the industrial sector. The consumption of gasoline rose by 9.9% due to consistently low fuel prices since late 2014, whereas that of LPG fell by 5.3%. This encourages NGV and LPG motorists to shift to liquid fuels. Jet fuel rose by 7.2% due to a rise in the number of tourists and flights. Fuel oil consumption climbed 10.5% due to soaring industrial consumption (PTT Public Company Limited, 2016).

It is evident from the data that the energy sector in Thailand, as well as in the world, will continue to grow with an increase in demand. Although this positive trend is predicted to continue over the next few years, there may be surprises on the way, for example, the booming shale oil in the United States, which resulted in the dramatic fall of the world oil price.

PTT Public Limited Company at a Glance

One of the strongest players in Thailand's oil and gas sector is PTT Public Limited Company (PTT). PTT is Thailand's state-owned, fully integrated petroleum and petrochemical company. Since its inception in the late 1970s, the company has envisioned to become Thailand's premier multinational energy company with a mission to look after its stakeholders, including the country, community and society, shareholders, customers, business partners, and employees, in a balanced manner (PTT Public Company Limited, 2016).

PTT was initially established as a state enterprise called the Petroleum Authority of Thailand on 29 December 1978. This was the period of the second world crisis of petroleum shortages. It was, therefore, critical for PTT to focus on its primary mission of ensuring the procurement of adequate oil for domestic consumption. It also made efforts to raise domestic production by seeking indigenous petroleum reserves to support its energy needs. In the process, Thailand was not only able to meet its domestic demand but also began exporting excess fuel capacity, supported by an increase in natural gas production, by 1987.

Following the privatization of the state enterprise "Petroleum Authority of Thailand", PTT Public Company Limited was registered on 1 October 2001 under the Corporatization Act B.E. 2542 (2012; see Table 2.1).

PTT's operations span the entire petroleum industry from upstream to downstream, with the core focus on incremental value addition, supported by innovation and technological advances. As an operating and holding company, PTT conducts business directly, as well as through the PTT Group companies (see Table 2.1).

One of the business units of PTT that faces intense competition is the oil marketing unit. This business unit is directly responsible for the distribution of petroleum products that are categorized into three core categories: liquid fuels and LPG, lubricating oil and lubricating products,

Table 2.1: Company's milestones

Year	Events
1978	Petroleum Authority of Thailand (PTT) was established on 29 December 1978.
1978–1982	• PTT played an important role in the second world oil crisis. • PTT began submarine gas pipeline from the Erawan gas field.
1983–1987	• PTT built its first gas separation plant. • The National Petrochemical Co. Ltd. was established. • PTT Exploration and Production Co. Ltd. was established.

(Continued)

Table 2.1: *(Continued)*

Year	Events
1988–1992	• PTT took delivery of its one trillion cubic feet of natural gas. • PTT commissioned a gas separation plant unit, Unit 2. • PTT pioneered the sale of "PTT Hi Octane Unleaded".
1993–1997	• PTT achieved the top position in the domestic oil market. • PTT operated and inaugurated a gas separation plant unit. • Natural Gas Sales Agreement governing the Yadana and Yentagun gas field in Myanmar was affixed.
1998–2002	• The operation of Yanada Natural Gas Pipeline Project started. • Thailand's first international petroleum and petrochemical research and development institute was established. • PTT launched gasohol sale at service stations.
2001	Following the privatization of the state enterprise "Petroleum Authority of Thailand", PTT Public Limited Company or "PTT" was registered on 1 October 2001 under the Corporatization Act B.E. 2542.
2003	• PTT started selling NGV. • PTT opened 7-Eleven convenience stores. • The District Cooling System and Power Plant Co. Ltd. was established.
2004	Forest Ecosystem Learning Center was established.
2005	• PTT built the fifth gas separation plant. • PTT Chemicals Plc was established. • PTT acquired shares of TPI Plc. • PTT Polymer Marketing Co. Ltd. was established.
2007	• The operation of PTT's third gas pipeline system started. • PTT engaged in Jet Jiffy business. • The Rayong Gas Separation Plant won Thailand Quality Award. • PTT invested in a palm oil business by establishing PTT Green Energy Co. Ltd. • PTT Aromatics and Refining Plc was founded with the amalgamation of Aromatics (Thailand) Plc and Rayong Refinery Plc.
2008	• PTT opened the first LNG plant in Southeast Asia. • PTT gained the largest marketing share of lubrication oil products.

(Continued)

Table 2.1: *(Continued)*

Year	Events
	• PTT expanded its international business to the Middle East. • The first LNG jetty and receiving terminal was constructed.
2009	PTT expanded overseas investments of PTT International Co. Ltd. by investing in an overseas coal business for the first time.
2010	• The Natural Gas Pipeline Division won the TQA Award. • PTT started selling LNG to the water transportation sector. • PTT Tank Terminal Co. Ltd. was established. • PTT FLNG Co. Ltd. was established to conduct a study on FLNG (floating LNG) technology production.
2011	• PTT started bioplastic business by setting up PTT MCC Biochem Co. Ltd. • PTT started using Amazon Bio Cup, which is made from biodegradable plastic and is 100% degradable. • Energy Solution Co. Ltd. was established to provide technical and engineering consultancy service. • The sixth gas separation plant was started. • The first LNG receiving terminal in Southeast Asia located in Mab Ta Phut Industrial Estate, Rayong Province, was commissioned. • Hydropower plant business of Xaiyaburi Power Co. Ltd. started its operation in Lao.
2012	• PTT and NECTEC conducted a research on the technology of power generation from the solar cell. • PTT and THAI Airway signed an agreement of Bio-Jet Development Cooperation. • The "Learning Institute for Everyone" was established.
2016	• PTT won the Outstanding State Enterprise Award, The Asset CEO of the Year and Asia's Outstanding Corporate Governance Award. • PTT got 192nd rank on the Fortune 500 list.
2017	• PTT won the Asia Marketing Excellence Award from the Asia Marketing Federation (AMF).

Source: Fortune (2017), PTT Public Company Limited (2012), and PTT Public Company Limited (2016).

and retail non-oil business products. PTT's retail service stations act as the primary distribution channel for the entire product line-up, catering especially to individual consumers. As of December 2016, PTT operated 1,530 service stations across the country (PTT Public Company Limited, 2016) (Figure 2.2).

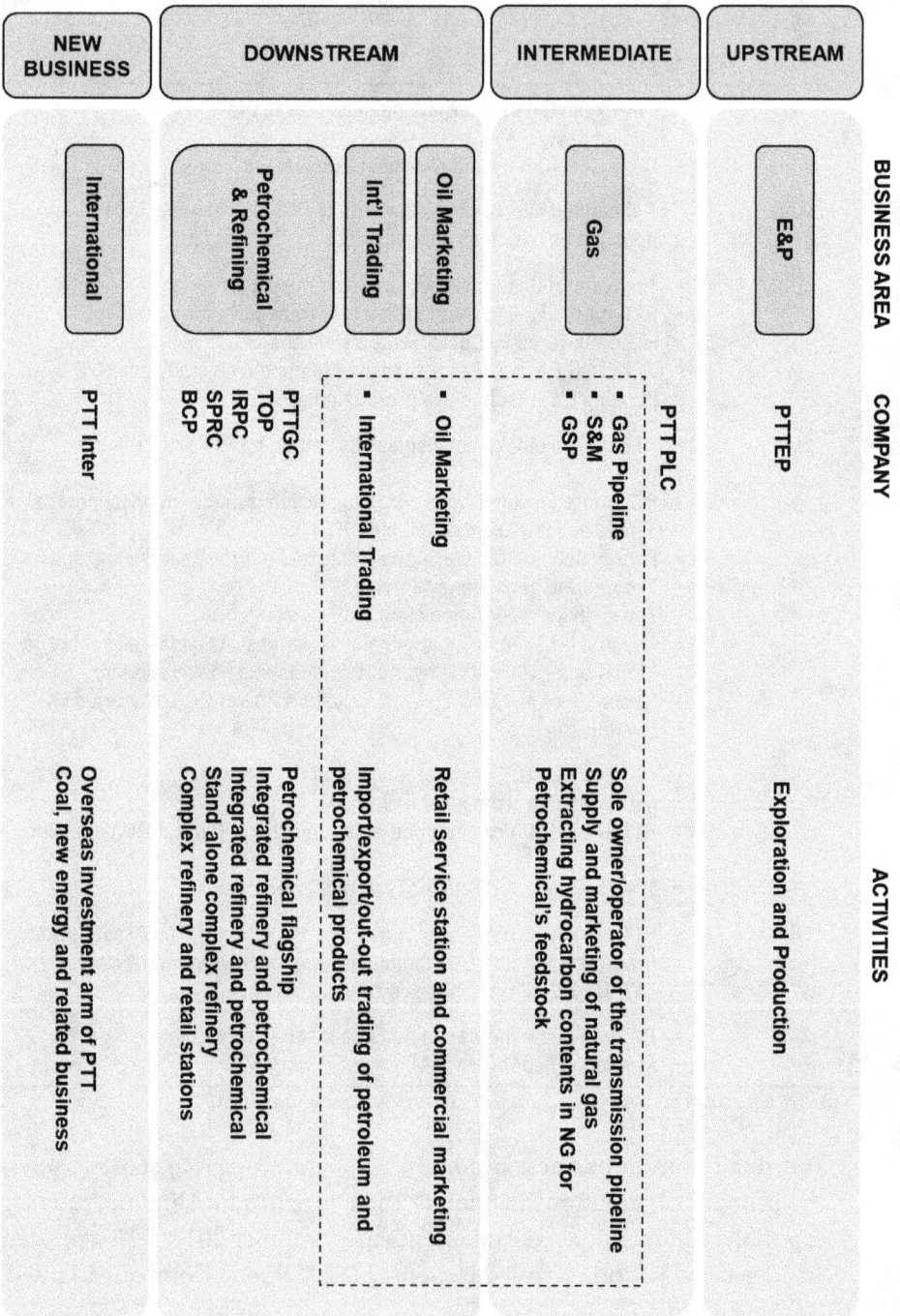

Figure 2.2: PTT's business portfolio.
Source: PTT (2013).

Dealing with the "New" Thai Consumers

In the oil marketing business, industry players are supposed to deal with individual consumers, who may not just be rational but also tend to be emotional when it comes to purchases, somewhat contrary to commercial buyers. What it calls for is consistent value innovation to touch the hearts of individual consumers. This could be daunting in today's environment of intense competition and especially with advances in digital technology, which have resulted in a more connected and demanding Thai consumer.

Compared with several other Asian countries, digitalization in Thailand is advanced. Of the approximately 68,297,547 people, about 57,000,000 are already Internet users, that is about 83.5% of the total population (Internet World Stats, 2017). According to a January 2017 release of data from the National Statistical Office of Thailand, more than 90% of Internet users in the country go online via their smartphones, far exceeding the rates for any other device. The second most popular device for Internet access is desktop, which is used by around half of the Internet users surveyed (eMarketer, 2017).

This massive technology adoption is also making fundamental changes to the way Thai consumers make purchasing decisions; social media is driving e-commerce and consumers actively search for a wide variety of products online (Bharadwaj *et al.*, 2017). It is increasingly clear that, in order to engage tech-savvy consumers in this digital age, companies need to adopt a new strategic approach. PTT is following the digital movement closely. Auttapol Rerkpiboon, Senior Executive Vice President, Oil Business Unit, PTT Public Company Limited, shared, "The world has entered the 'digital economy era', an age in which technology has a significant influence on the consumption of services and economic development. Thailand is not an exception. Any organization that conducts business in old, traditional ways will no longer thrive in the next five years" (Network Asia, 2016).

PTT management also appears to recognize that, in this new era, the spirit of customer centricity must complement effective utilization of innovative and new technologies, lest the company risks losing business growth that it strives for. Those strategies are outlined in PTT Group's business strategies (see Box 2.1).

> ### Box 2.1: PTT Group's Business Strategies.
>
> PTT Group defines its business strategies in "3D":
>
> - **Do Now:** Productivity improvement to be implemented immediately to strengthen the business amid energy price volatility
>
> - **Decide Now:** Sustainable growth to be achieved through 3- to 5-year investment decisions for organic growth, with a focus on leveraging competitiveness and business advantages of PTT Group
>
> - **Design Now:** Priming for leapfrogging growth by leveraging innovation and new technologies for the new S-Curve growth. This is characterized by customer centricity and opportunities derived from megatrends together with addressing the public sector's industrial drive to "Thailand 4.0"
>
> *Source:* PTT Public Company Limited (2016).

O2O Initiatives

One of the most strategic touch points owned by PTT to interact with individual consumers is the service stations located across the country. It is, therefore, PTT's constant endeavor to improve the customer experience at its service stations, by providing a more integrated service and not just filling up consumers' vehicles with fuels.

Currently, no less than 1,350 7-Eleven outlets are operational at PTT gas stations nationwide. PTT has also launched 18 "PTT Compact Model" service stations to multiply its service to communities on secondary roads. The number is set to rise along with the development of "Mini-Community Malls" to accommodate burgeoning urban growth. Moreover, utilizing its expansive network of service stations, PTT carries out public service through "Pracharath Sookjai Shops" at its 148 service stations, wherein the petrol station compounds serve as sales outlets for agricultural products, local enterprise products, foods and snacks, and souvenirs. Due to such initiatives, PTT continues to be the leader in the domestic retail oil market, with a 40.8% market share in 2016. The company has also been selected as the "most popular brand" in Thailand for the 13th year in a row by *BrandAge* Magazine, as well as the "No. 1 Brand Thailand" by *Marketeer* Magazine for the fifth consecutive year (PTT Public Company Limited, 2016).

Meanwhile, to increase customer loyalty, PTT has introduced the PTT Blue Card, which provides various rewards to consumers. PTT Blue Card represents a core component of the strategy, providing customers with exclusive benefits that strengthen their relationship with the brand and resulting in great brand loyalty and widespread word-of-mouth. Today, on average, Thai vehicle owners not only fill up their gas tanks at PTT stations but also buy their groceries using their PTT Blue Card and, in return, earn reward points, which can be exchanged for resort deals and complimentary meals.

To the customers, PTT Blue Card is a customer loyalty program that brings them rewards. With over 1.6 million cardholders and 150,000 transactions recorded per day, PTT Blue Card is a vital source of customer data (Network Asia, 2016). For the marketing team handling oil products, PTT Blue Card provides a rich database that can yield vital information on how to better understand PTT customers. Tailored promotion programs can be developed in order to continue winning the loyalty of the existing customers as well as adding new ones. With the program, PTT can derive new business insights to drive operational excellence in every aspect of its operations and make the organization customer-centric and data-driven. The impact is evident as the company has been able to create matching campaigns tailored to specific customer profiles. With personalized marketing activities, these deliver outstanding experiences for its customers and thereby drive retention rates and customer loyalty (Network Asia, 2016).

The customers' preference toward hand-held devices has not gone unnoticed by PTT. In order to provide a personalized experience in this age of widespread mobile penetration, the company has developed the PTT Blue Card app for smartphone and tablet users. This app helps customers register their accounts, check the accumulated points, redeem rewards, and check numerous promotions.

These initiatives by PTT corroborate the company's proactive approach in utilizing digital technology (big data analysis and smartphone application) to market a product such as vehicle fuel while also keeping in mind the personal touch and ensuring an integrated customer experience through its service stations. This is a form of customer management PTT aimed at maintaining brand loyalty through integrated online-to-offline (O2O) customer experiences. Furthermore, a greater focus on additional sources of revenue from its non-oil portfolio, including convenience stores, food courts, budget hotels, and Amazon coffee shops, does not only augment the customer experience but is also in line with the company's long-term strategy to remain competitive; such non-oil revenue is important as oil companies brace themselves for the potential shift toward electric vehicles in the future.

References

Bharadwaj, A *et al.* (October 2017). *Five Consumer Trends to Watch in Thailand.* https://www.bcg.com/publications/2017/globalization-go-to-markets-five-consumer-trends-watch-thailand.aspx [8 January 2018].

eMarketer (February 2017). *More Than 90% of Internet Users in Thailand Use Smartphones to Go Online.* https://www.emarketer.com/Article/More-than-90-of-Internet-Users-Thailand-Use-Smartphones-Go-Online/1015217 [31 December 2017].

Fortune (2017). *Fortune Global 500.* http://fortune.com/global500/ptt/ [30 December 2017].

Internet World Stats (2017). *Asia Marketing Research, Internet Usage, Population Statistics and Facebook Subscribers.* http://www.internetworldstats.com/asia.htm [31 December 2017].

Network Asia (September 2016). *The Digital Transformation Journey of Thailand's PTT.* https://www.networksasia.net/article/digital-transformation-journey-thailands-ptt.1474902005 [30 December 2017].

PTT (2013). *Conquering ASEAN Energy Frontier.* https://www.set.or.th/th/asean_exchanges/files/PTT.pdf [30 December 30, 2017].

PTT Public Company Limited (2012). *Background.* http://www.pttplc.com/en/About/pages/Background.aspx [30 December 2017].

PTT Public Company Limited (2016). *Annual Report 2016.* Bangkok: PTT Public Company Limited.

Thomas, Z, (January 2016). The global oil glut is squeezing the US shale industry. *BBC News.* http://www.bbc.com/news/business-35355286 [31 December 2017].

U.S. Energy Information Administration (EIA) (September 2017). *Full Issue PDF Volume 32, Issue 3 International Energy Outlook 2017.* https://www.eia.gov/outlooks/ieo/pdf/0484(2017).pdf [31 December 2017].

Ocean Park Hong Kong

With the largest number of skyscrapers and as one of the prominent financial centers in the world on one hand and three-quarters of the land as countryside on the other hand, this makes Hong Kong a uniquely attractive destination for travelers. This island, which is also famous for its Disneyland, is home to a much older theme and amusement park Ocean Park Hong Kong. This is the second largest theme park in Hong Kong, after the former. As a leading tourist destination, Ocean Park Hong Kong faces fierce competition to attract local visitors and those from Mainland China and other Asian regions. Creative strategies based on digital technology are required to get, keep, and grow its customers.

Hong Kong's Tourism Industry

Today, tourism is regarded as a major pillar of the Hong Kong economy. The industry caught the government's deeper attention when the country's economy severely suffered in the wake of the Asian financial crisis in 1997. The crisis brought to light the gaps in the economic structure, which was heavily reliant on the financial and the real estate industries. The need for diversifying the economy was well recognized. This was followed by the government calling for the development of industries based on knowledge and innovation and strengthening the contribution of service industries to the economy, including that of finance, logistics, and tourism (Loo and Yim, 2007).

In 2014, tourism contributed 5% to Hong Kong's GDP. The sector employs around 271,800 persons and accounts for 7.2% of the total employment (Hong Kong Special Administrative Region Government, 2016). In recent years, the country's tourism sector has been impacted by several factors, including the slowdown in the global economic growth and greater competition from regional tourist destinations. This was, in part, thanks to the depreciating currencies in those regions that made travel and tourism there more affordable. In 2016, the number of visitors in Hong Kong from around the world was 56.7 million, which represents a decline of 4.5% compared with the figure in 2015 (Hong Kong Tourism Commission, 2017). As a result, the direct contribution of travel and tourism in Hong Kong's GDP also declined to 4.6% in 2016 (World Travel & Tourism Council, 2017). In 2016, Hong Kong's top ten visitor source markets in the order of arrival numbers were the Chinese mainland, Taiwan, South Korea, United States, Japan, Macao, the Philippines, Singapore, Thailand, and Australia. Altogether these countries accounted for 92% of the total visitor arrivals (Hong Kong Tourism Commission, 2017).

Unlike some countries such as China, Hong Kong had few natural scenic endowments. Therefore, it had to develop its own attractions. The development of tourist attractions is also aimed at changing the perception of Hong Kong, from a mere business destination to a family destination. One such prominent tourist destination in Hong Kong today is Ocean Park.

Ocean Park: The Beginning and Development

Ocean Park Hong Kong is a marine-based leisure complex in the Southern District of the region and was opened to the public in 1977. The park was constructed by the Hong Kong Jockey Club, built on land provided by the government at a small fee. By 1987, Ocean Park ceased to be a subsidiary of Jockey Club and, therefore, began operations under its own statutory body, with a board appointed by the government. This is facilitated under the Ocean Park Corporate Ordinance. Ocean Park is now managed by Ocean Park Corporation, a financially independent, nonprofit entity. It became a public park for educational, recreational, and conservational activities (Loo and Yim, 2007).

Today, Ocean Park is renowned as Hong Kong's prominent recreational and educational park. Spread across 915,000 sq. m of land and with a diverse array of animals and attractions, rides, and thematic shows, Ocean Park is divided between two areas: the Summit and the Waterfront. The Summit is home to a number of thrill rides, whereas the Waterfront features Ocean Park's latest themed area, the Amazing Asian Animals, an educational and highly entertaining collection of exhibits that bring together some of Asia's rarest animals (Ocean Park Hong Kong, 2018a).

Since it was founded 40 years ago, the park has consistently attempted to rejuvenate and reinvent itself to serve its guests better. New attractions continue to be added to provide new experiences to visitors. As an example, in 2005, Ocean Park announced a HK5.5 billion Master Redevelopment Plan (MRP) to develop the Park into the world's best marine-based theme park, doubling the amount of animal and ride attractions, from 35 to over 80. This reinforces its commitment to become Hong Kong's must-visit tourist attraction and as a world-class landmark.

Ocean Park Hong Kong's journey is not one without challenges. The theme park witnessed several periods when visitor numbers went down. For example, the Asian financial crisis in 1997 began a spell of losses for the Park that lasted four consecutive years. The outbreak of the Severe Acute Respiratory Syndrome (SARS) in 2003 had also reduced the attendance at the Park by about 70% (Loo and Yim, 2007). However, through various efforts to develop attractions and promotions, Ocean Park managed to sail through these difficult times. Currently, this park has recorded various achievements and awards that show that its allure remains strong, especially in Asia (Table 2.2).

Table 2.2: Ocean Park's history and achievements.

Year	Events
1977	Opened in January 1977 by the Governor of Hong Kong, Sir Murray MacLehose, Ocean Park was constructed as a subsidiary of the Hong Kong Jockey Club.
1982–1984	The Jockey Club put in a further investment of HK240 million (around USD30 million) to develop new facilities.
1987	The Park ceased to be a subsidiary of the Hong Kong Jockey Club and became a statutory body incorporated under the Ocean Park Corporate Ordinance.
1997	• The Asian financial crisis hit Hong Kong. • Due to the Asian financial crisis, Ocean Park suffered losses for four consecutive years.

(Continued)

Table 2.2: *(Continued)*

Year	Events
2001–2002	The park began to post profits, owing to extensive efforts in creating new events and attractions for visitors, aggressive marketing, and promotional offers. The park recorded HK15.3 million in profit and attendance reportedly went up by 23%, amounting to 3.4 million.
2003	• Allan Zeman, known for leading the creation of the popular Lan Kwai Fong entertainment district of Hong Kong, was appointed Chairman of Ocean Park Corporation, a position he held for 11 years. • The outbreak of the Severe Acute Respiratory Syndrome (SARS) reduced the attendance at the Park by about 70%.
2005	• Hong Kong Disneyland was opened. • Ocean Park unveiled a Master Redevelopment Plan (MRP), under which older features at the park were rejuvenated and new areas were developed. • The number of attractions more than doubled, from 35 to over 80.
2006	Forbes.com named Ocean Park one of the "10 Most Popular Amusement Parks in the World".
2007	Forbes Traveler ranked Ocean Park as one of the "50 Most Visited Tourist Attractions in the world".
2009	• Amazing Asian Animals, Ocean Park's new, exclusive animal and edutainment area, showcasing several endangered species, was opened. • Ocean Express, a cable-based train system able to transport over 5,000 visitors per hour between the Summit and Waterfront, started its operations.
2011	• The new flagship attraction area Aqua City was opened. • The Rainforest, an integrated theme zone featuring over 70 exotic animal species, was opened.
2012	• A new attraction zone, Old Hong Kong, was opened, reminiscing visitors about the older view of Hong Kong between the 1950s and the 1970s. • Polar Adventure was launched, featuring animals such as penguins, Pacific walruses, spotted seals, and northern sea lions and with an aim to promote conservation efforts.
2014	A 20,000-sq.-ft shark aquarium was opened.

(Continued)

Table 2.2: *(Continued)*

Year	Events
2015	• Ocean Park achieved TripAdvisor's Certificate of Excellence. • It achieved Yahoo! Emotive Brands Award 2014–2015.
2016	It achieved "Top Ten Highest Attendance of Chinese Theme Parks in 2016" from the China Association of Amusement Parks and Attractions.
2017	• Ocean Park welcomed over 140 million guests since its inception. • It achieved TripAdvisor Travelers' Choice Awards for Amusement Parks (No. 2 in China and No. 3 in Asia).

Source: Ocean Park Hong Kong (2016, 2017, 2018a), and Loo and Yim (2007).

Customers and Competition

Ocean Park set to position itself as a family-friendly tourist attraction, offering something for everyone in the family, from children to grandparents. Although based on its original concept, Ocean Park segregates its visitors into three categories: locals, mainlanders (the tourists from the mainland China, visiting in group tours), and fully independent travelers (FIT). These three categories of visitors often possessed different characteristics and tourist behaviors when visiting Ocean Park. For example, local visitors came to the park around 10 a.m. and stayed until 2 p.m.; FITs arrived around the same time and remained in the park until it closed, whereas the group tours arrived in the afternoon and remained in the park for up to 3.5 hours. Among the three groups, mainlanders, because of their preplanned itineraries and a relatively shorter duration of stays, spent the least time in the park (Loo and Yim, 2007). The majority of tourists to Ocean Park, in recent years, have actually come from the mainland China, but, since 2015, the number of tourists from this region has declined (Ocean Park Hong Kong, 2017).

The onset of competition is one of the challenges that have partly contributed to falling visitor arrivals. It is also a challenge taken head-on by Ocean Park to continue to improve its services and offerings to the travelers. In 2005, the year when the rival Hong Kong Disneyland opened, Ocean Park unveiled a Master Redevelopment Plan (MRP), under which older features at the park were rejuvenated and new areas developed. Under the development plan, the number of attractions was more than doubled, from 35 to over 80.

That said, competition in the region in this space is thriving. Ocean Park continues to manage rising challenges as it wards off competition, which is increasing as a result of several new theme parks being built in the region, by international and domestic brands, especially in 2016–2017. This has led to a horde of choices for consumers with respect to content and entertainment options. As Asian tourists continue to be targeted, by both domestic and foreign brands, emerging projects in the region would continue to reinvest, leading to upgrades of facilities and expansion of established theme parks — thus fueling further competition. The mainland alone is expected to have 59 new theme parks by 2020 (Ocean Park Hong Kong, 2017). To meet visitors' ever-growing choices and expectations of the theme park experience, it is critical for Ocean Park to maximize its customer management initiatives.

Customer Management in the New Era

For customer-centric companies like Ocean Park, the ability to manage relationships with customers could provide them with an unrivalled competitive advantage to outperform the rivals. In doing so, creative approaches must be implemented to get new customers, keep customers loyal, grow loyal customers to give recommendations, and win-back lost customers (see Figure 2.3). In today's environment, the development of digital technology provides an opportunity for Ocean Park to con-duct customer management initiatives that integrate online and offline approaches to create more memorable experiences.

To attract new visitors' attention, Ocean Park has been creatively utilizing digital technology. For example, at the launch of Halloween Fest 2016, claimed as Asia's largest annual Halloween celebration, Ocean Park offered a unique activity by utilizing gamification. The company used an interactive mobile ad that recreated one of the haunted scenes in Ocean Park and turned it into a 360-degree panorama based on HTML5 technology. Mobile users were highly engaged by the interactive mobile ad through a mini-game and were then redirected to Hong Kong Ocean Park's YouTube channel to experience the 360-degree video (Hotmob Limited, 2016).

Not only that, customers taking part in the festival were engaged in unforgettable online and offline experiences. Making its debut during

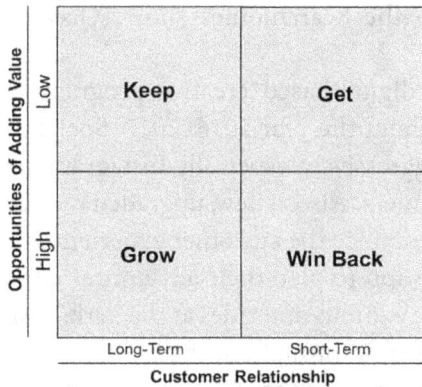

Figure 2.3: Customer value management.
Source: Kotler, Kartajaya and Hooi (2017).

Halloween Fest 2016, Halloween Ghost Hunt, a smartphone app, further enhanced and complemented the offerings during the Park's Halloween season and let guests win exclusive prizes. Halloween Ghost Hunt comprises three modules: Ghost Detector, Third Eye, and Ghost Hunter Game.

Ghost Detector worked like a radar that detected "ghosts" from as far as 3 metres and allowed the guests walking around the park to capture those ghosts that were also around the park in their cameras. This makes for an adrenaline-pumping adventurous activity for the visitors. Guests could also use the density map to determine where all these spirits were hiding and to locate them effectively. The feature "Third Eye" utilized AR technology to enhance the experience at the Legendary Palace. By simply activating the module and pointing their mobile cameras toward specific locations, spirits would appear on their phones' screens. This online-offline amalgamation of experience for guests celebrating Halloween created a truly unforgettable experience during the Halloween season. There were also some games adding to the fun. As visitors hopped from attraction to attraction, they could play these Halloween-themed games during break time while enjoying Halloween-special meals. These games were offered via the Ghost Hunter Game, while queuing up to enter the attractions. Guests could also collect points and win special prizes by playing these games, ranging from in-Park coupons for F&B items; limited, priority access to designated Halloween attractions; and exclusive access to the Scaremonies show (Ocean Park Hong Kong, 2018b).

Various other digital-based creative programs were developed at Ocean Park throughout the year 2016–2017. Social media platforms are being used more aggressively, especially Instagram, to share content and interact with consumers. Also, a new, upgraded mobile app was launched in 2016 to further enhance the customer experience. Guests could use an "eScheduler" in the app to plan their adventures and minimize queuing time for some of the exhibits and rides at the Park. Visitors could also win discounts and privileges throughout the Park, using the "eCoupon" feature. For visitors looking for more detailed information, the app's "Virtual Guided Tour" provided location-based video and audio facilities so as to help guests explore animal exhibits (Ocean Park Hong Kong, 2017).

By creating such memorable sensations, Ocean Park expected that customers who had the opportunity to visit would be willing to share their experience with people in their social network. This type of customer management leads to heightened advocacy from loyal and satisfied customers.

However, that is not to say that Ocean Park has abandoned the traditional approach. It is true that for companies in the business of delivering physical tangible experiences — online initiatives cannot fully replace the offline programs. Instead, both online and offline initiatives need to be synergized to create optimal results. To boost inbound visitor numbers, the Park continues to deepen its connection with mainland Chinese visitors, while gaining wider access to international markets to drive growth.

In 2016–2017, Ocean Park opened a new representative office in Shenzhen, South China, to better cater to the visitors from that region with an on-the-ground presence. This office works closely with the four other offices in Guangzhou, Shanghai, Beijing, and Chengdu, thus offering customized services to its customers. In order to undertake international marketing, Ocean Park works closely with the Hong Kong Tourism Board and other industry peers to promote Hong Kong as a preferred travel destination. As a result of this collaboration, Ocean Park has been able to successfully position itself as a must-visit attraction in the major markets across Asia and also recorded impressive year-on-year growth in visitor numbers from markets like Japan (29%), Indonesia (27%), the Philippines

(14%), and South Korea (5%) in 2017 (Ocean Park Hong Kong, 2017). This has helped Ocean Park preserve its iconic status as the oldest and the most family-friendly theme park in Hong Kong.

References

Hong Kong Special Administrative Region Government (2016). *Hong Kong: The Facts* https://www.gov.hk/en/about/abouthk/factsheets/docs/tourism.pdf [13 March 2018].

Hong Kong Tourism Commission (2017). *Tourism Performance,* http://www.tourism.gov.hk/english/statistics/statistics_perform.html [13 March 2018].

Hotmob Limited (2016). *Campaign Highlight of 2016,* http://www.hot-mob.com/updates/campaign-highlight-of-2016/ [21 March 2018].

Kotler, P, H Kartajaya and DH Hooi (2017). *Marketing for Competitiveness: Asia to The World.* Singapore: World Scientific.

Loo, G and B Yim (February 2007). Ocean Park: In the face of competition from Hong Kong Disneyland. *Harvard Business Case.* Boston: Harvard Business School Publishing.

Ocean Park Hong Kong (2016). *Annual Report 2015–2016,* http://media.oceanpark.com.hk/files/s3fs-public/ophk_ar15-16.pdf [21 March 2018].

Ocean Park Hong Kong (2017). *Annual Report 2016-2017,* http://media.oceanpark.com.hk/files/s3fs-public/ophk_ar16-17.pdf [21 March 2018].

Ocean Park Hong Kong (2018a). *General Facts.* https://www.oceanpark.com.hk/en/corporate-information/general-facts [21 March 2018].

Ocean Park Hong Kong (2018b). Ocean Park Halloween Fest 2016 Kicks Off! Ocean Park launches Asia's largest annual Halloween celebration. *Press Release.* https://www.oceanpark.com.hk/en/corporate-information/general-facts [21 March 2018].

World Travel & Tourism Council (2017). *Travel and Tourism Economic Impact 2017 China,* London: World Travel & Tourism Council.

Cinnamon Hotels and Resorts

The political and security situation in Sri Lanka has improved significantly over the years. This has put the tourism and hospitality sector into the spotlight for its increasingly important role in the country's economic development. Sri Lanka boasts of vast natural scenic beauty — from rainforests to beaches — which also attracts global brands to set up luxury hotel ventures. Amidst rising competition in the upscale segment, the Cinnamon Hotels and Resorts has emerged as a local player, offering unique experiences to its customers. Here, we discuss Cinnamon Group's creative efforts to get the attention of digital consumers who are increasingly connected with the internet today.

Tourism in Sri Lanka

Sri Lanka, with all its natural landscape, rich traditions, and diverse wildlife, has historically been a popular tourist attraction. In the twelfth century, Italian explorer Marco Polo claimed Sri Lanka to be the "best island of its size in the world" (*The Times, 2012*). Tourism in Sri Lanka today is one of the fastest-growing industries. The country reached 2,050,832 tourist arrivals in 2016, recording a year-on-year growth of 14%.

In terms of countries of origin, Western Europe was the largest contributor in 2016, with 643,333 arrivals — a 17% growth year on year. Two of the largest single-source markets were India and China, with 356,729 and 271,577 tourists in 2016, respectively. Per data from the Central Bank of Sri Lanka, tourism revenues in 2016 reached USD3.40 billion, up 14% from the USD2.98 billion in 2015 (John Keells Hotel PLC, 2017).

The high number of tourist arrivals from Western Europe — compared with other regions, especially Asia — is due to some policy decisions of the Sri Lankan government. Back in the 1980s, when Sri Lanka invested in building its tourism infrastructure, much of it was targeted at the western European market, as Asians in those days were not considered affluent enough to be active travelers. However, the situation today is quite different. Over the past decade, Asians — accounting for almost 60% of the world's population — have actually begun to travel a lot more, not only domestically but regionally. On the contrary, the economic situation in Western Europe is not the same as it used to be, and a segment, which could previously perhaps have afforded a holiday in another continent, may not be able to do so today or may wait longer (Kulamannage, 2013).

Sri Lanka's natural beauty comprises up to 1,600 km of coastline, which has many sandy calm beaches, overlooking bays, lagoons, sandbanks, and rocky headlands. Needless to say, Sri Lanka's beaches are a hit with domestic and international travelers alike. Marine recreational activities such as sea bathing and swimming, surfing, boating, snorkeling, deep-sea fishing, underwater photography, and scuba diving are available at most of these beaches and surrounding resort areas (Sri Lanka Tourism Promotion Bureau, 2018). Without a doubt, Sri Lanka's tourism and hospitality industries carry great potential, which can be further developed. Following the end of a three-decade-long civil conflict in May 2009, the tourism and the hospitality sectors have emerged as front-runners in Sri Lanka's economic activities (International Finance Group, 2013).

Cinnamon Hotels and Resorts: Inspired Living

Currently, the hospitality industry in Sri Lanka is dominated by hotels, targeting luxury and upper-upscale segments. Apart from domestic players, some global brands that have also entered the market include (Hospitality.lk, 2016) the following:

- Marriott International, with brands including Sheraton, Marriott, and Ritz-Carlton;

- Shangri-La Hotels and Resorts, which has properties in Hambantota and Colombo;

- Hyatt Hotel Corporation, which will launch its flagship property;

- Mövenpick Hotels and Resorts, which is soon to enter the market; and

- InterContinental Hotel Group's Crowne Plaza Colombo Beira Lake, which is currently in the planning phase.

Amidst the growing dominance of various global hospitality brands, Cinnamon Hotels and Resorts, managed by a Sri Lanka-based holding company John Keells Hotel PLC, is also in the hospitality sector. The brand is known to represent a new, vibrant Sri Lanka and, thus, pits itself against a number of global giants. Combining an old-world charm with world-class service and modern convenience, Cinnamon promises to offer a contemporary yet culturally rich look and feel to its customers.

Launched in 2005, the chain currently owns and manages a portfolio of more than 1,330 four- and five-star rooms in 13 hotels across Sri Lanka and the Maldives (see Table 2.3 for detailed information on the company's various milestones). As a pioneer in sustainable tourism in Sri Lanka, the multi-award-winning Cinnamon Hotels and Resorts portfolio

Table 2.3: Cinnamon Hotels and Resorts' milestones.

Year	Events
2002	After nearly two decades of ethnic conflict in the country, Sri Lanka signed a ceasefire agreement (CFA) with the LTTE. Consequently, many unexplored territories in the country became open for business.
2003	• John Keells Holdings purchased a 60.5% controlling share of Asian Hotels and two leading five-star hotels in Colombo, the former Oberoi and Trans Asia. • Many other properties were acquired, including one in the Maldives.
2004	• The brand Cinnamon was born, and it represents a collection of various hotels, including a second-tier series named Chaaya. The ceasefire agreement was breached, and the country was again at war. Cinnamon used the timeout due to the turmoil to plan its ventures outside Sri Lanka.
2005	Cinnamon came to be recognized as an emerging hospitality brand from Asia, with the launch of Cinnamon Hotels and Resorts. It was once again in the spotlight with the launch of Cinnamon Grand, the flagship city hotel.
2006	The second-tier brand Chaaya was launched with the establishment of the first flagship resort — Chaaya Village, Habarana.
2007–2010	Cinnamon Hotels and Resorts witnessed interest from several foreign investors. As peace was restored in 2009, new opportunities opened in the tourism sector, and Cinnamon was a front-runner to take advantage of the burgeoning trend. The Sri Lankan market once again became the primary focus of the group.
2011	• As tourism grew by a staggering 40%, international hotel chains began to invest in the Sri Lankan hospitality and tourism sector. • Cinnamon invests Rs. 5.4 billion (around USD3.1 million) to develop travel and tourism in the country, with a continuing focus on building the Sri Lankan brand.
2012	• Cinnamon's brand strategy and execution were conceptualized as a result of a comprehensive analysis of Sri Lanka's travel and tourism industry, with special emphasis on Cinnamon's identity and group offerings. • The results called for a consolidated approach, merging Cinnamon and Chaaya brands under the Cinnamon Hotels and Resorts umbrella.

(*Continued*)

Table 2.3: *(Continued)*

Year	Events
2014	The Cinnamon brand is further strengthened with a new credo aimed at delivering "Inspired Living" combined with new vibrant methods of brand storytelling. Cinnamon goes beyond a holiday brand or lifestyle company, evolving into an inspired way of life.
2015	• Cinnamon launched a whole new brand architecture under the Inspired Living banner as a vibrant lifestyle brand, which offers its customers the most unique travel experiences in South Asia. • Cinnamon Life, an all-encompassing lifestyle group that comes under the Cinnamon mother brand, further strengthened its position as a leader in lifestyle and hospitality.
2016	Cinnamon Hotels and Resorts organized some events of international significance, including the "Miss Intercontinental Pageant 2016" and the second Travel Bloggers Conference Asia and Awards 2016.
2017	Cinnamon launched the "Sri Lanka Photo Contest 2017", the country's largest crowd-sourced destination campaign to date.

Source: Cinnamon Hotels & Resorts (2015) and John Keells Hotel PLC (2017).

has obtained and continued to comply with numerous international certifications, including Green Globe, ISO 22000:2005, ISO 14001, and OHSAS 18001, among others (John Keells Hotel PLC, 2017).

To optimize its penetration in the upscale segment, Cinnamon Hotels and Resorts strives to offer premium accommodation in a variety of categories: lean luxury, rustic luxury, luxury, and signature luxury (see Table 2.4). Each property comes with its own personality, presence, and experience, but they all drive the same brand positioning: "Inspired Living". The idea is to make them the most happening places to enjoy a destination with a luxurious experience.

Getting into the Digital Travelers' Mind

In addition to building hotels and resorts at picturesque locations and with excellent facilities, Cinnamon realizes the importance of providing an experience that suits customers' needs. The need for more authentic and personalized experiences has driven demand for alternative hospitality offerings, such as homestays and apartments (John Keells Hotel PLC, 2017). This forms the basis of a customer-centric perspective, wherein firms strive to create value for customers and consider their points of

Table 2.4: Cinnamon's hospitality portfolio.

Categorization	Signature Luxury	Luxury	Rustic Luxury	Lean Luxury
Brand Name	Cinnamon White	Cinnamon Luxury	Cinnamon Signature	Cinnamon Red
Relationship with Master Brand	Co-brand	Master Brand	Endorsed Brand	Co-brand
Brand Driver	**Bespoke Luxury:** We enable you to enjoy the finest luxury in Sri Lanka's exclusive and unique locations	**Vibrantly Yours:** We enable people to discover new places in a setting that suits their style	**Simply Yours:** We enable people to discover new places in a comfortable setting that suits their style	**Cool Red:** We enable people to discover new places with less fuss and more independence
Value Proposition	Curated for you, more personal, more active, and luxurious. **I visit because:** • I feel so indulgent • I feel so inspired	More active and fun, more stylish. **I visit because:** • I feel energized • I feel inspired	More active and fun, more easygoing. **I visit because:** • I feel refreshed • I feel rejuvenated	More youthful, cool, bold and innovative in style. **I visit because:** • I feel at ease and can be myself • I feel inspired
Experience Drivers	Curated, Personal, Private, Active, Luxurious	Active, Fun, Stylish	Easygoing, Comfortable, Soulful, Charming	Youthful, Cool, Bold, Innovative

Source: Cinnamon Hotel Management Ltd. (2016); Mirror Business (2016).

views. With such a focus, the nature of the buying decision by consumers has come under closer scrutiny. Companies pay closer attention to the psychological and emotional — as opposed to strictly functional — types of "utility" (Quelch and Jocz, 2008).

Considering this perspective, customer management efforts — to get, keep, and grow customers — have become vital for a company to build a competitive advantage in dealing with the competition. However, the business landscape in the hospitality industry is no longer the same as it used to be decades ago. Digitalization has revolutionized the way travelers choose and determine accommodation during their travels. Travelers' decision-making processes are now being shaped long before they enter a resort or meet a hotel's salesperson. It is a new decision-making moment that plays out a hundred million times a day on mobile phones, laptops, and other wired devices of all kinds (Kotler, Kartajaya and Hooi, 2017).

Bearing that in mind, in order to beat the competition, Cinnamon focuses on improving the rate of bookings by online travel agents (OTAs) and through its own website, along with an increased attention on digital marketing (John Keells Hotels PLC, 2017). Digital initiatives are primarily aimed at gaining the attention of customers from leading markets in Europe, including the United Kingdom, France, and Germany. However, the fast-growing markets of China and India are also keenly eyed by Cinnamon, considering the looming downturn facing the European economy. For example, Cinnamon widely uses the social media web and mobile platforms to target the young, cosmopolitan, and wealthy middle-class Indians (Kulamannage, 2013).

In addition to the use of social media, Cinnamon also undertakes various creative digital initiatives. In the forever-connected, mobile-first world of today, digital initiatives in customer management must aim at creating something interesting and/or engaging, which can be shared by the users (Lecinski, 2014). Below are some tactics that Cinnamon Hotels and Resorts uses to win the heart of digital travelers.

Travel Blogger Conference Asia

As a travel industry participant, Cinnamon is aware that the point of view of every stakeholder whose presence can influence a customer's journey should be heard and valued. In today's digital world, travel bloggers play a strong influencing role in inspiring travelers through their journey accounts and experiences. To this end, Cinnamon hosted the first-ever travel bloggers gathering in 2015. Up to 50 bloggers from across the world came together to discuss the fast-growing travel writer industry trends and how it shaped today's tourists' decision-making. They were taken on a Sri Lankan tour, followed by an insightful discussion of their experiences in Sri Lanka. The conference itself was attended by 250 delegates, including representatives from leading media houses, media officials, hoteliers, and tourism regulatory bodies from all over Asia (Cinnamon Hotels & Resorts, 2015).

Cinnamon Hotels also organized the second Travel Bloggers Conference Asia and Awards 2016, hosting 60 of the best travel and video bloggers globally, with the intention of recognizing the contribution made by bloggers in creating awareness on travel and destinations. With the help of these events, which are able to generate wide attention in the global travel and tourism community, Cinnamon Hotels and Resorts benefits from branding exposure. This also brings attention to Sri Lanka as a paradise for new-age digital travelers (John Keells Hotel PLC, 2017).

Cinnamon Immersive Video

Cinnamon came out with an immersive video on six Cinnamon destinations, which was featured at the World Travel Mart (WTM) in London in November 2015. The first-ever immersive virtual reality video took the viewers on a virtual tour of six Cinnamon destinations, played through virtual reality headsets, and showing Sri Lanka's natural landscapes.

It was the first time that such immersive videos had been released about a hotel chain in Sri Lanka. Technology and innovation in the hospitality industry were increasingly put to good use by Cinnamon when it launched such videos and several other forms of content, such as blogs, social media posts, and mobile advertising (Cinnamon Hotels & Resorts, 2015).

Online Travel Agent Training Module

Cinnamon also launched a specialized Online Travel Agent training module at the WTM in 2015. This was aimed at providing training to OTAs to better serve customers and keep them updated on the changing behaviors of online customers. To popularize the island, the training module contained information on Sri Lanka's natural beauty and travel potential. It also featured Cinnamon Hotels' unique offerings in terms of reimagining the tourism and hospitality scenario in the country. The platform presented in the module linked over 97,000 travel agents globally with the largest eLearning library providing 200 courses through software (Cinnamon Hotels & Resorts, 2015).

Treasure Hunt

With an aim to popularize Sri Lanka in the world, a familiarization drive was planned for 57 travel agents. This was in the form of a treasure hunt across the island, with a series of clues relating to the country's prime destinations to solve. This was done in order to explore the island in a fun, playful way through a treasure hunt. The week-long hunt eventually culminated into a grand event at Cinnamon Bay in Beruwala, where all attendees were given the experience to take a memorable Sri Lanka island tour. The treasure hunt event is organized annually (Cinnamon Hotels & Resorts, 2015).

Through such initiatives, it is clear that Cinnamon actively targets today's tech-savvy travelers and online travel agents from different countries; the company vies for their attention, both online and offline. Not only that, unique experiences that the target audiences earned during the events promoting Sri Lanka and Cinnamon hotels are expected to be spread through word of mouth, as well as online reviews and recommendations.

References

Cinnamon Hotel Management Ltd. (2016). Entry submission document prepared for the SLIM Brand Excellence Award 2017.

Cinnamon Hotels & Resorts (2015). Investor profile. https://london.wtm.com/__novadocuments/321266?v=636205021606900000 [15 February 2018].

Hospitality.lk (2016). Sri Lankan Hotel Performance in 2016, http://hospitality.lk/sri-lankan-hotel-performance-2016/ [16 February 2018].

International Finance Group (2013). Ensuring sustainability in Sri Lanka's growing hotel industry. https://www.ifc.org/wps/wcm/connect/30f331004fddd89eb9d8ff23ff966f85/Mapping+Report++-+Ensuring+Sustainability+in+Sri+Lanka%E2%80%99s+Hotel+Industry.pdf?MOD=AJPERES [16 February 2018].

John Keells Hotel PLC (2017). *Annual Report 2016–2017*. https://www.keells.com/resource/other-group-company-financial-reports-2016_17/KHL_2016_17.pdf [15 February 2018].

Kotler, P, H Kartajaya and DH Hooi (2017). *Marketing for Competitiveness: Asia to the World*. Singapore: World Scientific.

Kulamannage, S (March 2013). JKH's Indian make over. *Echelon*. http://www.stingconsultants.com/wp-content/uploads/2014/08/Cinnamon-hotels-case-study.pdf [15 February 2018].

Lecinski, J (2014). *ZMOT: Why It Matters Now More Than Ever.* https://www.thinkwithgoogle.com/marketing-resources/micro-moments/zmot-why-it-matters-now-more-than-ever/ [16 February 2018].

Mirror Business (July 2016). John Keells to enter boutique hotel market with "Cinnamon White". *Mirror Daily.* http://www.dailymirror.lk/112861/John-Keells-to-enter-boutique-hotel-market-with-Cinnamon-White- [15 February 2018].

Quelch, JA, and KE Jocz, (2008). Milestone in marketing. *Business History Review* 82(Winter), 827–838.

Sri Lanka Tourism Promotion Bureau (2018). Pristine Sri Lanka. *Sri Lanka: Wonder of Asia.* http://www.srilanka.travel/pristine-sri-lanka [15 February 2018].

The Times (October 2012). Sri Lanka: An island paradise. https://www.thetimes.co.uk/article/sri-lanka-an-island-paradise-f20tkrp6bsw [15 February 2018].

CHAPTER 3

HUMAN-CENTRIC PERSPECTIVE: DOING GOOD BY DOING WELL IN THE CONNECTED WORLD

We believe that companies concerned with social problems can obtain greater economic benefits. Citing the words of Bill Gates, "they can do good and do well at the same time". This basic idea also underlines the emergence of the concept of human-centric marketing or Marketing 3.0. This concept asserts that we can combine economic objectives with social objectives in "one package" while gaining a sustainable competitive advantage.

The call for corporations to take a more active role and make greater contributions toward resolving social and environmental problems has long been heard and resonated, although differing in magnitude in various parts of the world. In this case, companies in Asia can provide an additional value to the larger community by addressing three major issues in their business model: sociocultural issues, economic problems, and environmental challenges.

- *Promoters of the social transformation process*
  Here the role of a company is to contribute towards the creation of sociocultural changes in the society. Addressing social challenges should not be viewed only as a tool of public relations or as a way to diffuse criticism of some negative fallout from the company's practices. On the contrary, companies should act as good corporate citizens and deeply address social problems by reviewing their business models and implementing appropriate measures. The key initially is to identify the sociocultural challenges that exist and the possible consequences thereof.

- *Poverty problem resolution catalyst*
  A popular saying goes, "give a man a fish, and he'll eat for a day. Teach a man to fish and he'll eat for the rest of his life". This proverb may also be illustrated through the concept of human-centric marketing and how it contributes to resolving economic problems in Asian countries. The jargon is "from aid to entrepreneurship". Businesses accelerate poverty reduction efforts by empowering communities in the lower income segments, rather than merely doling out relief funds for consumption.

- *Contributors to the resolution of environmental problems*
  Considering the speed and intensity of environmental degradation in today's world, these challenges can be more effectively tackled by linking them to the business model of the company. Businesses are often involved in environmental issues; big corporations produce industrial waste, and regulatory pressures compel them to meet standards and minimize the effect on the environment. Some companies may act under pressure to do what is necessary before being exposed and publicly embarrassed by environmentalists. At the other end are the companies that believe that they could take advantage of this public interest in environmental causes by aggressively marketing their products and services as "green".

In this era of an increasingly connected world, companies find it easier to collaborate with various stakeholders, both online and offline, to achieve business and social objectives. With a human-centric spirit, collaboration is built with an aim to realize transformation that is positive and beyond a mere transactional business relationship. Various economic, social, cultural, and environmental problems that Asian nations battle also present opportunities for creative enterprises to develop novel solutions through their business models. The cases of Thailand's Ampol Food Processing Ltd., Pakistan's Ferozsons Laboratories Limited, and India's Indian School of Business discussed in this chapter will provide examples of how a human-centric perspective can be realized more effectively in this new era by utilizing technology that enables connectivity and collaboration among various stakeholders.

Ampol Food Processing Ltd.

Social and environmental changes brought about by the growth and development of an industry are inevitable. If instead of being viewed as a burden or impediment, these changes are embraced and treated as opportunities to bring positive changes to the surrounding community, such steps are sure to leave a lasting positive effect on the sustainability of a company over the long term. Ampol Food Processing Limited in Thailand is one such company that demonstrates how a firm can establish an authentic and meaningful linkage between its business objectives and social mission. With its human-centric marketing principles, Ampol Food processing has emerged as a responsible business.

Thailand's Food Processing Industry

Thailand is one of the Asian countries that have exhibited significant economic and social developments over the past four decades. During the boom periods of 1960–1996, Thailand's economy grew at an annual average rate of 7.5% and grew at about 5% in the post-Asian financial crisis period (1999–2005). Such a rapid growth created millions of jobs and reduced poverty considerably. Between 2005 and 2015, the average growth of the country slowed down to 3.5% and further down to 2.3% during the period 2014–2016. The country's economy now seems to be on its way to recovery, with growth to reach 3.9 percent in 2017.

With sustained strong growth and rapid poverty reduction, particularly in the 1980s, Thailand moved from a low-income country to an upper-income country within a generation. The level of poverty in the country has reduced considerably over the last 30 years, from 67% in 1986 to 10.5% in 2014, during the high-growth period and improving agricultural prices. However, challenges loomed in the form of some degree of poverty and inequality, along with dwindling economic growth, falling agricultural prices, and natural calamities such as droughts. According to 2014 estimates, up to 80% of the country's 7.1 million poor reside in rural areas. Up to 6.7 million were living within 20% above the national poverty line and are susceptible to falling back into poverty (The World Bank, 2017b). Such socio-economic challenges need to be dealt with by various stakeholders in Thailand, including the government, nonprofit organizations (NGOs), as well as the private sector.

The country's economy now seems to be on its way to recovery, with growth reaching 3.9% in 2017. Thailand's economic growth is mainly attributable to industries and services (see Table 3.1), but it is the agriculture sector that engages a large amount of labor (Table 3.2). The agricultural sector in Thailand is highly competitive, diversified, and specialized, and its exports are quite famous internationally. Rice is the country's most important crop, with some 60% of Thailand's 13 million farmers growing it (SCB Economic Intelligence Center, 2017). Thailand is a major exporter of rice and other agricultural products such as tapioca, rubber, grain, and sugar. It also exports fish and other seafood products.

With growing industrialization in Thailand since the 1960s, the agriculture sector has witnessed a shift toward the food processing industry. This shift has earned considerable government support and is expected to provide greater added value to the economy. Rather than simply exporting agricultural and fishery products in the raw form, producers are encouraged to sell the processed products at higher prices for greater returns.

Thailand's abundant natural resources also lend it a strong comparative advantage to compete with other countries in the global food processing industry. About 80% of the raw materials for the food processing industry in Thailand are supplied domestically. By utilizing its rich natural resources, supported by technological advances and stricter implementation of international standards for food safety and hygiene, Thailand has managed to retain its top spot as the world leader in the food processing industry. The Thai government is also strongly committed to helping food industry players to continuously improve technology and production methods in order to meet international quality standards. These initiatives

Table 3.1: Thailand's gross domestic product by industry sectors (billion bahts).

	2010	2011	2012	2013	2014	2015	2016
GDP at current market prices	10,808	11,307	12,357	12,921	13,204	13,673	14,361
Agriculture, forestry, and fishing	1,137	1,311	1,422	1,462	1,330	1,192	1,197
Mining and quarrying	367	401	483	497	496	430	398
Manufacturing	3,343	3,279	3,457	3,565	3,651	3,753	3,938
Electricity, gas, steam, and air-conditioning supply	264	270	292	314	332	344	406
Water supply; sewerage, waste management, etc.	38	38	42	48	52	55	
Construction	303	307	341	345	337	380	402
Wholesale and retail trade; repair of motor vehicles and motorcycles	1,516	1,571	1,710	1,731	1,797	1,937	2,216
Transportation and storage	607	616	666	694	721	780	1.031
Information and communication	312	350	413	473	498	598	
Hotel and restaurants	222	243	265	291	303	328	682
Financial and insurance activities	581	645	745	871	961	1,044	1,115
Real estate activities	294	306	318	319	325	335	915
Professional, scientific, and technical activities	196	214	259	267	268	260	

(*Continued*)

Table 3.1: (Continued)

	2010	2011	2012	2013	2014	2015	2016
Administrative and support service activities	172	189	228	234	232	237	
Public administration and defense; compulsory social security	640	681	733	766	802	839	874
Education	418	454	503	528	558	587	613
Human health and social work activities	206	219	236	251	271	288	281
Arts, entertainment, and recreation	45	51	60	65	66	70	265
Other service activities	130	142	163	175	182	186	
Activities of households as employers; undifferentiated goods- and services-producing activities of households for own use	18	21	23	23	25	28	28

Source: Asian Development Bank (2017).

have been so successful that processed food exports now exceed primary agricultural exports (Thailand Board of Investment, 2013).

In addition to abundant raw materials, the following factors benefit Thailand's food processing industry:

- *Competitive workforce*: According to the Thai National Food Institute, approximately 800,000 individuals are employed by Thailand's food industry. Numerous training programs launched by the government and assistance from support organizations also help enhance the quality of labor continuously (Thailand Board of Investment, 2013).

Table 3.2: Thailand's labor force (in thousands).

	2011	2012	2013	2014	2015	2016
Labor Force	38,360	38,746	38,661	38,576	38,548	38,267
Employed	37,953	38,324	38,217	38,077	38,016	37,693
Agriculture, forestry, and fishing	12,485	13,164	13,042	12,733	12,272	11,747
Mining and quarrying	50	68	62	69	79	66
Manufacturing	6,001	6,269	6,294	6,393	6,454	6,289
Electricity, gas, water supply, etc.	197	172	191	223	188	217
Construction	2,204	2,335	2,388	2,269	2,282	2,352
Wholesale and retail trade; repair of motor vehicles and motorcycles	6,357	6,195	6,200	6,185	6,176	6,331
Hotel and restaurants	2,923	2,551	2,536	2,568	2,644	2,729
Transportation and storage	1,122	1,087	1,144	1,192	1,216	1,199
Information and communication	231	272	265	248	242	231
Financial and insurance activities	461	493	526	527	539	546
Real estate activities	945	160	165	159	194	186
Others	4,979	5,559	5,405	5,512	5,732	5,799
Unemployed	254	254	282	323	341	377
Unemployment rate,%	0.7	0.7	0.7	0.8	0.9	1.0
Labor force *annual change,* %	-0.7	1.0	-0.2	-0.2	-0.1	-0.7
Labor force participation rate,%	72.1	71.8	71.1	70.3	69.8	68.8
Male	80.3	79.9	80.4	79.3	78.6	77.6
Female	64.3	64.2	63.2	62.0	61.6	60.6

Source: Asian Development Bank (2017).

- *Strong business climate*: Thailand is one of the fastest growing economies in Asia, and it was ranked 46th by the World Bank's Ease of Doing Business 2017 report, up three spots from last year. It is among the top three countries in Southeast Asia (The World Bank, 2017).

- *Hub of Asia*: Thailand also wins in terms of its bilateral and multilateral cooperation, robust infrastructure, vast availability of raw materials, skilled labor, government assistance, and central location among ASEAN member countries, especially considering its proximity to India and China. Furthermore, the launch of the ASEAN Economic Community (AEC) in 2015 will expand the market of Thai food to around 600 million consumers in Southeast Asia (Thailand Board of Investment, 2013).

In 2016, Thailand rose to become the world's 13th leading food exporter, up by two ranks from the previous year. Among other Asian countries, Thailand is at the third spot, following China and India. Today, Thailand's F&B processing industry is one of the most developed in Southeast Asia, with more than 10,000 factories, exporting 50% of the production (Food Ingredients Asia [FI Asia], 2017).

Ampol Food Processing

Ampol Food Processing Ltd. is one of the largest manufacturers and exporters of processed food in Thailand. The company was established in 1988, with an initial capital of around 90 million baht. The company's vision is to produce and distribute domestic agricultural processed goods and products (Ampol Food Processing, 2017a). The company began its business with the export of vegetables and fruits to other countries around the world. Later, the company introduced the first UHT coconut milk under the brand "Chaokoh", which was well accepted and warmly welcomed by the public. It is now a well-known brand in more than 65 countries around the globe.

It was in 1996 that Ampol Food Processing turned its attention to the health beverage market, which was just starting to warm up in response to consumers' increasing preference toward healthy foods and beverages. The company's first batch of health drinks came to the market in the form of Fit C Konjac Drink with 25% fruit juice, Pro-Fit Job Tears Cereal Drink, and V-Fit Young Rice Milk Cereal Drink. These products were developed by the Institute of Nutrition, Mahidol University, followed by the Good-Life range of products, including Seasoning Sauce Less Sodium and Less Saturated Fat Cereal Coconut Milk. Following the success of several products, Ampol Food Processing today has more than 700 employees and records a consistently growing income (Ampol Food Processing, 2017a).

Ampol Food Processing Ltd. owes its success in part to its technologically advanced business processes. The company is certified by ISO 9001: 2000, ISO 14001 on Environmental Friendliness, OHSAS/TIS 18001 with HACCP and GMP on Security and Sanitation from BVQI, together with the certification of the Ministry of Public Health Food and Drug Administrative Committee. All these certifications underline the company's unrelenting focus on product quality and customer service (Ampol Food Processing, 2017a).

A Responsible Company

In business, Ampol Food Processing is not just focused on profits. The company is also stringent when it comes to upholding the principles of social and environmental responsibilities, as reflected in its organizational values and policies. In its "Code of Business Ethics", Ampol Food Processing expressly declares its commitment to society and the environment, as listed in the following three points:

1. Support and help the society and the community in which the company operates, to have better living standards.
2. Take responsibility for ensuring that all standards on environmental protection are met in areas in which the company operates.
3. Provide responsive communications to the surrounding communities who are affected by the company's activities.

Like other companies recognized as responsible entities, Ampol Food Processing also believes that cognizance of social issues and environmental concerns will eventually not only have a positive impact on external stakeholders but also support the long-term sustainability of the company. The idea is in line with the concept of human-centric marketing. This concept asserts that we can combine economic objectives with social/environmental objectives in "one package", making a positive impact on the society and the environment, while also creating a sustainable competitive advantage for the firm.

The call for corporations to play a more active role and make a greater contribution toward resolving social and environmental problems has long been heard and resonated although with differing magnitude in various countries. The different concerns that companies commit to and their initiatives toward those ends vary, depending on the real problems on the ground that exist in different parts of the world. In the case of Thailand, the big shift from agriculture to food-processing industries, while on the one hand added great value to the country's economy, is also capable of causing huge environmental challenges if not managed properly, especially due to increased waste production.

Ampol Food Processing has set to avoid such environmental costs by pledging to do business responsibly and undertake various social–environmental projects, especially in the area of waste reduction. Ampol Food Processing has taken some initiatives that particularly have a positive impact on the society:

- **Magic Box**
  This project stems out of the environmental concerns related to global warming and entails recycling of UHT cartons to transform them into shift boards. These shift boards are assembled into student desks and chairs, which are sent to schools across 76 provinces in Thailand. In addition to reducing waste from cartons, the Magic Box project also supports the improvement of educational facilities in disadvantaged areas.

- **Fuel pellet projects**
  These projects involve the production of fuel pellets from coconut fiber. These wood pellets made from coconut fiber, created in cooperation with the Suranaree University of Technology, become biomass briquettes, which can be used as fuel to produce electricity for factories. This carbon-neutral source of energy not only reduces the cost of electricity costs but also provides a cleaner alternative energy source.

- **Biomass energy projects**
  These projects include producing renewable energy from biomass by employing the gasification technology, in order to produce biogas. Biogas is a clean alternative source of fuel that can provide electric power for machines in Ampol Food Processing factories.

- **Recycling Bank**
  This project creates waste management systems for all kinds of waste in the company. Waste material in various forms is accommodated here for later reuse or recycling. Such a centralized shelter enables easier and more controlled waste management, thereby also reducing its environmental cost.

Saving Thailand from the "Coconut Crisis"

In addition to the initiatives mentioned earlier, there is another landmark project by Ampol Food Processing that has a strong impact on Thailand's agricultural future. This project is not just for its external stakeholders. It is also quite advantageous to Ampol itself, in order to ensure its business sustainability in the future.

As stated earlier, "Chaokoh", the UHT coconut milk is Ampol's flagship product, which is exported to more than 65 countries. The availability of large quantities of fresh coconuts is essential to ensure the supply of raw materials for Ampol Food Processing. The problem is Thailand could potentially experience a "coconut crisis" that may threaten the supply of this commodity.

Thailand, currently a leading producer and exporter of coconuts, could eventually have to begin importing coconuts to meet its domestic demand especially when there are natural calamities that continue to erode supplies. From the way this crisis is unfolding and worsening, Thailand could even go on to become a 100% coconut importing country in the future (Ampol Food Processing, 2017b). This is partly due to the severe drought in the Prachuap Khiri Khan Province, Thailand's biggest coconut plantation region in September 2010. The severe drought destroyed a plantation area of more than 400,000 Rai (one Rai is equal to 1600 km^2 or 0.16 ha).

Even though coconuts can grow in any part of the country in Thailand, sandy neutral soil and scattered rain throughout the year provide the optimum climate for a good yield. However, in Prachuap Khiri Khan, rainfall — which is otherwise sufficient to support good coconut crops — has been relatively scant in recent years. The area is also devoid of any artificial rain, and the low supply of irrigation water has detrimentally affected coconut supply in the area.

In addition to low rainfall, resulting in drought conditions, the situation is further exacerbated by infestations from various plant insects, such as the Coconut hispine beetle and Coconut black-headed caterpillar. According to a farmer, who described the situation in Tubsakae district, Prachuap Khiri Khan Province, "the amount of coconut production has been immensely reduced. Crop yields have gone down to as low as 8,000 nuts from 70,000 nuts. This has resulted in many farmers in this area becoming bankrupt because of the parasitic attack".

In order to address the infestation issues, several local institutions, such as the National Biological Control Research Center, National Research Council of Thailand, Kasetsart University, and Thailand Coconut Farmers Association — together with Ampol Food Processing — have encouraged farmers to educate themselves about the protection of coconut yields from infestations. This is important as most farmers in the area have a lack of knowledge and are clueless about the approaches to deal with insect outbreaks and protect their yields.

Thus, in order to save Thailand from a looming coconut crisis, these agencies have collaborated to conduct research and implement educational programs for the farmers in areas with potential outbreaks. Although such efforts will not produce immediate results, the educational initiatives will equip the local coconut farmers with knowledge to deal with infestations and also serve to improve their confidence in dealing with crisis situations.

These efforts and initiatives present fine examples of human-centric marketing or Marketing 3.0 practice, which has been undertaken by Ampol Food Processing. By recognizing and addressing several social and environmental issues at such a vast scale and with sizeable impact, Ampol Food Processing has won strong recognition for its various activities. It won the 2015 Asia Responsible Entrepreneurship Award (AREA) in the Green Leadership Award category from Enterprise Asia. AREA, an award for entrepreneurs in Asia, recognizes and honors Asian businesses that work toward sustainable and responsible entrepreneurship in several categories, such as Green Leadership, Investment in People, Health Promotion, Social Empowerment, SME CSR, and Responsible Business Leadership (Enterprise Asia, 2017).

References

Ampol Food Processing (2017a). *Chairman Message*. http://www.ampolfood. com/en/about01.php [2 October 2012].

Ampol Food Processing (2017b). *APF for Thai Agriculture*. http://www. ampolfood.com/en/social05.php [29 December 2017].

Asian Development Bank (2017). *Key Indicators for Asia and the Pacific 2017*. Mandaluyong City: Asian Development Bank. https://www.adb.org/sites/ default/files/publication/357006/tha.pdf [30 September 2017].

Enterprise Asia (2017). *Reduce Waste by Using 3R: Ampol Food Processing*. https: //enterpriseasia.org/area/projects/ampol-food-processing-ltd/ [29 December 2017].

Food Ingredients Asia [FI Asia] (2017). *Thailand's Food Industry Set to Prosper*. https://www.figlobal.com/asia-thailand/visit/news-and-updates/thailands-food-industry-set-prosper [25 September 2017].

SCB Economic Intelligence Center (2017). Healthy Baking Thai Organic Foods have Healthy Growth Potential (6 February 2017). *Bangkok Post*. http://dx. doi.org/10.1094/cfw-62-2-e85

Thailand Board of Investment (2013). *Thailand's Food Industry*. Bangkok: Thailand Board of Investment.

The World Bank (2017a).*Doing Business in 2017: Equal Opportunity for All*. Washington: World Bank Group.

The World Bank (2017b). *The World Bank in Thailand*. http://www.worldbank. org/en/country/thailand/overview [2 October 2017].

Ferozsons Laboratories Limited

In 2016, more than 1,300 under-five children with diarrhea died each day around the world. In Pakistan, 9% of under-five children lost their lives to diarrhea. Ferozsons, a Pakistan-based pharmaceutical company along with PanTheryx, has successfully created a special food for dietary use, which is safe for adults and under-five children with diarrhea. With this innovative product, the deaths reportedly caused by diarrhea have gone down and Ferozsons has also improved its margins by solving a social health problem.

Ferozsons Laboratories Limited: A Company Overview

Founded in 1956, Ferozsons Laboratories Limited is one of the first pharmaceutical manufacturing companies in Pakistan, which operates businesses in the fields of gastroenterology, hepatology, cardiology, and oncology, as well as having an emerging presence in endocrinology and the mother and child health space. It seeks to attain market leadership by putting patients first and utilizing every opportunity to earn trust and credibility from patients, Ferozsons has succeeded in distributing, selling, and co-manufacturing reputable products by maintaining exclusive agreements with several international partners, such as the Bagó Group, Biofreeze, BioGaia, Boston Scientific, GE Healthcare, Gilead, Kadmon, and PanTheryx (see Table 3.3 for detailed information about the company's milestones).

Pakistan's Healthcare Challenge

Pakistan — the country where Ferozsons is headquartered — faces considerable challenges in the health sector. According to UNICEF, in 2016, almost 8% of all deaths of under-five children in the world were caused by diarrhea (UNICEF, 2018). That amounts to nearly 1,300 children dying due to diarrhea every day — or 480,000 every year. According to data from Ferozsons Laboratories Limited (2018), in Pakistan, one in every ten children dies before turning five years, making pediatric diarrhea the second most major cause of death in under-five children (Table 3.4).

Even though the disease represents a major pediatric health challenge in the country, it is preventable and treatable. It can be prevented through safe drinking water and adequate sanitation and hygiene. Besides causing deaths, diarrhea is also a major factor in triggering malnutrition in under-five children. According to the World Health Organization (WHO, 2018), there are nearly 1.7 billion cases of childhood diarrhea each year across the world.

The global diarrhea health issue, accompanied by the associated water, sanitation, and hygiene problems, is a pressing challenge for gov-

Table 3.3: Ferozsons' Milestones

Year	Events
1956	Established as one of the first national companies to set up a pharmaceutical manufacturing plant in Pakistan
1960	Listed on the Karachi Stock Exchange with an authorized capital of PKR10 million and became one of the first national pharmaceutical companies to do so
1961	Started work on two new manufacturing facilities dealing in the production of soap chemicals and glycerin
1963	Launched "Dew" bath soap in the local market, along with Pakistan's first detergent soap "707", which became one of the most preferred products in the category
1964	Became a preferred supplier to foreign missions and international organizations, including the United Nations, the Government of USA, and British Crown Agents
1988	Launched Cimet (Cimetidine), which became one of the top-selling antiulcerants in the country
1991	Entered into an agreement with Procter & Gamble, Pakistan, for the manufacturing of its famous brand, Vicks VapoRub
1995	Collaborated with Laboratories Orgasynth of France to launch Diabetron, an oral antidiabetic treatment
2002	Entered into strategic partnerships with two major international companies Curatis Pharma GmbH, Germany, and Bago Group, SA, Argentina, for import and marketing of a range of biological products related to oncology and liver disease
2006	Signed an agreement for a joint venture with the Argentinian group Bago to establish BF Biosciences Limited, Pakistan's first biopharmaceutical manufacturing company
2008	Acquired distribution rights for Boston Scientific, Inc. USA, the world's leading manufacturer of interventional medical devices
2014	Partnered with Gilead Sciences, Inc., to bring Sovaldi, the miracle hepatitis C Virus cure, in the country — Pakistan became the first country to implement the access program under which thousands of patients receive the drug
2016	Signed an agreement with GE Healthcare FZE and became the channel partner to market and sell value segment medical devices in Pakistan
2017	Partnered with PanTheryx Inc., United States, to exclusively market the breakthrough nutritional product for childhood diarrhea DiaResQ®, which is featured in the Innovation Countdown 2030 report jointly issued by PATH, USAID, and NORAD

Table 3.4:   Estimates of Cause of Child Death due to Diarrhea in Pakistan.

Years	Total neonatal deaths	Total post-neonatal deaths	Neonatal deaths due to diarrhea	Post-neonatal deaths due to diarrhea	Under-five deaths due to diarrhea	Neonatal death rate from diarrhea (per 1,000 live births)	Post-neonatal death rate from diarrhea (per 1,000 live births)	Under-five death rate from diarrhea (per 1,000 live births)	% Neonatal deaths due to diarrhea	% Post-neonatal deaths due to diarrhea	% Under-five deaths due to diarrhea
2000	266,517	228,120	3,792	61,019	64,811	1	14	15	1	27	13
2001	260,345	224,016	3,793	57,735	61,528	1	13	14	1	26	13
2002	256,088	219,348	3,769	54,675	58,444	1	12	13	1	25	12
2003	252,542	214,741	3,752	51,970	55,722	1	12	12	1	24	12
2004	250,106	212,210	3,741	49,831	53,573	1	11	12	1	23	12
2005	248,634	210,421	3,728	48,059	51,788	1	10	11	1	23	11
2006	250,224	209,170	3,705	46,089	49,794	1	10	11	1	22	11
2007	252,630	206,549	3,683	44,818	48,501	1	9	10	1	22	11
2008	256,442	201,501	3,648	43,887	47,535	1	9	10	1	22	10
2009	260,457	197,785	3,618	43,216	46,834	1	9	9	1	22	10
2010	263,406	197,745	3,587	42,158	45,745	1	8	9	1	21	10
2011	264,557	195,660	3,576	40,573	44,149	1	8	8	1	21	10
2012	263,859	194,159	3,543	38,637	42,179	1	7	8	1	20	9
2013	260,764	193,818	3,477	39,570	43,047	1	7	8	1	20	9
2014	257,937	183,907	3,379	37,381	40,760	1	7	8	1	20	9
2015	253,261	178,688	3,265	35,441	38,706	1	7	7	1	20	9
2016	248,449	175,131	3,138	33,724	36,862	1	6	7	1	19	9

Source: UNICEF (2018).

90

ernments in developing countries. This is also creating opportunities for businesses to provide solutions to this social health issue. One of the concepts in Marketing 3.0 is how a company can earn a profit by solving social problems around them. In Pakistan, Ferozsons — as a leading pharmaceutical and medical technology company — has seemingly embraced the concept of Marketing 3.0 for not only undertaking product innovations and collaborations but also working toward the resolution of social problems. This has resulted in significant profits for the company.

In this connectivity era, a company should also be collaborating with other partners to increase its effectiveness in developing products or services. Each company and country has different resources and specialization. By undertaking collaboration with other companies that have different specializations, a better, low-cost product or service can be developed. Ferozsons has benefited with several such collaborations, one of which involves a partnership with PanTheryx, a medical nutrition company.

Collaboration to Solve Healthcare Problem

PanTheryx is a US-based medical nutrition company co-founded by Tim and Bimla Starzl while they were conducting deep statistical research on pediatric diarrhea in developing countries such as India. The company's major work was directed toward creating an inexpensive therapeutic treatment based on the bovine colostrum, which could be administered orally and reach the gastrointestinal tract to help in treating diarrhea. With a focus on the research, development, and commercialization of such immunological products, PanTheryx offers medical foods for the dietary management of people with special medically determined nutrient requirements, food for special dietary use that addresses the dietary needs of children with infectious diarrhea, and dietary supplements to support intestinal health. Using technology in this modern era, PanTheryx has become the world's premiere producer and supplier of bovine colostrum, which is transformed into a nutrient with powerful benefits for human health (PanTheryx, 2018).

Ferozsons and PanTheryx worked together to launch DiaResQ® in Pakistan to reduce the high number of deaths due to diarrhea. DiaResQ® provides nutritional oral rehydration to the diseased as it is rich in nutrients such as zinc, which helps in intestinal repair. Most children suffering from diarrhea in Pakistan are also reported to be malnourished. Per a study from the *British Medical Journal (BMJ)*, DiaResQ˚ was shown to be effective in the treatment of acute diarrhea among children that is caused by most of the common pathogens (*Pakistan Observer*, 2017). This treatment is considered safe for children as young as one-year-old. It is not a drug or antibiotic; it is a food for special dietary use that works with the body's natural immune response to support digestive health and rapidly restore the normal intestinal function. Hence, it provides fast and safe relief from diarrhea. Besides reducing the number of deaths from diarrhea, DiaResQ˚ also improves the overall quality of life for families across Pakistan.

In Reimagining Global Health, a report from the Innovation Countdown 2030 initiative selected DiaResQ˚ as one of the 30 leading healthcare innovations that have great promise to transform global health by 2030. DiaResQ˚ also helps accelerate progress toward the new health targets proposed in the United Nations Sustainable Development Goals (PanTheryx, 2015). This potential is aptly identified by Ferozsons as an answer to a healthcare challenge in Pakistan. This also proves that a mutual collaboration can create improvement in the overall quality of life for the community while also increasing the sustainability of the company.

References

Ferozsons Laboratories Limited (2018). *Ferozsons Launched DiaResQ.* https://ferozsons-labs.com/ferozsons-launched-diaresq/ [8 August 2018].

Innovation Countdown 2030 (PATH). The IC2030 Report, Reimagining Global Health. http://ic2030.org/wp-content/uploads/2015/07/ic2030-report-2015.pdf [8 August 2018].

Pakistan Observer (April 2018). Ferozsons partners with PanTheryx to introduce DiaResQ. https://pakobserver.net/ferozsons-partners-with-pantheryx-to-introduce-diaresq/ [8 August 2018].

PanTheryx (2015). *PanTheryx's Product, DiaResQ®, Selected as a Leading Healthcare Innovation with Great Promise to Transform Global Health.* https://diaresq.com/buzz/diaresq-selected-as-leading-healthcare-innovation/ [8 August 2018].

PanTheryx (2018). *About PanTheryx.* https://pantheryx.com/our-story/ [8 August 2018].

UNICEF (2018). *Diarrhoeal Disease.* https://data.unicef.org/topic/child-health/ diarrhoeal-disease/ [8 August 2018].

World Health Organization (2018). *Diarrhoeal Disease.* http://www.who.int/ news-room/fact-sheets/detail/diarrhoeal-disease [8 August 2018].

Indian School of Business

The students of a business school, which has a strong concern for social and environmental issues, are expected to apply their business skills to tackle the issues and contribute to social and environmental improvements. ISB works as the academic partner for the Goldman Sachs 10,000 Women Entrepreneurs Certificate Program, which conducts management education for "under-served women", to create thousands of women entrepreneurs around the world. ISB was established with a clear social mission to provide a top-notch professional educational service. This is an example of the implementation of the Marketing 3.0 concept, which advocates the shift from just satisfying and addressing customers' needs toward making the world a better place through value-based marketing.

The Indian School of Business at a Glance

The Indian School of Business (ISB) is a postgraduate business school in India, which has a vision to be an international top-ranked, research-driven, independent management institution that grooms future leaders for India and the world. The top eight competitors of ISB are Indian Institute of Management Calcutta (IIMC), Indian Institute of Management Indore (IIM-I), Faculty of Management Studies (FMS), Stanford University, Birla Institute of Management Technology (BIMTECH), Princeton University, Great Lakes Institute of Management, and Indian Institute of Management Udaipur (IIM-U) (Owler, Inc., 2018).

ISB was founded to fulfill the needs of visionary young leaders who not only understand the developing economies but also present a global perspective of leadership. ISB is a nonprofit organization and is funded entirely by private corporations, foundations, and individuals from around the world who believe in its vision (Indian School of Business, n.d.[a]; Table 3.5).

Table 3.5:   ISB's milestones.

Year	Events
1995	The idea for the School was conceived.
	An ISB Board was formed.
1997	An association with The Wharton School and The Kellogg School of Management was established.
1998	A MoU was signed with the Government of Andhra Pradesh for the setting up of ISB in Hyderabad.
1999	ISB foundation stone-laying ceremony held.
2000	An association with the London Business School was formed.
2001	• The first class of Post Graduate Program in Management was started in the campus, with 128 students. • The first student Exchange Program was commenced. • The Centre for Executive Education (CEE) was inaugurated. • ISB was inaugurated by the former Prime Minister of India, A B Vajpayee. • The first Centre of Excellence, Wadhwani Centre for Entrepreneurship Development (WCED), was inaugurated.
2003	• The Artist-in-Residence program was launched. • The Business and Arts program was launched.
2004	• ISB Women's Initiative was launched. • The Centre of Analytical Finance (CAF) was inaugurated. • The first Global Social Venture Competition started. • ISB K-HUB was launched.
2005	The Centre for Global Logistics and Manufacturing Strategies (GLAMS) was launched.
2006	• The Srini Raju Centre for Information Technology and the Networked Economy (SRITNE) was inaugurated. • The first Global Logistics Summit was held. • The Thomas Schmidheiny Chair on Family Business and Wealth Management was instituted.
2008	• ISB became the first Indian B-school to be ranked in the top 20 in the Global Top MBA rankings by Financial Times, London. • The Centre for Leadership, Innovation, and Change (CLIC) was inaugurated. • The Indu Centre for Real Estate and Infrastructure was inaugurated.

(Continued)

Table 3.5: *(Continued)*

Year	Events
2009	• The Centre for Emerging Markets Solutions (CEMS) was inaugurated. • The Case Development Centre was launched. • Post Graduate Program in Management for Senior Executives (PGPMAX) was launched.
2010	• ISB signed an MOU with MIT Sloan School of Management. • ISB Mohali foundation stone-laying ceremony was held. • ISB inked an MoU with the Fletcher School, Tufts University, for the Bharti Institute of Public Policy.
2011	• The Young Leaders Program was launched. • The Fellow Program in Management was launched. • ISB inked an MoU with the Wharton School for the "Max Institute of Healthcare Management". • ISB became South-Asia's first business school to earn AACSB accreditation.
2012	• ISB commenced the Post Graduate Program in Management at Mohali. • ISB launched MFAB — Management Program for Next Generation Leaders of Family Businesses.
2017	ISB received the EQUIS accreditation and re-accreditation from AACSB.
2018	ISB launched the Executive Fellow Program in Management.

Source: Indian School of Business (n.d.[b]).

Integrating Business and Social Mission

Education is very important for every country in the world, whether it is a developed or developing country. Education-related problems greatly affect the development of a country, and India is no exception. India faces several education problems, including the high cost of education. Universities, professionals, and technical education have very high costs (*Bee Bulletin*, 2017). Some business people use the privatization vehicle to establish private universities and to make profits.

The Indian School of Business, as a nonprofit organization, tries to solve educational problems and challenges in India by utilizing knowledge and expertise to engage with the business community, the government, and the society. It seeks to contribute to the welfare and development of the community at the local, national, and global levels. Through its educational programs and collaboration with other institutions, ISB strives to solve educational problems and help in the economic development of India.

Given the cost and income levels, some parents are unable to provide their children with high-level education. Parents with limited education funds prefer to prioritize education for their sons as they think that boys will be on their side for a longer period than girls who will marry and live with their husbands' families. In fact, women education is no less important than male education. Women should be provided with an equal right and equal access to education because they have a big potential to build their career and future prospects. In the short and the long terms, they can improve the economy of their families and contribute to the nation's economic growth.

ISB is the academic partner for the Goldman Sachs 10,000 Women Entrepreneurs Certificate program in India, which provides management education to "under-served women". Through this global program, more than 10,000 women from around 56 countries are given practical business education, business advice, and avenue for networking. The graduates are expected to take part or even set up a sustainable business so that their welfare condition can be improved. Over the years, the program has been upgraded and expanded, and it provides online education in collaboration with Coursera (Goldman Sachs, 2018). This improvement gives an opportunity to women in distant locations who cannot attend the program, due to geographical constraints.

This institution was established with a strong social mission, and it also provides a top-notch professional educational service. ISB is the first business school in South Asia to receive the Association to Advance Collegiate Schools of Business (AACSB) accreditation. Moreover, since 2008, ISB has consistently featured in the Global Top MBA rankings. In 2017, ISB was listed as one of the leading business schools across the world. This ranking is published annually by The Financial Times (FT). Leading the top-ranking institutions across the country, ISB has secured the 27th position in global rankings (*India Today*, 2017).

ISB's business model is in line with the concept of Marketing 3.0 that discusses the shift from just satisfying and addressing customers' needs toward making the world a better place through value-based marketing (Kotler, Kartajaya and Hooi, 2010). ISB provides a good example of how organizations can apply their business skills to remain sustainable and solve social problems at the same time.

References

Bee Bulletin (January 2017). Issues and challenges of Indian education. https://beebulletin.com/issues-challenges-indian-education/ [15 August 2018].

Goldman Sachs (2018). *Goldman Sachs 10,000 Women Launches Online Education Partnership with Coursera.* https://www.goldmansachs.com/citizenship/10000women/news-and-events/coursera-launch.html [14 August 2018].

Indian School of Business (n.d.[a]). *About ISB.* https://www.isb.edu/about-isb [14 August 2018].

Indian School of Business (n.d.[b]). *Net Impact Club.* https://www.isb.edu/net-impact-club [14 August 2018].

India Today (January 2017). FT Ranking 2017: World's best MBA institutes ranked, ISB leads from India. https://www.indiatoday.in/education-today/news/story/ft-ranking-2017-958065-2017-01-31 [14 August 2018].

Kotler, P, H Kartajaya and I Setiawan (2010). *Marketing 3.0: From Products to Customers to the Human Spirit.* Hoboken, NJ: Wiley.

Owler, Inc. (2018). *ISB's Competitors, Revenue, Number of Employees, Funding and Acquisitions.* https://www.owler.com/company/isb [14 August 2018].

References

CHAPTER 4

MARKETING 4.0: MOVING FROM TRADITIONAL TO DIGITAL

Technology is not only revolutionizing the way industry players conduct business but also changing the pattern of customers' decision-making processes. In the preconnectivity era, a customer's journey to buying a product or service was relatively simpler and shorter and could be described with help of the 4A process: Aware, Attitude, Act, and Act Again. This funnel-shaped process demarcates various points in the customer journey: customers become aware of a brand, develop an attitude toward it — of like or dislike — based on which they decide whether to purchase it and also consider if it's worth a repeat purchase. The shape of the funnel represents a decline in the number of customers as they move from one stage to another — people who like the brand would naturally be aware of it; those who buy like it; and those who buy again would have already purchased it once.

Today, in the era of connectivity, the customer journey is no longer a straightforward funnel-like process. The changes brought about by the technology-driven connected world calls for redefining the customer path. The customer path has now transformed into a 5A process: Aware, Appeal, Ask, Act, and Advocate.

In the "Aware" phase, customers are passively exposed to a long list of brands due to their prior experience, marketing communications, and/or recommendation from others. Then, they tend to process the messages they are exposed to, creating either a short-term memory or an amplifying long-term memory and eventually becoming attracted only to a short list of brands. That marks the "Appeal" stage. Eventually, prompted by their curiosity, customers actively search for more information on the brands they are attracted to from their friends and family, from the media, and/or directly from the companies. This represents the "Ask" stage. Reinforced by more information, customers decide to "Act". They buy a particular brand and interact deeper with a brand through purchase, usage, and/or service processes. With technological developments, a purchase can now be made online or through mobile and doesn't necessarily need a face-to-face interaction. Over time, customers may develop a strong sense of loyalty toward a brand, which can be reflected from retention, repurchase, and ultimately recommendation to others. This is the "Advocate" stage. In the connectivity era, advocacy is a major attribute of the customer journey that companies should leverage, since positive advocacy and recommendations from personal acquaintances or opinions posted online are emerging to be the most trusted form of information.

The changing pattern of customers' decision-making processes as mentioned above demands companies to rethink their traditional marketing practices. In this transition and adaptation period to the digital economy, a new marketing approach is required to guide marketers in anticipating and leveraging on the disruptive technologies while maintaining the human-centric approach of Marketing 3.0. We call this approach 4.0. Marketing 4.0 is a marketing approach that combines online and offline interaction between companies and customers. In the digital economy, digital interaction alone is not sufficient. In fact, in an increasingly online world, offline touch is a powerful tool to strengthen customer engagement. These are lessons we can learn, for example, from GO-JEK (Indonesia), Alibaba (China), and Carousell (Singapore).

GO-JEK

GO-JEK started out as a modest application-based transportation service provider in Indonesia, but today it is one of the few unicorn tech startups in the country that has expanded its reach in various service sectors — from food delivery to logistics and grocery shopping. GO-JEK recorded massive business growth within the first few years in business, which caught the attention of several online and offline businesses. In response to GO-JEK's high-speed growth, some online transportation companies operating in Indonesia are trying to consolidate. Considering the competitive business environment, GO-JEK must develop a creative business strategy with an integrated online-offline approach.

GO-JEK: The Beginning and Massive Growth

Established in 2010 as a motorcycle ride-hailing phone service, Indonesia's GO-JEK has evolved into an on-demand mobile platform and a cutting-edge app, providing a wide range of services, such as transportation, logistics, and food delivery, as well as many other on-demand services. On the back of strong growth and rapid progression, the company is further advancing the development of mobile payment (e-money) solutions for its app users.

GO-JEK was founded by Indonesian businessman Nadiem Makarim — a Harvard Business School alumnus who gave up a lucrative multinational consultant job to establish the company. Originally, the company was set up as a fleet of motorcycle drivers to offer rides to passengers on their motorbikes, take their couriers, or deliver food. This idea didn't kick off immediately; the company only got the much-needed jumpstart after being launched as an app in 2015. The app became an instant hit among the Indonesian users who began to use the service for rides. It has expanded its reach to dozens of cities across Indonesia. Since then, there has been no looking back for GO-JEK, which has now expanded its services to offer everything from food delivery, logistics, and grocery shopping to doorstep masseur and beauticians. Today, the GO-JEK army of motorists with their chic green jackets can be easily spotted on Indonesia's streets, fetching riders and bringing Indonesians their food, packages, and groceries.

This massive growth in GO-JEK's app users, fleet of drivers, and services did not go unnoticed by investors. In October 2015, the company obtained an undisclosed amount of funding from Sequoia Capital and other investors. Over the next 1 year, it officially achieved unicorn status after raising USD1.2 billion through a funding round led by the Chinese Internet behemoth Tencent (Pratama, 2016). Google, Singapore's Temasek, and the Chinese online platform Meituan-Dianping also reportedly participated in a new funding round for GO-JEK in January 2018 (*CNBC*, 2018). Some of GO-JEK's extraordinary milestones since its establishment until its massive success in Indonesia are listed in Table 4.1.

Backed by a strong injection of funds, GO-JEK is well positioned to strengthen its business and support its services by making strategic acquisitions. In February 2016, the company announced the acquisition of C42 and CodeIgnition, two engineering startups from India. In December 2017, it acquired three local startups — Kartuku, Midtrans,

Table 4.1: GO-JEK's milestones.

Year	Events
2010	Established by Nadiem Makarim in 2010 with a fleet of 20 motorcycle riders
2014	Investors' interest stirred due to Uber's strong rise in the online transportation business
January 2015	• Launched its smartphone applications for Android and iOS users, with a basic service portfolio, including transportation, courier, and shopping, in Jakarta and adjoining satellite cities • Amassed a rider base of 800 motorcyclists
March 2015	Expanded to Bali with 300 riders
April 2015	• Launched Go-Food services • Expanded to Bandung, West Java
May 2015	• Malaysia's Grab entered Indonesia • GO-JEK gathered 3,000 riders
June 2015	• Expanded to Surabaya, East Java
August 2015	• Held a massive recruitment drive in Jakarta • Gathered 30,000 riders • Expanded to Makassar
September 2015	Launched Go-Mart
October 2015	• Obtained an undisclosed amount of funding from Sequoia Capital and other investors • Launched Go-Glam, Go-Box, Go-Massage, and Go-Clean services

(*Continued*)

Table 4.1: *(Continued)*

Year	Events
December 2015	• Expanded to Yogyakarta, Medan, Palembang, Semarang, and Balikpapan • Indonesia's Minister of Transportation, Ignasius Jonan, banned all online transportation services • The ban was lifted 1 day later and GO-JEK resumed normal operations • Launched Go-Tix, an event ticket booking service
January 2016	Enabled ride-hailing via Line app
February 2016	• Announced its acquisition of C42 and CodeIgnition, two engineering startups from India • Amassed 200,000 riders
March 2016	A large-scale protest by Jakarta's taxi drivers against online transportation services
April 2016	Introduced Uber-like cars with the launch of Go-Car
May 2016	• Announced collaboration with Blue Bird, a major taxi company in Indonesia • Expanded to Malang, Solo, and Samarinda
July 2016	Launched Go-Auto services
August 2016	Officially became a unicorn after obtaining another USD550 million investment
May 2017	Raised a new funding of USD1.2 billion led by Chinese Internet giant Tencent
December 2017	• Acquired three local startups — Kartuku, Midtrans, and Mapan — to boost Go-Pay
January 2018	Google, Singapore's Temasek, and Chinese online platform Meituan-Dianping reportedly participated in a new funding round for GO-JEK

Source: Pratama (2016), Reuters (2017), Russel (2017), and CNBC (2018).

and Mapan — to strengthen Go-Pay, its mobile payment services (*Reuters*, 2017). Such strategic acquisitions bolster its backend operations and organic growth. Through a significantly expanded userbase, GO-JEK has successfully branched into a variety of services other than the original online ride-hailing transportation. Box 4.1 illustrates the diverse portfolio of services from GO-JEK.

Today, Jakarta-based GO-JEK is the largest Indonesian unicorn. As of February 2018, the company is valued at about USD5 billion. The additional funds and backing of well-known investors, including Google, Singapore's Temasek Holdings, and Chinese technology giant Tencent Holdings, will help GO-JEK better compete in Southeast Asia's cut-throat market, where incentives to drivers and passengers are used to build loyalty (Daga, 2018).

Box 4.1: One App for All Your Needs

- Go-Ride: A two-wheeler transportation solution that provides speed and ease of booking and destination with a maximum distance of 25 km

- Go-Car: A service to get comfortable four-wheel transportation for individuals and groups

- Go-Send: An instant courier service for documents or items with a maximum weight of 20 kg, wherein a GO-JEK driver functions as a courier

- Go-Mart: An instant shopping service to buy goods from a variety of stores that are already available in the app with the help of GO-JEK drivers

- Go-Shop: A shopping service that makes it easy for customers to buy any item from any store within the same area

- Go-Food: A solution that allows application users to order food and beverages from the restaurants listed on the app. These are purchased and delivered by GO-JEK riders

- Go-Med: A service for customers who want to buy drugs, vitamins, and other medical supplies from licensed pharmacies that are already available on the GO-JEK app

(Continued)

Box 4.1: *Continued*

- Go-Tix: Solutions to find interesting activities, concerts, as well as purchase movie tickets

- Go-Box: A service that allows GO-JEK app users to order delivery trucks, from pick-ups to single-axle box trucks, to ship items from the place of origin to the destination

- Go-Massage: A professional masseur service that lets the users order doorstep massage services by entering data, the time of reservation, and duration

- Go-Clean: A professional solution to get cleaning services for homes, apartments, or shops

- Go-Glam: Various top-notch beauty services supported by top beauty professionals

- Go-Auto: Auto care, maintenance, and emergency repair services for customers' vehicles

- Go-Pay: An e-payment solution that can be used to make payment for any transactions through the GO-JEK application. As a next step, Go-Pay is being developed for a wider set of transactions, including bills payment

Source: Go-Jek (2018).

Competition with Conventional and Digital Players

The emergence of GO-JEK and other online ride-hailing apps has certainly led to a disruption in the land transportation industry, especially in Indonesia. As the company began to gain a massive business penetration, unfavorable reactions began to pour in, decrying the existence of online transportation apps. Somewhat surprisingly, a kneejerk reaction was also demonstrated by some in the "ojek" driver community, who failed to view GO-JEK as a lucrative opportunity to boost their income and efficiency. For conventional taxi drivers, GO-JEK understandably posed a mounting threat with the rise of Go-Car. To counter the rise of such online ride-hailing apps, and particularly GO-JEK, detractors staged large-scale protests not only in Jakarta but also in other big cities.

In order to defuse the looming tension, the Indonesian government made several attempts to mediate and issue revised regulations to provide a win–win solution for both parties. One of the new regulations that can allow transportation companies to lower the tariff is expected to stir healthier competition among conventional and online transportation companies.

GO-JEK, on its part, has attempted to join hands with conventional taxi operators in Indonesia by launching a new service called Go-Blue Bird — named after the largest taxi operator in Indonesia, Blue Bird. Under the collaboration, users can book a Blue Bird taxi through the GO-JEK app and Blue Bird taxi drivers can also obtain orders from passengers looking for a ride. This partnership represents a long-term commitment by Blue Bird and GO-JEK to jointly innovate and provide the best services to their community, as well as improve the well-being of drivers (Marzuki, 2017). As a mutual benefit, Blue Bird taxi drivers have the opportunity to acquire new passengers, while GO-JEK can also offer an additional fleet of transport to its users. Such a win–win collaboration could defuse the tensions previously occurring on the part of taxi drivers.

GO-JEK's close competitors would certainly be fellow app-based online transport businesses. Malaysia's Grab and Uber are its main rivals who are stirring competition in Indonesia's online ride-hailing transportation industry. Grab is a Malaysia-based technology company that offers ride-hailing and logistics services through its app in the home country and neighboring Southeast Asian nations such as Singapore, Indonesia, Philippines, Vietnam, Thailand, Myanmar, and Cambodia. As a regional player, Grab enjoys deeper pockets to fund its expansion in the region. Uber is a peer-to-peer ridesharing, food delivery, and transportation network company headquartered in San Francisco, California, with operations in 633 cities worldwide.

In March 2018, Grab announced the acquisition of Uber's Southeast Asia operations. This game-changing deal represented the biggest-ever acquisition in this space in Southeast Asia. Under the terms of the acquisition, Uber's ridesharing and food-delivery businesses will be integrated into Grab's existing transportation and payment platform. This combined entity aims to be the number one online-to-offline (O2O) mobile platform and one of the major companies handling food delivery in Southeast Asia (Grab, 2018).

Integrating Online and Offline Campaign

To counter the increasingly fierce competition, GO-JEK focused its attention on the very diverse range of services it offers to its customers and the ways to meet their everyday needs. All GO-JEK services (e.g., Go-Ride, Go-Car, Go-Box, Go-Send, Go-Mart, Go-Food, Go-Auto, Go-Med, and Go-Busway) provide solutions to problems faced by people in all major Indonesian cities, be it the ease of finding an Ojek (the motorcycle taxi) to wade through the infamous traffic snarls or a cab at the doorstep, delivering items easily and securely or buying groceries sitting at home. Unfortunately, not many users are aware of all these features.

In fact, customers need to be "aware" of a service, show interest (appeal) in the benefits it offers, know more information (ask) about the service or product, and then take an "action" (download the app, opt to use a service). If they are "wowed" by the experience, they would often voluntarily share their stories with those around them (advocate). This is the 5A model (aware-appeal-ask-act-advocate) that represents a new customer path in the digital age (Kotler, Kartajaya and Hooi, 2016).

This is why, GO-JEK continues to intensively work on introducing new services or enhancing the existing ones with new features that appeal to the current and new customers. To target those who have not yet downloaded the GO-JEK app and build awareness, the company carries out massive publicity drives through various media — online and offline. It uses various attractive offers, especially discounted rates, to stir the interest of potential customers and customer education to make the existing users of the GO-JEK app try out the diverse range of services on offer.

As a technology company, GO-JEK takes full advantage of the digital media to introduce its services and benefits. However, as its competitors — especially Grab — are also proactive in campaigning on the digital and social media, it is re-emphasizing the importance of the word-of-mouth strategy (WOM) in order to attract the attention of its target audience. The main keys are story and placement.

GO-JEK uses two types of story-based contents in its creative campaigns to stimulate WOM response from the audience: authentic stories told by drivers and stories that contain the elements of fun and emotion. In the "For My Country" campaign, for example, the company presents an inspiring and emotional story from seven GO-JEK drivers. The company also encourages customers to create and share their personal stories (user-generated content) through social media. Funny experiences and inspirational and touching anecdotes from customer interactions with GO-JEK drivers are widely shared on various social media platforms. Many of these stories become viral that keeps the interest of people in GO-JEK alive while also educating potential customers about the app and its services. In addition to stories, placement is also a key determinant of the success of campaigns in the digital and social media because each social media has different characters and audiences (Wulandari, 2016).

Despite a strong online presence through various campaigns on digital media, GO-JEK continues to utilize traditional media. The company invests heavily in outdoor advertising through billboards and print media, mostly advertorials, to boost its offline campaign. Below-the-line advertising is also conducted to engage target customers, especially in fairs, festivals, and music events.

Along with its digital media campaigns, GO-JEK pays special attention to the importance of creativity in campaigning. For example, some billboards installed by the company do not apply the rule of thumb commonly used by other advertisers. Instead of using attractive pictures and flashy words, it actually uses texts like those in classified print ads. Such creative execution of traditional campaigns then creates word of mouth on social media, triggered by audiences documenting such unique billboards and sharing the messages. Such integration of online and offline campaigning helps the company acquire new customers and stand its ground against competitors, who are also aggressively expanding their reach in Indonesia's lucrative tech-savvy user market.

References

CNBC (January 2018). Google and Singapore's Temasek are coming in as new investors in Indonesia's Go-Jek, sources say. https://www.cnbc.com/2018/01/18/google-and-singapore-temasek-to-invest-in-go-jek-says-report.html [27 March 2018].

Daga, A (February 2018). Go-Jek raises $1.5b as ride-hailing market heats. *Jakarta Globe.* http://jakartaglobe.id/business/go-jek-raises-1-5b-as-ride-hailing-market-heats-up-sources/ [27 March 2018].

Go-Jek (2018). *About.* https://www.go-jek.com/about/ [27 March 2018].

Grab (2018). Grab Merges with Uber in Southeast Asia. *Press Center.* https://www.grab.com/sg/press/business/grab-merges-with-uber-in-southeast-asia/ [27 March 2018].

Kotler, P, H Kartajaya and I Setiawan (2016). *Marketing 4.0: Moving from Traditional to Digital.* New Jersey: John Wiley & Sons, Inc.

Marzuki, Y (April 2017). Blue Bird, Go-Jek collaborate to launch Go-Blue Bird. *Digital News Asia.* https://www.digitalnewsasia.com/business/blue-bird-go-jek-collaborate-launch-go-blue-bird [27 March 2018].

Pratama, AH (August 2016). Go-Jek: A unicorn's journey. *Tech in Asia.* https://www.techinasia.com/how-go-jek-became-unicorn [27 March 2018].

Reuters (December 2017). Indonesia's Go-Jek acquires three companies to boost payment services. https://www.reuters.com/article/us-gojek-indonesia/indonesias-go-jek-acquires-three-companies-to-boost-payment-services-idUSKBN1E9088 [27 March 27, 2018].

Russel, J (May 2017). Indonesia's Uber rival Go-Jek raises $1.2 billion led by Tencent at a $3 billion valuation. *Tech Crunch.* https://techcrunch.com/2017/05/03/go-jek-tencent-1-2-billion/ [27 March 2018].

Wulandari, D (December 2016). Strategi WON Go-Jek. *Mix.* http://mix.co.id/marcomm/brand-insight/marketing-strategy/strategi-wom-go-jek [28 March 2018].

Alibaba

Alibaba has become a major global electronic marketplace (GEM) in the world in just a few years. Its business, which is initially focused on e-commerce, has now expanded its wings to various services, such as financial technology, logistics, and education. This development is inseparable from the initiatives of its founder, Jack Ma, who continues to strive to innovate by utilizing the omnichannel approach (online-offline integration).

Alibaba Group and E-Commerce in China

The rapid expansion of e-commerce in China has become a worldwide phenomenon and formed a significant business network, for both foreign and domestic firms. Being the biggest market in the world, China's e-commerce market has increased by 50% annually since 2011 and is expected to continue to soar up to USD1 trillion by 2019 (The Canadian Trade Commissioner Service, 2017). The reasons for the rapid growth of China's e-commerce market are the size and the growth of the country's economy; the relatively rudimentary standing of its traditional retail sector when the Internet first reached the country; and government policies on investments, infrastructure, and taxation that favoured the progress of e-commerce and related services. (International Trade Centre, 2016).

One of the leading e-commerce players in China is Alibaba.com. In fact, currently, it has become one of the largest e-commerce businesses in the world. This has enabled many people to make buying and selling transactions easily. Alibaba.com is one of the core businesses of the Alibaba Group. Currently, Alibaba Group (2018a) has the following businesses:

1. Taobao Marketplace (China's largest mobile commerce destination)
2. Tmall (China's largest third-party platform for brands and retailers)
3. AliExpress (a global retail marketplace)
4. Alibaba.com (a leading wholesale marketplace for global trade)
5. 1688.com (a leading online wholesale marketplace in China)
6. Alimama (a leading online wholesale marketplace in China)
7. Alibaba Cloud (one of the world's top three IaaS providers)
8. Cainiao Network (a logistics data platform operator)
9. Ant Financial Services Group (a financial service provider focused on serving small and micro enterprises and consumers)

Led by Jack Ma, the Alibaba Group was established in Hangzhou in 1999 by 18 people. The company's founders promoted a belief that the Internet would level the playing field by enabling small enterprises to utilize innovation and technology to grow and compete more effectively in the local and the global economies. Several years after its founding, a number of investors, including SoftBank, were attracted by the growth of the Alibaba Group and began injecting capital. Large funds from these investors were used to develop other companies under the Alibaba Group.

Alibaba's Business Growth

Innovations and ideas from Alibaba were not always fully supported. When Jack Ma wanted to set up his own online payment system, which is now known as AliPay, many people doubted and ridiculed him. However, Jack Ma's enthusiasm and optimism are exemplary. He finally proved that his online payment business can be successful, and it has since become one of the biggest payment platforms in the world. In 2016, AliPay became the most frequently used payment platform in China (Ernst & Young & DBS, 2016). In May 2018, the Ant Financial Services Group, the operator of Alipay, raised USD10 billion in funding from a clutch of global and local investors (CNBC, 2018).

With the continued expansion of the Alibaba Group, it began to invest in many other companies, especially in Asia. Some of them are Tokopedia and Lazada (Indonesia), BigBasket (India), and Ele.me and Cainao (China) (Millward, 2017). Table 4.2 shows the business development of the Alibaba Group.

Alibaba achieved its success through effective marketing strategies (segmentation, targeting, and positioning) augmented by creative marketing tactics such as product development, pricing, distribution, and marketing communications. Through these activities, Alibaba has won a long-term relationship with its suppliers and buyers, which is beneficial to the company. Not stopping there, Alibaba continues to innovate to capture opportunities that arise from technological developments and changes in customers' behavior. Interestingly, Alibaba did not only focus on online businesses, but it also began to make acquisitions of conventional retailers. Alibaba realized that now the company must be able to provide integrated experiences for customers, both online and offline.

Omnichannel Marketing Strategy

The group's e-commerce business continues to show significant growth. In 2017, an estimated 1.66 billion people worldwide purchased goods online, and the number continued to increase (Statista, 2017). The dynamic changes in public spending patterns also pose a challenge to retail entrepreneurs. Many breakthroughs are made by companies. One of these is conducting online-to-offline (O2O) marketing. This means retail entrepreneurs using online channels to encourage consumers to go to

Table 4.2: Alibaba group's milestones.

Year	Events
1999	Alibaba Group was founded by Jack Ma and Alibaba.com launched in Hangzhou. Subsequently, the Alibaba Group launched a China marketplace 1688.com for domestic wholesale trade.
2000	The Alibaba Group raised USD20 million from an investor group led by SoftBank.
2003	Taobao Marketplace was launched.
2004	Alipay, a third-party online payment platform, was launched.
2005	The Alibaba Group formed a strategic partnership with Yahoo!.
2006	The Taobao University program was launched, providing e-commerce training and education to buyers and sellers.
2007	Alimama monetization platform was launched.
April 2008	Tmall, a dedicated platform for third-party brands and retailers, was launched.
Sep 2008	Alibaba Group R&D Institute was launched.
2009	Alibaba Cloud Computing was founded.
2010	Juhuasuan (a sales and marketing platform for flash sales), AliExpress, and Mobile Taobao were launched.
2011	The Alibaba Group established Alibaba Foundation.
2012	The Alibaba Group officially launched its mobile social networking app, Laiwang (currently known as DianDianChong).
Oct 2014	Ant Financial Services Group, a related company of Alibaba Group that operates Alipay, was formally established.
Oct 2014	Taobao Travel became the independent platform Alitrip, currently known as Fliggy.

Source: Alibaba Group (2018b)

offline channels. However, this method poses many challenges, including a difficult-to-track return on investment of channels, rising costs, and disjointed customer experience (PWC, 2017). Meanwhile, businesses that only focus on online strategy also face tough challenges in the future. Jack Ma, the founder of Alibaba Group, said, "In the future, pure e-commerce will be reduced to a traditional business and replaced by a new concept of retail — the integration of online, offline, logistics and data across a single value chain" (Weinswig, 2017).

One of Jack Ma's innovations to deal with this problem is to use omnichannel marketing in the Alibaba Group. The difference between O2O and omnichannel marketing is that O2O only focuses on marketing, whereas omnichannel marketing covers a broader spectrum of marketing and operational processes, including promotion, channels of distribution, and customer service and fulfillment. Omnichannel strategies are intended to improve operational efficiency, customer experiences, and overall profitability. These strategies are in line with the reports published by PWC (2017). The reports highlight nine trends in the retail and the consumer product sectors in China. One of the trends is "new retail", namely the increasing maturity of businesses in using data analytics and omnichannel technologies to create a seamless consumer journey between online and offline channels.

One example of the application of "new retail" in Alibaba is the integration of offline loyalty programs with Tmall, which allows customers to claim benefits wherever they shop and enables brands to capture end-to-end consumer data. Another activity carried out by the Alibaba Group to realise Jack Ma's hopes for the "new retail" model is the aggressive acquisition spree of numerous types of traditional Chinese retailers, including Bailian Group (the largest brick-and-mortar retailer by store numbers in China), Sun Art Retail Group (China's top hypermart operator), Yintai Group (high-end retailer), Suning Commercial Group (Electronics retailer), and Hema Xiansheng (high-tech supermarket) (*The Straits Times*, 2017).

With these acquisitions, Alibaba offers a new shopping experience to its customers. For example, consumers who shop at Hema Xiansheng can make purchases directly in the store using the mobile app. Henceforth, the items will be sent within 2 hours. Various forms of this kind of convenience are offered to consumers to make them more loyal to the company.

To maintain its excellence in the digital era, various innovations need to be continued by the company, notably by integrating online and offline initiatives. The following are examples of other breakthroughs made by Alibaba:

- Alibaba set up Taobao University as a platform for e-commerce training and education. Taobao aims to make buyers and sellers their loyal partners. The Alibaba Group also focuses very much on the sound evaluation system, in which both sellers and buyers can give feedback on business transactions that appear on each other's platform (website), hence providing better and clearer references for the next business partner.

- The group expanded its business to various fields, such as financial technology, education, and logistics. Various programs that integrate these services will provide total solutions to customers.

References

Alibaba Group (2018a). *Our Business.* https://www.alibabagroup.com/en/about/businesses [4 August 2018].

Alibaba Group (2018b). *History and Milestone.* https://www.alibabagroup.com/en/about/ [4 August 2018].

The Canadian Trade Commissioner Service (2017). *An Introduction to E-Commerce in China.* http://thegrinlabs.com/wp-content/uploads/2017/05/China-eCommerce-Guide2016.pdf [2 August 2018].

CNBC (2018). China's ant financial raises 10 billion at 150 billion valuation. *CNBC.* https://www.cnbc.com/2018/05/29/chinas-ant-financial-raises-10-billion-at-150-billion-valuation.html [4 August 2018].

Ernst & Young & DBS (2016). *The Rise of FinTech in China.* https://www.ey.com/Publication/vwLUAssets/ey-the-rise-of-fintech-in-china/$FILE/ey-the-rise-of-fintech-in-china.pdf [4 August 2018].

International Trade Centre (ITC) (2016). *E-Commerce in China: Opportunities for Asian Firms.* Geneva: ITC.

Millward, S. (December 2017) Alibaba's biggest investments in 2017. *Business Standard.* https://www.business-standard.com/article/companies/alibaba-s-biggest-investments-in-2017-117122600203_1.html [4 August 2018].

PWC (2017). How retailers and brands are innovating to succeed in the most dynamic retail market in the world. *PWC.* https://www.pwccn.com/en/retail-and-consumer/publications/total-retail-2017-china/total-retail-survey-2017-china-cut.pdf [2 August 2018].

Statista (2017). Number of digital buyers worldwide. *Statista.* https://www.statista.com/statistics/251666/number-of-digital-buyers-worldwide/ [4 August 2018].

The Straits Times (November 2017). Alibaba invests $3.9b in china's top grocer. https://www.straitstimes.com/business/companies-markets/alibaba-invests-39b-in-chinas-top-grocer [4 August 2018].

Weinswig, D (2017). Alibaba's new retail integrates e-commerce, stores, & logistics: Is this the next gen of retail? *Forbes.* https://www.forbes.com/sites/deborahweinswig/2017/04/14/alibabas-new-retail-integrates-e-commerce-stores-logistics-is-this-the-next-gen-of-retail/ [4 August 2018].

Carousell

Carousell is a Singapore-based e-commerce company that has successfully expanded globally, especially in Malaysia, Indonesia, and Taiwan. In view of Asian consumers' shifting shopping behavior in the digital world, the market potential of this sector appears to be promising. That said, the competition that Carousell faces is also getting stiffer. The entry of other online marketplaces in the Asian market, especially in Singapore, is presenting consumers with a lot of choices. Moreover, traditional retailers have also jumped into the game by establishing an online presence. Considering the scenario, Carousell must continue to innovate in order to create a superior customer experience and drive engagement.

E-Commerce in Singapore

Singapore is one of the most technologically and economically advanced countries in Southeast Asia. With mobile penetration reaching 149.8% (Department of Statistics of Singapore, 2016) and Internet penetration reaching 81.3% (Internet World Stats, 2016), it can be concluded that the majority of Singaporeans are digital consumers and inevitably Singapore is a land of digital talents. The survey conducted by the IMD World Competitiveness Center reinforces the idea by putting Singapore at the top position in terms of digital competitiveness. The ranking measures the ability of economies to explore and adopt digital technologies that transform government practices and business models (Leong, 2017).

Therefore, it is hardly surprising to see a plethora of technology companies flocking to Singapore, either to tap on the digital users or to benefit from the digital resource pool. A number of major global e-commerce players, including Rakuten from Japan and Taobao from China, have chosen Singapore as the location of their regional headquarters. A high level of technology adoption in the community, strategic location, conducive business climate, and strong IT infrastructure are some of the factors contributing to Singapore's position as an ideal test bed for the launch of new e-commerce services before further rollout in the region (Lu, 2015).

There are various types of e-commerce businesses in Singapore, but the majority are business-to-consumer (B2C) platforms, for example, Qoo10, Lazada, Rakuten, and Omigo. Carousell, in contrast, is an example of a consumer-to-consumer (C2C) type of e-commerce. Other types of e-commerce transactions, such as business-to-business (B2B) and business-to-government (B2G), are also growing in Singapore, but not as fast as the B2C or C2C types of transactions — a trend observed in almost all major e-commerce markets.

E-commerce in Singapore is well developed, in terms of transactions, as well as facilities such as payment methods and logistics for the delivery of goods and services. Table 4.3 lists some examples of popular online businesses in Singapore operating in different industries.

Despite the advanced e-commerce infrastructure and digital-savvy consumers, the volume of online transactions in Singapore is not too high. Kearney and CIMB ASEAN Research Institute (2015) reported that online sales account for approximately 4% of total retail sales in Singapore. Nevertheless, one can expect the growth of online shopping sales and the development of the e-commerce industry in the country. Analysts predict that by 2020, transactions conducted by consumers in Singapore will mostly be online (Choudhury, 2014). As for businesses, the emergence of e-commerce is being viewed as an intelligent solution to overcome business constraints that are commonly encountered in Singapore, namely high rental costs and limited manpower. This rising trend of the combination of demand and supply is what makes the future of e-commerce in Singapore very promising. This vast potential and opportunity were recognised by three students from the National University of Singapore (NUS) — Siu Rui Quek, Lucas Ngoo, and Marcus Ta — when they decided to establish SnapSell, which was ultimately rebranded into Carousell.

Carousell: Early Challenges and Business Expansion

Carousell is an online consumer-to-consumer (C2C) marketplace for buying and selling new and second-hand goods. The idea originally surfaced when the three founders carried out a pitch at the Start-up Weekend Singapore event in March 2012. They won the competition. While winning the competition further reinforced their idea, it also caused a dilemma to the founders. They found themselves at a crossroad between continuing their university education and taking the risks to support SnapSell, as that would mean having no jobs or income for a

Table 4.3: Some popular online businesses in Singapore.

Year of Market Entry	Firms	Industry
2007	PropertyGuru	Property
2009	Reebonz	Luxury products and services
2010	Smooch the Label	Fashion
	Qoo10	B2C marketplace
	Clozette	C2C marketplace
	Luxola	Beauty and cosmetics
	Groupon	Marketplace for daily deals
	Deal.com.sg	Marketplace for daily deals
2011	MyRepublic	Telecommunications
	NoQ Store	Books
	Bellabox	Cosmetics/Groceries
	Vanity Trove	Beauty
	RedMart	Groceries
2012	iCarsclub	Car rental marketplace
	Kwerkee	Home and lifestyle
	Zalora	Fashion marketplace
	Carousell	C2C marketplace
	Food Panda	Food
2013	Taobao	B2C and C2C marketplace
	HipVan	Home furnishing and fashion
	Omigo	B2C marketplace
2014	Rakuten	B2C marketplace
	Lazada	B2C marketplace
	ShopBack	Marketplace for daily deals
2015	Honestbee	Groceries

Source: Lu *et al.* (2015), Tay (2015), and Tegos (2015).

certain period. Finally, in May 2012, the three decided to leave the comfort zone and concentrate on developing the business (Yin, 2016).

The start-up began operations with a capital of SGD20,000, which was sourced from the savings of the founders. The next milestone was in the form of some additional fund injection from their university, the National University of Singapore (NUS) and the Government of Singapore. During the early period, the founders decided to rebrand SnapSell to Carousell. The new name was picked with the intention to provide greater emotional appeal to consumers.

In the early days, Carousell experienced slow growth. In fact, the startup even witnessed times of just half a dozen registrations in a day, while the active user base during this period hovered at around 400 people. Such statistics were hardly encouraging for Carousell, a technology startup where things are expected to move swiftly, especially in the early stages. Nevertheless, the founders of Carousell did not give up. They worked to get detailed feedback from the active users. A variety of marketing communications and customer relationship management programs were launched to encourage the active users to revisit the app and recommend it to the people around. Slowly but surely, the number of users began to grow.

However, the growth had not been able to make money for the company. To attract a wider base of users, Carousell began to offer several complimentary services, for which collaboration with various parties, especially investors, became necessary. In early 2013, Carousell announced an official collaboration with Singapore Press Holdings (SPH) STClassified. The partnership was mutually beneficial. Items listed at the Carousell app for sale would also be placed on STClassified marketplace, helping Carousell users reach a larger pool of prospective buyers and allowing STClassifieds to reach out to the mobile-savvy young generation (Yin, 2016). The next collaboration with *SPH* Magazine was in the form of developing a mobile app called SheShops Marketplace, to sell fashion and beauty items. The partnership with *SPH* Magazine became an important turning point in Carousell's journey. The startup steadily gained ground, as it further strengthened its positive image. This makes it easier to cooperate with investors.

In November 2013, Carousell earned an injection of USD1 million from Rakuten, Golden Gate Ventures, 500 Startups, and several angel investors. The seed funding allowed the company to strengthen its expansion in the Southeast Asian market, especially in Malaysia as it is geographically the closest (Yap, 2013). The Southeast Asian market was indeed encouraging. Fierce competition made it inevitable for Carousell to begin expanding its customer base outside the domestic market, especially when the demographic potential outside Singapore is much greater. A widespread penetration of smartphones in Malaysia made e-commerce opportunities in the country look promising in the future.

In November 2014, Carousell announced an investment of USD6 million from Sequoia India. Subsequently, the Singapore-based startup launched its services in the second country outside Singapore: Taiwan. In fact, the founders were even optimistic that Taiwan could eventually become their number one market. With a larger population, as much as five times the population of Singapore, and a highly mature e-commerce ecosystem, Taiwan was a very attractive market. Moreover, Taiwanese people were considered some of the world's biggest spenders on the mobile platform (Horwitz, 2014).

Indonesia was the third target market in Carousell's expansion bid outside the domestic market, beginning in January 2015 (Yin, 2016). Although demographically Indonesia had a huge population — ranked fourth in the world, after China, India, and the United States — its Internet usage was still not as advanced as that of Singapore. Moreover, millions of Indonesians did not have a bank account. Another difficulty was the geographical condition in the form of an archipelagic state that made the delivery of goods difficult compared with that in Malaysia or Taiwan. Regardless of the challenges, a growing Internet and mobile penetration in Indonesia presented great opportunities for online retailers like Carousell.

Delivering the Digital Experience

Although the market potential in Southeast Asia is huge, Carousell has to deal with strong competition from other e-commerce players and brick-and-mortar retailers, which, in the case of the latter, means possessing a retail presence. This fierce competition gives strong motivation to Carousell to continue to innovate towards improved service quality and customer experience.

Following the so-called pure play approach, Carousell is the only online company with no brick-and-mortar presence. From the beginning, the company has remained focused on developing a superior digital customer experience. The development and the improvement of the app are continuously undertaken since its launch in 2012 at the Singapore Apple App Store. Along with the development of smartphone technology, sellers wishing to use Carousell marketplace need to spend only a small amount to put their products up. It's as simple as just taking pictures of goods via smartphones, doing some editing for desired effects, and adding descriptions and prices, and their products are already showing up in the marketplace.

To further improve the experience, Carousell seeks to make buyer–seller interactions more effective and engaging. This has come in the form of a feature in the app, which allows buyers to follow their favorite sellers. The existing buyers get notifications when a seller puts up new products for sale. Buyers can also like and comment on sellers' posts, and if buyers find the product information interesting and useful to them, they can also easily share it through social media such as Facebook, Twitter, Pinterest, and Google Plus (Yin, 2016).

To expand its reach to more users, at the end of 2015, Carousell launched a web platform. This new platform allowed sellers and buyers to make transactions through their desktops. A larger screen display than the smartphone garnered positive response from some users, especially facilitating the buyers in finding the products they need.

Not only positioning itself as a marketplace, Carousell is also trying to build an online community to enhance the social relationship between buyers and sellers. Through the Carousell Group feature launched in January 2016, users can join groups according to their interests. This has resulted in the formation of various communities, involving fans of certain brands, such as "Apple Fans" and "Nike Sports Club". Some users also form groups based on the same interests, such as "Boards Games Club" and "Coins and Currency Collectors" (Yin, 2016). With this kind of communitization strategy, the loyalty of users is expected to increase, which is likely to be followed by an increase in recommendations that will arise through interactions among community members.

Going Omnichannel?

Carousell's success in developing digital experience found its own challenge with the development of an omnichannel trend. Omnichannel or

O2O (Online to Offline) is a hot topic in the Asian retail market at the moment, and it will only get hotter as new technologies and innovations accelerate the opportunity for retailers. O2O Commerce is about connecting the online digital world with the offline world by integrating Internet-connected devices. The goal is to optimize customer experience across all touch points, both online and offline.

Online channels can indeed facilitate transactions and offer more diverse product choices and practicality in the purchase process. However, the offline touch is still useful in providing greater emotional appeal to customers. In a report titled *Digital Disconnect in Customer Engagement*, Accenture claims that human interactions remain a vital component of customer satisfaction, even in the digital age. This holds true for all regions, including the Asia-Pacific (Hont *et al.*, 2016).

As a case in point, e-commerce companies in Asia are beginning to realize the importance of integration between online and offline experience for shoppers. Even though rising e-commerce adoption is encouraging, a hard-hitting business reality is that a large section of Asian customers is still wary of online payment methods. Moving beyond the conventional cash-on-delivery model, Zalora, a Singapore-based online fashion retailer, offers a unique payment method. The websites provide a cash-on-collection option, a concept that has already gained popularity in Taiwan and Japan. Collaborating with some convenience store chains, Zalora gives its customers an option of picking up and paying for their items at an outlet of their choice (Kotler, Kartajaya and Hooi, 2017).

Commenting on this integration of online and offline interaction, Achyut Kasireddy former Managing Director of Fonterra Brands (South West Asia) says, "differentiating online and offline is really a false distinction. It's much more important to get the offline and the online working together seamlessly" (The Economist Corporate Network, 2015).

Carousell itself has started using offline promotion programs to attract users. An example is the activities the company undertook to gain greater penetration in Malaysia, its first foreign market. Carousell's team in Malaysia went to bazaars and flea markets and ran various roadshows to introduce the mobile marketplace to the target customers (Yin, 2016). Those offline approaches complemented their online marketing communications through various social media — such as Facebook and Twitter — as well as digital magazines.

Tighter competition — both from e-commerce companies and traditional retailers who began to venture online — has made Carousell keep its guards up at all times. Innovations must continue to create a more memorable experience for customers, both online and offline.

Let us wait to see what kind of further surprises will come from the young founders of Carousell.

References

Choudhury, AR (September 2014). More Singaporeans turn to virtual stores for shopping. *The Business Time*. http://www.businesstimes.com.sg/top-stories/more-singaporeans-turn-to-virtual-stores-for-shopping [5 September 2017].

Department of Statistics of Singapore (2016). *Latest Data*. http://www.singstat.gov.sg/statistics/latest-data#8 [5 September 2017].

Horwitz, J (December 2014). Carousell's entry into Taiwan presents big opportunities and big challenges. *Tech in Asia*. https://www.techinasia.com/carousells-taiwan-entry-means-islands-ecommerce-industry [5 September 2017].

Hont, R, D Klimek and S Meyer (2016). Digital Disconnect in Customer Engagement. *Global Consumer Pulse Research,* Accenture.

The Economist Corporate Network (2015). *Asia's Digital Disruption: How Technology is Driving Consumer Engagement in the World's Most Exciting Markets.* The Economist Intelligence Unit.

Internet World Stats (2016). *Singapore: Internet Statistics and Telecommunications.* http://www.internetworldstats.com/asia/sg.htm [5 September 2017].

Kearney, AT and CIMB ASEAN Research Institute (2015). *Lifting the Barriers to e-Commerce in ASEAN*. https://www.atkearney.com/documents/10192/5540871/Lifting+the+Barriers+to+ecommerce+in+ASEAN.pdf/d977df60-3a86-42a6-8d19-1efd92010d52 [5 September 2017].

Kotler, P, H Kartajaya and DH Hooi (2017). *Marketing for Competitiveness: Asia to the World*. Singapore: World Scientific Publishing.

Leong, G (May 2017). Singapore tops new ranking of digital competitiveness. *The Straits Times*. http://www.straitstimes.com/business/economy/singapore-tops-new-ranking-of-digital-competitiveness [5 September 2017].

Lu, LW (2015). *E-Commerce in Singapore: How It Affects the Nature of Competition and What It Means for Competition Policy*. Singapore: Competition Commission of Singapore.

Tay, D (February 2015). Here are the top 10 most well-funded internet companies in Singapore. *Tech in Asia*. https://www.techinasia.com/top-10-most-funded-internet-companies-singapore [5 September 2017].

Tegos, M (October 2015). 14 Popular ecommerce sites in Singapore. *Tech in Asia*. https://www.techinasia.com/14-popular-ecommerce-sites-singapore [5 September 2017].

Yap, J (November 2013). NUS Alumni Received Million Dollar Investment to Expand Carousell Mobile App. *Vulan Post*. https://vulcanpost.com/1832/nus-alumni-received-million-dollar-investment-expand-carousell-mobile-app/ [5 September 2017].

Yin, WK (2016). *Carousell: How to Thrive Amid Fierce Competition?* Singapore: Nanyang Technopreneurship Case Center.

Part II

Marketing Is Creating?

Marketing is about creating, enhancing, communicating, and delivering value to companies' stakeholders. To develop a consistent value, strategic marketing concepts must be implemented. This involves the analysis of internal competitive conditions and the external environment in order to formulate a strategy to position an organization's brand, products, and services in the minds of its stakeholders. Next, the strategy needs to be translated into a set of tactics, which are more down to earth and practical.

In summary, there are three dimensions of marketing architecture: strategy, tactic, and value. First, you must explore the market by performing segmentation. You then need to target certain segments. You can target one, two, several, or all segments within the market, depending on your competitive situation and competitive advantage. Then, you must position your company in the customer's mind: what exactly are your offerings?

However, positioning needs to be supported by solid differentiation, which afterward can be translated into the marketing mix (product, price, place, and promotion). Finally, the selling tactics, the only element that "captures the value" back from the market, is the transaction-oriented element. Brand should be created as the *value indicator*, and the value of the brand should be enhanced continuously through the service strategy. Last but not least comes process, the *value enabler*. No matter how strong you are in the other eight elements, they will not be effective unless you have good processes and systems.

All of the above refer to the practices used in Legacy Marketing — a concept developed when connectivity among various stakeholders involved in the process of value creation was not as strong as today. However, a lot has changed over the past two decades. The digital technology revolution that is fast unwrapping in the world and, especially in Asia, makes the vertical Legacy Marketing approaches not entirely relevant anymore. This is why the marketers of today need to understand how the entire concept of marketing has undergone a fundamental transformation, considering that the world has become more connected and horizontal. This has led to the birth of what we call New Wave Marketing. The following chapters demonstrate examples of how some Asian companies practice New Wave Marketing strategies, tactics and values.

CHAPTER 5

MARKETING STRATEGIES FOR VALUE EXPLORATION

In the legacy era, marketing strategy is known to consist of three main elements: segmentation, targeting, and positioning. Segmentation can be defined as the way companies look to market their products and services creatively. We call segmentation a "mapping strategy" as it primarily deals with mapping the market in order to determine segments.

Having mapped the market and segmented it into groups of potential customers with similar characteristics and behaviors, companies can then choose segment(s) to target more effectively. This is called targeting. Targeting is defined as a means of allocating corporate resources effectively by choosing the right target market(s). We term targeting as a "fitting strategy" because it entails adjusting the company's resources with the needs of the target market.

The last element of the marketing strategy is positioning. Positioning is the way by which a company occupies a position in the minds of its customers. Positioning is also described as a "being strategy" as it helps establish an identity among its customers. After mapping a market for segments and adjusting its resources in line with the target segment, the company must define the image it wants to build to achieve credibility in the eyes of its target market(s).

That's how companies would typically develop a marketing strategy in an era when the world had not yet been hit by the wave of horizontalization that arises from advances in information technology. However, technological advancements have dramatically changed customer behavior, thus demanding a new business approach. The cases presented in this chapter — Korea's Acer, Japan's Table for Two, and Philippines' Century Pacific Food — show how the three elements of marketing strategy have undergone a fundamental shift in the digital era: segmentation has evolved into communitization, targeting has become confirmation, and positioning has transformed into clarification.

Acer

Acer is a Taiwan-based multinational company with a presence in over 160 countries in the world. Over the years, Acer has transformed from a hardware company to an advanced software and service-oriented company. In an effort to improve customer experience and earn customers' loyalty in the digital era, Acer strives to optimize the communitization strategy, both offline and online. This case attempts to discuss the types of communities utilized by Acer, which is on a mission to "break barriers between people and technology".

Technology and Horizontal Era

Technology firms occupy a central position in advanced economies. They drive economic growth, spark productivity gains, and trigger the creation of new industries and innovative products. Many will agree that technology firms are distinguished from others in their emphasis on technological activities. Many such companies continue to make huge investments in the advancement of their technological prowess. The biggest motivation is the need to maintain and improve competitive position, reduce costs, and respond to customer desires. When competition gets tighter, product innovation must always be followed by targeted promotional activities.

In addition to effectively promoting their products, technology companies must also be able to communicate with consumers using means and ways that are in line with the times. In this horizontal era, consumers should no longer be perceived as kings, but as "partners" or "friends". In essence, customers are no longer objects, but subjects that need to be involved more actively in a company's value-creation process. Hence, there is a shift from segmentation to communitization, targeting to confirmation, positioning to clarification, among others (Kotler, Kartajaya and Hooi, 2017).

Acer has been quick in acknowledging changes in customer interaction patterns in this horizontal era. In addition to product innovation by utilizing the best technology, it also has a communitization strategy that works well to ensure that its customers maintain their loyalty toward the brand. Amidst a rising tendency of customers to share information and influence decision making within their social circle and beyond, the emergence of online and offline communities is a phenomenon that must be closely observed and utilized by marketers.

Acer: History and Milestones

Stan Shih, a Taiwanese entrepreneur who studied electronic engineering, with his wife and four other partners, founded a company called Multitech in 1976. Multitech — Acer's predecessor —was formed with a capital of USD25,000. In 1980, Multitech introduced the Dragon Chinese-language terminal, which won Taiwan's top design award. In 1983, the company introduced an Apple clone and its first IBM-compatible PC. Eventually, Multitech set up AcerLand, Taiwan's first computer franchise, in 1985. In 1987, the company's name was changed to Acer, which was derived from a Latin term, meaning sharp, acute, able, and facile. The company was listed the following year on the Taiwanese Stock Exchange (Slob, 2005).

Now, Acer is one of the largest technology companies in the world, and its products include desktops, laptops, tablets, smartphones, displays, tablets, and smart cameras. Acer's top product lines include gaming PCs and accessories, marketed under the Predator and Nitro brands (Acer, Inc., 2018a). In a bid to develop technology products which continue to meet the evolving market needs, Acer no longer concentrates only on hardware; it also develops software and services related to information and communications technology (ICT; see Table 5.1).

Table 5.1: Acer's milestones.

Year	Events
1976–1986	Commercialized microprocessor technology
1987–2000	Created a brand name and globalized
2001–2007	Transformed from manufacturing to services
2008–2013	Enhanced its worldwide presence with a new multibrand strategy
Beyond 2014	Transforming into a hardware + software + services company

Source: Acer Group (2018).

Acer's Communitization Strategy

In a world that is becoming increasingly horizontal, consumers and marketers are more aligned. Consumers are no longer willing to be treated as a target or recipients of passive marketing. They now want to be positioned as people with a more active role. This calls for *segmentation* to be turned into *communitization* and, consequently, *targeting* should become *confirmation*. This has happened at Acer.

The company has developed what it calls the "Acer Community" — a peer-to-peer social support platform that aims to connect Acer users and "make the most of its products". Acer users can share information, reviews, and cool tips and tricks on how to use its products and services, with the company acting as an occasional provider of knowledge articles, moderation services, and topic assistance. For customers, the Acer Community is a useful online resource, acting as a low-cost, low-maintenance solution fielded by the company to solve customer concerns. The community also succeeds in today's digital era that is dominated by the millennial generation, which tends to demand solutions to their problems instantly and trusts their friends more than any communication from companies. Thus, the community plays an important role for Acer. In fact, data in 2012 shows that up to 70% of the users in the Acer Community visit the platform looking for answers, whereas the remaining 30% spend time in the community to help others. A community survey by Acer also shows that up to 40% of visitors find the community useful in finding solutions and answers to their problems. Up to 10% of people are unable to find solutions to their problems in the community and contact the official Acer Support department (Speyer, 2018).

In today's New Wave era, segmentation does not work in the way it used to traditionally; businesses, therefore, need to engage in what is known as "communitization", which relates to viewing consumers as a part of a community where people care for each other, share common purposes, live by a set of common values, and also share some identity. Communities can be created by the company (by design) or can be formed by virtue of an initiative coming from consumers (by default) (Kotler, Kartajaya and Hooi, 2017). In pursuing communitization, a marketer must understand the general model of the community that may be formed. According to marketing professors Susan Fournier and Lee (2009), there are three forms of community affiliation: pools, hubs, and webs.

Pools

A pool is a type of community that is created most naturally, as a result of members coming together due to shared values and/or interests in pursuing a common activity. The bond between the members of such a community, however, is not too strong. Examples of such communities are schools and universities. The similarity of activities between students makes them feel like they are part of a large community that can be approached by companies like Acer. However, due to the superficial nature of the bond, members in this kind of community do not always have a strong relationship. This kind of community affiliation can be leveraged more effectively through community activation with the help of marketing events, such as a promotion activity organized by Acer at schools or universities. Acer Education, for example, offers various promotions and contests to generate interest in its education products. For example, in August 2018, Acer announced Acer STEAM Lab Makeover, a contest for K-12 schools in the United States, to transform their classrooms with immersive technology. The winning school would receive 10 Aspire 7 laptops and 10 Acer Windows Mixed Reality headsets, valued at USD13,000 (Vocus PRW Holding, 2018).

Hubs

A hub is a type of community wherein members are connected with one another due to fondness or association toward a particular individual or group. An example of hubs is the Acer user community of gamers. As of 2015, there were about 1.8 billion gamers in the world and 1.2 billion of them already used PCs and notebooks (Entertainment Software Association, 2015). This number is predicted to rise further. Harnessing the power of emotional connections between gamers and the use of certain software, personal computers and game applications are some examples of how technology businesses can utilize hub-like communities.

One of the Acer products that target the gamer market is Predator. Predator is a gaming laptop that is loved by gamers. However, this interest in a product risks fading away, and it is likely that the gaming community will also have sporadic activities, like pools. This is why Acer holds various events to keep the interest alive in this community, one of which is through Acer Predator Meetup. Such activities are expected to strengthen the interactions among the members of the community so that they can remain popular and generate interest in Acer's gaming hardware and software products.

Webs

A web represents another type of community, which is considered the strongest and the most stable. The members of a web-shaped community can nurture strong bonds with each other and engage in extensive discussions and sharing. A web community can occur both online and offline. Social media platforms, such as Facebook and LinkedIn, and instant messaging groups are some of the platforms that facilitate the creation of web communities. Customers become part of web-like communities that are associated with a brand, product, or service reflecting a brand's strong positioning. On its part, Acer also strives to maintain this type of community, for example, the Acer Community. This community is accessible through a specific website used by its customers. The company meticulously maintains the Acer Community forum to provide a peer-to-peer sharing and exchange platform to its users.

The original concept is geared toward facilitating interactions between customers and the company. For example, if customers go to Acer.com and enter a serial number, they get personalized support for that product. Acer also sees its community as not just simply customer-generated but also a company-moderated source of knowledge for their customers. In encouraging the development of the Acer Community into a real "web" community, Acer strives to encourage customers to share their experiences and interact with other customers (Acer, Inc., 2018b). Questions from Acers users are frequently answered by fellow customers, with little intervention from the support staff of the company. The Acer Community has played a strong role in nurturing a wave of loyal Acer customers, who not only love its products but also provide substantially useful information to fellow users, thereby assisting the company in the process.

References

Acer Group (2018). *Milestones and Innovations.* https://www.acer-group.com/ag/en/TW/content/history [15 August 2018].

Acer, Inc. (2018a). *Acer Gaming.* https://www.acer.com/ac/en/US/content/acer-gaming-products [15 August 2018].

Acer, Inc. (2018b). *Acer Community.* https://community.acer.com/en/#_ga=2.20 4935638.715439811.1534317935-1663435118.1534317935 [15 August 2018].

Entertainment Software Association (2015). *Essential Facts about the Computer and Video Game Industry.* http://www.theesa.com/wp-content/uploads/2015/04/ESA-Essential-Facts-2015.pdf [15 August 2018].

Fournier, S and L Lee (April 2009). Getting brand community right. *Harvard Business Review*, 87(4), 105–111.

Kotler, P, H Kartajaya and DH Hooi (2017). *Marketing for Competitiveness: Asia to the World.* Singapore: World Scientific.

Slob, B (2005). *Acer Incorporated.* Amsterdam: Centre for Research on Multinational Corporations (SOMO). https://www.somo.nl/wp-content/uploads/2005/12/Acer-incorporated.pdf [15 August 2018].

Speyer, A (2018). How Acer reduced costs and increased their community ROI by 500% using Vanilla Forum. *Vanilla Forum.* https://blog.vanillaforums.com/case-study-how-acer-reduced-costs-and-increased-their-community-roi-by-500-using-vanilla-forums [15 August 2018].

Vocus PRW Holding (August 2018). *Acer Invites K-12 Schools to Apply for STEAM Lab Makeover.* https://www.prweb.com/releases/acer_invites_k_12_schools_to_apply_for_steam_lab_makeover/prweb15676225.htm [21 August 2018].

Table for Two

Table For Two is recognized as one of the fastest growing nonprofit organizations in the world. Within a few years, this Japan-based social contribution initiative has successfully formulated active chapters in 22 countries in Europe, the Americas, Asia-Pacific, and Africa and the Middle East. Its unique and inspirational programs have succeeded in mobilizing various parties, from school cafeterias to restaurants and events, to contribute. One of the secrets of its success is a communitization strategy that involves various business and social communities in various countries.

Table For Two: Mission and Early Growth

Table For Two (TFT) is a non-profit organization that aims to tackle the contradictory issues of malnutrition in developing countries and obesity or overconsumption in developed countries. This problem represents two parties with contrary nutritional conditions but who sit on the same "global table", and neither of them is in good health. One side of the table refers to developed economies such as the United States where people are increasingly suffering from lifestyle-borne disorders. The rise in average incomes and the availability of globalized food items have led people in these countries to consume a variety of food products that may not be healthy. This has resulted in a large number of people suffering from lifestyle health problems. The other side of the table constitutes developing countries, especially those in sub-Saharan Africa, where a large number of people struggle with hunger and malnutrition every day, in part owing to limited incomes, low agricultural productivity, and unfair food distribution. TFT seeks to correct this imbalance through a unique "calorie transfer" program, providing healthy meals to both sides of the "table".

The idea first came to the fore in 2006 during the World Economic Forum conference in Davos. It was proposed by a group of Young Global Leaders (YGLs) who found an opportunity in tying together two pieces of the puzzle, with one relating to solutions addressing obesity and other lifestyle-related ill choices and the other relating to malnutrition. Masa Kogure, the founder and Executive Director, created TFT in Japan in 2007 (Chao, 2012).

TFT cooperates with companies, universities, schools, and public service institutions to implement its idea of tackling hunger in developing economies and eliminating lifestyle diseases in developed societies. As part of the TFT program, companies, cafeterias, restaurants, or event organizers who participate offer meals on their menu which are low-calorie, healthier, and more balanced on the nutritional scale. These meals are dubbed TFT meals. People, patrons, or employees and customers who opt for these meals are charged extra, for example, 20 yen in Japan or 20 cents in the United States, which is donated to support children's school meals in underprivileged areas such as Africa. The 20-yen donation is equal to the price of one school meal for a child in a developing country; so, one meal is donated to a child for every TFT meal eaten in a developed country (Yoneda, 2010).

At the end of 2007, several months after TFT's establishment, only 11 companies and organizations were participating in the program. Despite the slow progress in the beginning, the goodwill of the founders of TFT resulted in the non-profit maintaining the momentum. In the following year, in April 2008, a new medical care system was introduced in Japan requiring companies to institute specific health checkups for employees between the ages of 40 and 74 years old (Yoneda, 2010). Japan, despite having one of the lowest obesity rates in the world among its population, was concerned about the rising obesity and implemented what was called the "metabolic law" — instating penalty for companies with more than 10% of their employees with a waist size of more than 33.5 in. (men) and 35.4 in. (women). The government also made it mandatory for companies and organizations to provide health counselling to employees with the metabolic syndrome and those prone to developing a lifestyle-related disorder such as cardiovascular diseases or diabetes (Chao, 2012).

Because of the new health-check requirements, TFT began to receive many more inquiries from executives in charge of employee benefits and looking for easy-to-accomplish health measures. As a result, the number of participating companies and organizations rapidly increased to 98 by the end of 2008 and to 212 by the end of 2009. By March 2010, 241 entities were participating in the TFT program (Yoneda, 2010). The number of participating members continued to grow. By 2012, the charity had 530 participating entities in Japan, including corporations, government offices, universities, hotels, and restaurants (Hollingworth, 2012).

As of March 2018, by collaborating with over 700 corporations, universities, restaurants, and organizations implementing TFT programs in their establishments and products, TFT has served over 56 million healthy meals to both sides of the "table" (Table for Two, 2018a).

Global Expansion

TFT, which expanded year by year, is probably one of the fastest growing non-profit organizations in Japan. The charity is even eager to strengthen its presence beyond Japan. Although developed countries in the West, where obesity in children is a growing concern, represent strong potential "markets" for TFT, the challenges faced in targeting these countries are not small by any measure. One of the main difficulties faced overseas is working with suppliers and caterers to ensure that the meals are sufficiently nutritious and meet the requirements of being between 750 and 950 calories.

Another challenge is the necessity to customize the programs offered in various markets to match the expectations of donors, who are TFT's customers. In Britain, for example, only two corporations participated in the scheme, and the British chapter is thinking about donating a part of the proceeds from the meals to the local community, instead of Africa, as a way of enticing more companies and public bodies into the program (Hollingworth, 2012).

Based on the initial concept, although TFT facilitates "calorie transfer" from developed countries to developing countries in Africa, there are still local issues that need to be addressed. As an example, donations solicited in Hong Kong are dedicated to providing lunches in the poor areas of the western part of the mainland China. Similarly, donations raised in Vietnam are devoted to lunch programs in the same country. In the Middle East region, the situation is different, where the help received is dedicated to Jordan's support for the Syrian refugees (Table for Two, 2016a).

As of March 2018, TFT already exists in more than 20 countries in the world. Table 5.2 shows the list of TFT active chapters. Most are managed independently from TFT Japan.

Table 5.2:   TFT's global chapters.

Europe	North America and South America	Asia-Pacific	Africa and the Middle East
France	The United States	China	Ethiopia
Italy		Hong Kong	Kenya
Norway		Japan	Malawi
Switzerland		Korea	Rwanda
The United Kingdom		Mongolia	Saudi Arabia
		Myanmar	South Africa
		The Philippines	Tanzania
		Vietnam	Uganda

Source: Table for Two (2018b).

Table For Two's Communitization Strategy

As a non-profit organization, TFT also requires a marketing strategy to attract donations from its target organizations. With limited resources, it has to map which segments need to be targeted. Therefore, potential partners need to be grouped based on certain criteria so that TFT can select the cluster or group to be prioritized. This is the practice of traditional segmentation as a part of a marketing strategy.

In today's New Wave era, instead of applying the same old way of segmentation, organizations need to practise what is known as Communitization, which is aimed at viewing consumers as a group of people who care about each other and share common goals and concerns, values, and identity. Such communities can be formed because of a company's efforts or the community's own initiative (Kotler, Kartajaya and Hooi, 2017). There are three forms of community affiliation — pools, hubs, and webs — which could be relevant for TFT (Fig. 5.1).

Pools

A pool is the most organic and natural form of community. Pools are formed by means of shared values and/or interests among its members or by virtue of the same activity. An example of TFT's targeted community pools, in almost all the countries where it operates, is schools. The similar nature of activities occurring in schools across the world renders them as one community. If a cooperation is established between TFT and

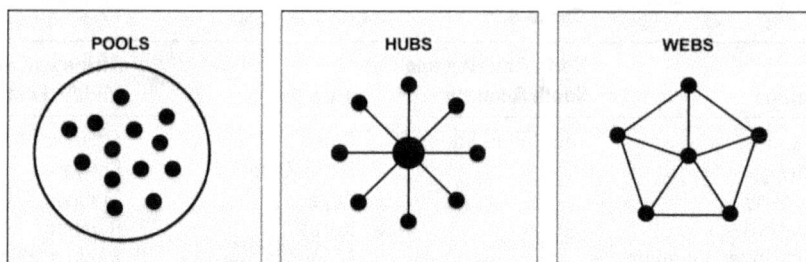

Figure 5.1: Community affiliation.
Source: Fournier and Lee (2009).

a school in any region, then it becomes easy for the members of the school, both teachers and students, to be involved in TFT's programs. To penetrate this school community, TFT needs to participate in events attended by their representatives. As an example, in 2015, ten thousand school officials from across the country attended the National Catholic Educational Association (NCEA) conference in the United States where TFT had an exhibit. Following the conference, 50 schools initiated TFT activities (Table for Two, 2016a).

Another example of pools is a community based on a hobby. In 2016, TFT and Golf Digest Online (GDO), the largest portal golf shop in Japan, launched a unique campaign called "Let's support vegetable gardens in Africa by having a birdie!" Golf lovers could simply use a golf scorecard app by GDO, and GDO would donate JPY10 when they record a birdie (Table for Two, 2016b).

Hubs

The second type is a hub community. Such communities are usually formed due to the admiration of its members toward a particular individual or group. This approach to a hub community was implemented by TFT USA in 2015. This independently managed TFT, along with New York's Japan Society, organized a talk by Professor Jeffrey Sachs on Sustainable Development goals. More than 100 people attended the event where TFT provided a healthy meal (Table for Two, 2016a).

Professor Jeffrey Sachs, who is known for his concern for poverty in developing countries, is a figure who has become an idol of social activities for businesspersons with the same interests. These people form part of the communities that are expected to participate in TFT events as well as to donate to the organization's social activities.

Another example is an event that was held in the United States in the same year. In Chicago, the author of *Onigiri Recipe 101*, Reiko Yamada, held an *onigiri* contest event where participants could create their own unique *onigiri*. This event was part of the World Food Day Celebration organized by TFT. The fans of Reiko Yamada were the community targeted for this event (Table for Two USA, 2015).

Pools and hubs, however, have shortcomings due to the nature of bonds that tend to be weak. If there is no continuous effort, the people within the community will be more or less like a crowd, with no real bonding between each other or no sense of belonging toward the community. This is why TFT always follows its efforts to build a deeper interaction, both between the organizations and their members in the communities and amongst members themselves. If this effort succeeds, it results in the formation of a third, more solid type of community, the web.

Webs

Webs represent the most powerful and stable form of community, because its members are able to develop a close relationship or engage in intensive interactions with one another. Communities such as these can be formed either online or offline, or a combination of both.

One of the potential communities as donors or supporters toward TFT are the Japanese companies and communities abroad. That is why many TFT activities abroad continue to present a Japanese cultural identity. On World Food Day 2015, TFT USA held the "One Million Itadakimasu" (or bon appetit!) Campaign. This campaign carried the theme "Transform the world with Japanese food", with a target of donating one million meals to needy children. The campaign featured a popular Japanese dish *onigiri*, which is a kind of rice ball. Major events were organized in New York City, Washington DC, Chicago, and California. An interactive website was also created for TFT fans and supporters to visit and donate meals.

As a non-profit organization based in Japan, TFT is driven to promote Japanese food culture and how it is best enjoyed through its campaigns, together with its commitment to deliver millions of meals to children in need. TFT supporters and donors, for example, can share photos of their own *onigiri* food experience on the site as an activity. Sponsor companies (San-J, Zojirushi America, Japan Block Fair, BentOn, Onigilly, Udemy) committed to donating five meals per photo submitted, while, in Washington DC, healthy TFT items with donation are made available at

Hana Japanese Market, Tako Grill, Sushi Express, Sushi Taro, and Rice Bar. On the occasion of the World Food Day, campaigns called "Brown Bag" talk and "Making Onigiri with a Difference," were run at events held at the Japan-America Society of Washington DC. In California, Japanese catering with donation was made available at the Sushi Chef Institute and various *onigiri* events were held (Table for Two USA, 2015).

The Japanese diaspora abroad typically represents a form of "pool" community, united by a common cultural identity. With TFT activation, both offline and online, interactions among the members of the community continues to grow stronger, resulting in the creation of a more solid form of "web" community. With this kind of communitization strategy, TFT continues to expand its activities to various countries rapidly and with a strong impact on the issues it is committed to.

References

Chao, R (April 2012). Table for two: How Japan is eating healthy to help children in Africa eat enough. *Asia Society.* https://asiasociety.org/blog/asia/table-two-how-japan-eating-healthy-help-children-africa-eat-enough [31 March 2018].

Fournier, S and L Lee (April 2009). Getting brand community right. *Harvard Business Review.*

Hollingworth, W (November 2012). Table for two NPO eyes larger overseas presence. Japan Times. https://www.japantimes.co.jp/news/2012/11/14/national/table-for-two-npo-eyes-larger-overseas-presence/#.Wr8O4hubIU [31 March 2018].

Kotler, P, H Kartajaya and DH Hooi (2017). *Marketing for Competitiveness: Asia to the World.* Singapore: World Scientific.

Table for Two (2016a). *Annual Report 2015.* http://usa.tablefor2.org/documentdownload.axd?documentresourceid=71 [31 March 2018].

Table for Two (May 2016b). *Global News Letter Vol. 32:* http://usa.tablefor2.org/documentdownload.axd?documentresourceid=65 [31 March 2018].

Table for Two (2018a). The Solution. http://www.tablefor2.org/home [31 March 2018].

Table for Two (2018b). *Where.* http://www.tablefor2.org/where [31 March 2018].

Table for Two USA (October 2015). *Table for Two Celebrates World Food Day 2015 with "One Million Itadakimasu (or bBon appetit!)" Campaign.* http://usa.tablefor2.org/documentdownload.axd?documentresourceid=58 [31 March 2018].

Yoneda, Y (April 2010). Table for two: Promoting healthier meals locally and school lunch donations internationally. *JFS Newsletter No. 92.* https://www.japanfs.org/en/news/archives/news_id029935.html [31 March 2018].

Century Pacific Food, INC.

This case tells the story of a company that started its journey as a small fish cannery enterprise in Mindanao, Southern Philippines. The company was named Asia's Marketing Company of the Year in 2017, a recognition from the Asia Marketing Federation (AMF). Century Pacific Food, Inc. is the largest canned food company in the Philippines and has been in operations for over 40 years. In addition to consistent product innovation, the company's success is also driven by its creative and horizontal marketing strategies. The company demonstrates how firms can implement a "clarification strategy" with messages that are multidimensional, customer-oriented, and delivered through ameans of communication that actively involves various parties.

Company at a Glance

Century Pacific Food, Inc. is a Philippines-based company that produces and distributes canned food products. The company was established in 1978 by its founder Ricardo S. Po, Sr., as Century Canning Corporation. It pioneered a tuna canning facility in the country mainly for export. By 1983, Century Canning Corporation became one of the largest fish canneries in the country, exporting canned tuna and sardines to the United States, Europe, and rest of the world. In 1986, the company launched its flagship Canned Tuna product in the domestic market, and by 1995, the company entered the meat processing business with the launch of Argentina Corned Beef.

Eventually, Century Pacific Food began to diversify its product portfolio and entered into the business of manufacturing powdered milk in 2001. In the same year, the company introduced Japanese fast-food restaurant chain Yoshinoya in the Philippines. The diversification continued with instant coffee, creamer, and soup mixes manufactured by Snow Mountain Dairy Corporation, which was set up in 2003 (refer to Table 5.3 for more information on Century Pacific Food's products and brands).

It is evident that a major factor driving Century Pacific Food's success is rapid product innovation with an inherent focus on fulfilling the evolving needs of customers. The company has succeeded in establishing a vast and diverse portfolio of products, which come in many variants and sizes. These come under various brands, thus catering to a large set

Table 5.3: Century pacific food's business segments.

Product Categories	Revenue Contribution (2016)	Brands or /Products
Marine Canned tuna, canned sardine, and other seafood-based products that captivate the Filipino consumers with their high quality, health, convenience, and affordability	37%	• Century Tuna • Century Quality • 555 • Blue Bay • Fresca Tuna • Lucky 7 • Kamayan
Meat Corned beef, luncheon meat, and Vienna sausage that offer delicious taste and affordability	27%	• Swift • Argentina • Shanghai • 555 • WoW! Ulam • Lucky 7 • Hunt's
Milk and Mixes Condensed milk, evaporated milk, and all-purpose cream, which are basic household necessities	11%	• Birch Tree Full Cream • Birch Tree Fortified • Angel • Kaffe de Oro • Home Pride
Tuna OEM Tuna products for many of the leading retail tuna brands around the world	15%	• Frozen tuna loins • Pouched tuna • Canned tuna
Coconut OEM High value, organic, certified, and conventional coconut products for both export and domestic markets	10%	• Aqua coco • Coconut water • Desiccated coconut • Virgin coconut oil • Organic coconut flour

of preferences and price points. This helps the company appeal to a larger consumer base.

Varying price points also allow Century Pacific Food to reach both the price-conscious consumers and the upper-income markets that seek premium options (Century Pacific Food, Inc., 2016). For example, Century Tuna is positioned as an upscale product, whereas the 555 brand is a mass product for budget-conscious consumers. Century Pacific Food has come up with products that suit the local consumer palates: Freska Tuna canned flavors, for example, are more in line with the tastes of consumers in North Luzon, and Blue Bay Tuna and Sardines are flavored for the Visayas region (Flores, 2011).

Local Domination and International Expansion

Armed with a wide array of products targeting all segments — from the mass market to the premium market — Century Pacific Food has succeeded in cementing its dominance as the top and largest canned food producer in the Philippines. Based on financial data from the first quarter of 2017, the company's brands were market leaders in various categories. In the canned and preserved food category, the company has captured 35% market share, while its closest competitor Purefoods has clinched 11%, followed by Del Monte (9%) and Liberty Gold (8%). Century Pacific Food also dominates the canned meat category, with a market share of 37%, followed by Purefoods, with a market share of 30%. In the categories of corned meat and luncheon meat, Century Pacific Food is in the top spot again, with a market share of 46% and 34%, respectively. The strongest dominance enjoyed by Century Pacific Food, however, is in the canned tuna category, with 82% market share, while its nearest rival CDO-Foodsphere manages only 16% market share (Century Pacific Food, Inc., 2017).

The company's strong position is not limited to the domestic market. Having pursued strong regional and international expansion, today Century Pacific Food brands are available in 59 countries (CNPF Corporate Presentation, 2017). The company has made a significant investment in its worldwide sales and distribution infrastructure, which has lent it a massive export presence and international manufacturing facilities. Its products are available at large global supermarket chains including Walmart and Carrefour.

Its flagship Century Tuna is a leading canned fish brand in China, Vietnam, and the Middle East. In 2016, Century Pacific Food acquired the distributor group of Century Tuna in China, thereby further strengthening its foothold in the market. Century Tuna is now recognized as the number one retail canned tuna brand in the country (Century Pacific Food, Inc., 2017). Its stronghold in China is particularly interesting as the company has established strong relationships with major local retailers, thus tapping this one-billion-consumer market to its advantage.

Century Pacific Food is also a well-known brand in North America, the Middle East, and Europe. The company works closely with several international partners to manufacture private labels and branded products to be sold internationally. Some of its international customers include Subway, Princes (United Kingdom's leading canned food importer), and Vita Coco, the world's largest coconut water brand by the US-based All Market, Inc.. Century Pacific Food's Kamayan Shrimp Paste is a product sold exclusively for export markets and is a top brand in the United States. Locally called Bagoong, this heritage Filipino brand has established its presence in the United States since the 1980s, when it first entered the market. The brand is currently being sold in leading Asian food stores across the West and East coast, catering primarily to large Filipino communities.

Century Tuna: Case of Clarification

One of the biggest contributors to the success of Century Pacific Food, especially in the domestic market, is the Century Tuna brand. The company has managed to position Century Tuna as a classic product for a "healthy lifestyle", owing to Tuna's numerous health benefits. Even the tagline "Think Healthy, Think Century Tuna" reflects the focus on healthy fish, available in a variety of flavors and appealing to different tastes. The growth in per capita income in the Philippines over the past few years has led to an expanding middle class, who are careful about health issues. Previously, Century Pacific Food marketed tuna based on taste, but the shift in the preferences of the health-conscious segment has resulted in a new positioning for Century Tuna. It not only appeals to the middle-class consumers concerned about eating and living healthily but also helps create a differentiation for Century Tuna from other similar offerings.

Gregory Banzon, Century Pacific Food Vice President-General Manager for Tuna, once said: "It was just a question of taste then. The health aspect came later and was an added layer to the message to help grow the brand" (Century Pacific Food, Inc., 2017).

In its brand-building efforts, Century Pacific Food seems to have adopted a new form of positioning strategy, which is more horizontal, inclusive, and social. This is referred to as "Clarification". The concept was built around the basic assumption that no single message could tell the whole multidimensional story of a mega-brand like Century Tuna, which means different things in different regions to different people in different situations with different needs. A brand's story cannot be a simple-minded, over-simplification of a complex brand idea (Kotler, Kartajaya and Hooi, 2017).

The concept of clarification moves away from the traditional notion of positioning, which tends to focus quite a lot on a single message that is repeated relentlessly to garner retention in consumers' minds. Instead, clarification is implemented through a multidimensional approach, which involves delivering messages through a set of varying channels aimed at different audiences. It works in the same way an editor approaches the creation of a magazine, with its array of different contents and stories aimed at readers with a variety of interests, but with a coherent editorial framework (Light, 2014).

The clarification strategy adopted by Century Pacific Food for its Century Tuna brand has three main characteristics, which distinguishes it from traditional positioning listed in Table 5.4 (Kotler, Kartajaya and Hooi, 2017).

Multidimensional message

In clarification, the tagline does not only consist of a message that is delivered repeatedly across the various media but also serves as a "cover story" that gets translated into various forms of content. In this case, Century Tuna uses several different themes of clarification for its customers, depending on the benefits offered. In order to set Century Tuna apart from other similar canned products, Century Pacific Food educated consumers on the benefits of regularly eating tuna, along with the general benefits of leading a healthy lifestyle with exercise and eating healthily.

Table 5.4: Positioning vs. clarification.

Positioning	Clarification
A single message	A multidimensional message
Company-oriented content	Customer-oriented content
One-way communication	Multiple-way communication

This effort culminates into a biannual staging of the country's biggest model search, the Century Tuna Superbods Contest, which has been ongoing since 2006 (Century Pacific Food, Inc., 2017). The Superbods campaign is also promoted through various media by roping in brand ambassadors who tell their own personal stories related to healthy living and body transformation. Brand ambassadors are selected from artists, musicians, or sportsmen who are already popular in the Philippines.

For one of its campaigns, Century Tuna used the theme "Be ABSolutely summer ready" which was promoted through commercials and billboards (Cruz, 2015). The campaign featured artists and brand ambassadors sharing the importance of a healthy lifestyle associated with summer vacation moments. In 2017, Century Pacific Food also used the #CenturyTunaNoExcuses campaign theme to encourage consumers to start a new, healthier lifestyle.

A closer look at the campaigns reveals that all the messages essentially are inspired by the same "cover story", which confirms Century Tuna as a "healthy-lifestyle product." This serves as an example of how Century Pacific Food has used multidimensional messages in its clarification strategy for Century Tuna.

Customer-oriented content

The approach that the process of clarification advocates includes the use of content that is more tailored to customer needs. Often, the content is not even directly related to the products on offer, but it could provide real benefits to customers (Kotler, Kartajaya and Hooi, 2017). In devising its marketing strategy for Century Tuna, Century Pacific Food not only creates promotions that effectively convey the functional and the emotional benefits of consuming its products but also makes a variety of content with practical, useful information for consumers to help them live a healthier lifestyle.

As an example, to make it easier for consumers to get information on how to lead a healthy lifestyle, the Century Tuna website (www.centurytuna.ph) is filled with workouts conceived by professional trainers. There are also daily meal plans based on the use of Century Tuna by fitness nutritionists, chefs, and weight-loss consultants.

Century Tuna has even published a book focused on body transformation. The book titled *Century Tuna Superbod Abs* features several of its fitness endorsers, with Century Tuna endorser James Reid, a Filipino Australian singer and actor, on the cover of the book. The book containing information on flat-belly meals and exercise challenges was launched in 2015 and made available at various book stores (Cruz, 2015). This type of content is considered customer-orientated as it provides direct benefits to customers rather than simply promoting the company, as in the case of company-oriented content.

Multiple-way communication

Traditionally, a company's product or brand positioning was established based on one-dimensional communication, which flowed from the company toward customers, who are treated as passive recipients of the information. However, with technological advances, the interaction has grown not only into a two-way communication (between a company and its customers) but also into a multiple-way communication (among customers). Mobile and digital technology has made it easier for customers to share information with the people around them (friends, families, and also followers). Customers are not only making purchasing decisions based on their own preferences or reviews from their friends and family but are also actively searching for reviews online and feedback from social media and online forums (Kotler, Kartajaya and Hooi, 2017).

In the case of Century Tuna, Century Pacific Food has creatively managed to trigger conversations among its brand ambassadors and customers, and the endeavor is clearly targeted at creating and strengthening the "brand story". Through the challenge campaign, Century Tuna challenges customers to experience the 90 days of fitness challenge. Customers are encouraged to share their experiences through social media, further fueling interest among followers and fans.

One such story that quickly became viral and received appreciation from customers is the body transformation program undertaken by TV host and Filipino celebrity Raymond Gutierrez. Raymond completed the 90-day challenge for Century Tuna's #noexcuse campaign and ended up losing 65 pounds. The celebrity host documented his weight loss journey in a Rappler video and now weighs 195 pounds. He was even called an inspiration by many on social media, and he admitted that his online engagement with the followers also fueled his own motivation to work harder. His weight loss journey video went viral and got 1.2 million views within 5 days. Such positive comments of appreciation that flooded Raymond's video post in turn also created a horizontal communication between Raymond and his new "fans" (Rappler.com, 2017). This serves as a good example of how a brand can benefit from creative clarification, as done by Century Tuna, by facilitating a multiple-way communication among its customers and brand ambassadors.

References

Century Pacific Food, Inc. (2016). Five reasons to invest in CNPF. *Business Highlight*. http://www.centurypacific.com.ph/webinvestor.php?d=cD02JnBjPTAmYmQ9MTk5&cat=investment [9 January 2018].

Century Pacific Food, Inc. (2017). *2016 Annual Report*. http://www.centurypacific.com.ph/investorpdf/Century%20Pacific%20Food%20Inc%202016%20Annual%20Report.pdf [8 January 2018].

Century Pacific Food, Inc. (May 2017). *Corporate Presentation*. http://www.centurypacific.com.ph/investorpdf/Financial%20Reporting/CNPF%20Corporate%20Presentation_May%202017n.pdf [8 January 2018].

Cruz, JAT (2015). Century Tuna's strategy: Selling a lifestyle with abs. *Business World Online*. http://www.bworldonline.com/content.php?section=Weekender&title=century-tunas-strategy-selling-a-lifestyle-with-abs&id=105806 [9 January 2018].

Flores, WL (October 2011). Success strategies of Tuna King Ricardo Po Sr. *The Philippines Star*. http://www.philstar.com/business-life/740181/success-strategies-tuna-king-ricardo-po-sr [8 January 2018].

Kotler, P, H Kartajaya and DH Hooi (2017). *Marketing for Competitiveness: Asia to the World*. Singapore: World Scientific.

Light, L (July 2014). Brand journalism is a modern marketing imperative. *Advertising Age*. http://adage.com/article/guest-columnists/brand-journalism-a-modern-marketing-imperative/294206/ [9 January 2018].

Rappler.com (May 2017). *Raymond vs Raymond*. https://www.rappler.com/brandrap/health-and-self/168281-raymond-gutierrez-no-excuses-century-tuna [11 January 2018].

CHAPTER 6

MARKETING TACTICS FOR VALUE ENGAGEMENT

Marketing tactics, the second component of the marketing architecture, consist of three main elements: differentiation, marketing mix, and selling. Differentiation is the core tactic of a company that describes the uniqueness that it offers to the target market. This uniqueness is then created through the 4Ps — product, price, place, and promotion (marketing mix). Further, selling is an effective tactic to build and maintain long-term relationships based on mutual benefits with customers.

In the Legacy era, it was common for Asian companies to bombard their audiences with messages through advertisements in various media. Some companies even concoct a not-so-authentic differentiation in order to be able to stand out from the crowd. Technology has, however, transformed the company-customer relationship in Asia and the world, making it increasingly inclusive and horizontal. The positions of the two have become increasingly aligned. Customers can easily access information about a company from various sources, so what's right can be easily identified by customers. In today's New Wave era, a company should be able to cultivate an authentic uniqueness, one that cannot be easily copied by its competitors. We call this codification.

This chapter also deals with the transformation of the marketing mix elements: from product to co-creation, price to currency, place to communal activation, and promotion to conversation. In the New Wave era, the product development process takes a more "horizontal" route. Companies keenly provide several opportunities to their customers, so that they can be actively involved in various product development stages. This effectively means that the final product could be the result of co-creation between the company and its customers. Advances in technology have also enabled companies to provide customers with greater freedom in conducting price customization. The price to be paid is determined by the subscribers according to the features of the products they need and offerings from competitive products. We call this flexible approach of pricing as currency.

The new technology also transforms the way companies promote to customers. As the user-generated content trend catches up, companies are focusing on putting across messages that are sufficiently creative in order to be able to trigger conversations among customers. This is contrary to the traditional unidirectional advertising where messages flow from a company to its customers. These conversations help catapult marketing messages into viral content that goes on spreading fast and wide as customers share it with people connected to them.

The final element of the marketing mix is place. It is typically the physical platform that connects companies and their customers, so that they can get their product or experience a service. As with the fundamental transformation of other elements, the Internet has also led to the creation of alternative distribution channels. Together with the ease to make online payments, online distribution channels are thriving across industries and, as a result, more companies can sell their products directly to customers. However, what needs to be noted is that this New Wave era calls for companies to be smarter in devising the right combination of online-offline approaches, especially for target customers who are turning increasingly communal, due to the shift from segmentation to communitization. Therefore, companies — at a tactical level also — need to implement the right initiatives, one of which is the utilization of the community that is aligned with the company's distribution channel, in terms of purpose, values, and identity. This is called communal activation.

The three cases discussed in this chapter — Dilmah Tea from Sri Lanka, Cathay Pacific from Hong Kong, and BlueBird from Indonesia — will show how Asian companies can implement the New Wave marketing tactics in a digital business context.

Dilmah Tea

Sri Lanka — formerly known as Ceylon — is considered one of the best tea-producing countries in the world. Tea producers and exporters face intense competition to grow their business by sourcing exotic raw materials for this very popular beverage in this world. Amidst such a competitive situation, Dilmah Tea has emerged as an authentic local brand from Sri Lanka due to the quality perceivably lacking amongst other players. Starting from the founder's personal commitment, these in-built authenticities have eventually become the company's brand DNA.

The Story of the Ceylon Tea Industry

Sri Lanka — known as Ceylon until 1972 — is an exquisite tropical island country in South Asia. Often considered a gateway to South Asia, owing to its strategic location as a bridge connecting the eastern and western routes, Sri Lanka prides itself on its natural beauty, biodiversity, spices, gems, and vast lush tea plantation (Herath, 2004). The tea industry in Sri Lanka is quite vibrant and accounts for one of the main sources of foreign exchange reserves, contributing as much as 2% of GDP (Sri Lanka Export Development Board, 2014). As of 2016, tea remains one of the main export products of Sri Lanka, besides textiles (Hong Kong Trade Development Center, 2017).

The tea industry in Sri Lanka gradually developed into what it is today. Initially, tea was exported in the form of raw materials to various countries; however, eventually, Ceylon tea, which is processed, packaged, and branded by the company came to be sold at higher prices. In subsequent developments, more local producers began attempting to provide greater value through processing and packaging before the tea was exported. This value-added tea is now a major strength of the Ceylon tea industry (Herath, 2004).

However, with the emergence of many branded teas, the issue of quality came to the fore as a challenge for Ceylon tea producers and exporters in Sri Lanka. With several companies now relying on marketing campaigns to promote their products using the name "Ceylon Tea", consumers became more aware of the "Ceylon" tea brand than really knowing where Ceylon originates from (Herath, 2004). In order to offer more competitive prices; however, some of these players have not shied from compromising on quality by blending the authentic Ceylon tea with other inexpensive tea types. This eventually gave rise to the phenomenon of blended tea, increasingly popular among tea producers in Sri Lanka.

Realizing the gravity of the situation, some tea producers brought it upon themselves to revive the charm of the authentic and legendary Ceylon tea. This idealism has come to be realized through the production of Ceylon tea that does not use any blending techniques (not mixing it with teas from other origins). Traditional "orthodox" methods are used, which help preserve the distinctive aroma of Ceylon tea. A pioneer of that effort is Dilmah Tea.

Dilmah Tea: Bringing the Single-origin Ceylon Tea Back

At a time when large advertising budgets and wide promotion of so-called Ceylon tea brands from big corporations flooded the market, quality constantly suffered due to the availability of all the blended tea options. The return of the traditional tea was much called for. Merrill J. Fernando spearheaded the effort in 1988 when he launched Dilmah — a brand name he chose as an amalgam of the names of two of his toddler sons: Dilhan and Malik (Dilmah Ceylon Tea Company, 2017a).

Born in 1930 in Pallansena, a village near Negombo, Merrill Fernando worked as a Ceylonese tea taster after moving to the Sri Lankan capital, Colombo. He also went on to work at big tea companies, including Lipton and Tetley. Eventually, he was sent to London for training in the 1950s, where he discovered how Ceylon teas were routinely blended with other tea types to make them more cost competitive. This served as a pivotal moment for Fernando in his quest to change the face of the Sri Lankan tea industry (Hicks, 2015).

Fernando's determination to kick-start a transformation in Sri Lanka's tea industry grew stronger when he found evidence of several big corporations deserting the single-origin tea in favor of blends, which made greater business sense. The aftermath was evident too; from the 1950s, when Sri Lankan tea was globally popular as a beverage, it was now being replaced by less-expensive teas from other countries, which were even preferred by buyers from the United States, Europe, and Australia. Even though those companies made more profits, producers and traders from Sri Lanka suffered a massive blow to their margins (Bajaj, 2010).

This moved Fernando to establish Dilmah, a 100% original, pure, and single Ceylon tea. At its incorporation, there was a fair share of cynics who doubted Dilmah's ability to compete with big brands who had been there for much longer, grown more powerful, and had deeper pockets. However, with time, the concept of the single-origin tea offered by Dilmah has lapped up the market, as tea lovers began to favor Dilmah over the blended tea. Today, Dilmah is Sri Lanka's most recognized international brand of tea (Rosenfeld, 2015). The brand now sells in over 100 countries around the world — from Estonia, the United Kingdom, Turkey, Poland, Hungary, and Chile to the United States, South Africa, New Zealand, Australia and Pakistan, Indonesia, and Japan. In 2009, Dilmah was considered the sixth largest tea brand in the world (Bajaj, 2010).

With Ceylon Tea Trails — a set of luxury boutique bungalows, which were set up by revamping old tea plantations — Dilmah also ventured into tourism. These five-star bungalow resorts offer a unique period-era experience, with gourmet cuisines and butler service amidst lush tea fields and mountains. Dilmah plans to open two more such bungalows, along with 10 timeshare villas. The company has also set up what it calls "tea bars" to offer tastings and classes on tea, a memorable experience for tea connoisseurs. All these efforts weaved nicely into Dilmah's brand story and why it commands a premium price amongst other teas (Bajaj, 2010).

Dilmah's Authenticities: Toward DNA Codification

The success of Dilmah as the choice of tea for consumers home and abroad cannot be separated from the authenticity that the brand stands for. In today's New Wave era, a company should be able to cultivate an authentic uniqueness — one that cannot be easily copied by its competitors. Gilmore and Pine (2007) advocated three key drivers behind the demand for authenticity. First is the overabundance of commercial experiences. Customers today are better adept at telling a real experience from a phony one. An experience which appears to be conceived forcibly, does not impress customers today and mostly considered as "trying too hard". A "fake" experience would likely be remembered as a waste of time, whereas a truly authentic and sincere experience would be treasured for life.

Second, with the proliferation of machines all around us, our social lives are increasingly impersonal, which also makes people yearn for something that's more authentic, genuine, and from the heart. This is the paradox of our time: high-tech (machine-to-machine) mechanism creating the demand for high-touch (human-to-human) interaction.

Finally, several big scandals have been unearthed in recent times, resulting in a loss of faith among consumers. Consumers, therefore, look up to organizations that come across as truthful, sincere, and authentic today — the more socially and environmentally responsible entities, which actually believe, and work toward and in accordance with their missions, visions, and values.

To seal its image as a flagbearer of authenticity, Dilmah began with following the concept of single-origin tea, as the family-owned company refused to conduct business in line with industry trends. Apart from the flagship single-origin teas, other specialties offered by Dilmah are garden fresh and unblended teas. Box 6.1 lists some of the authenticities that have made customers fall in love with and be loyal to Dilmah tea.

Box 6.1: Dilmah's Authenticities

1. *Pure Ceylon Tea Leaves*
   The Ceylon tea, named after the geographical region where the tea plant is grown, is an authentic tea from Sri Lanka that benefits from the area's unique topography and environment. Dilmah claims that it pays special attention to how the finest tea leaves are picked, thus not only preserving the taste but also doing fair business by protecting the heritage of the tea industry and encouraging the artisanal style of tea making.

   (Continued)

Box 6.1: *Continued*

2. *Unblended Tea*

   Another factor that adds to its authenticity is the fact that Dilmah tea is devoid of any blends, thus providing uncompromised original quality. As opposed to blended teas, which have become popular because of their inexpensive price tags, Dilmah refuses to compromise its tea's freshness and authenticity by blending it, even if its prices are higher, which limits its market reach.

3. *Freshness*

   The flavor, aroma, and characteristics of a tea are heavily dependent on how fresh the tea leaves are. As the tea ages, it absorbs moisture, which can release toxins — not only degrading its flavor but also reducing the amount of antioxidants in it. Dilmah, therefore, is extremely particular about the production process and its supply chain to maintain the freshness of the tea it produces.

4. *Single-origin Tea*

   In picking tea leaves, the origin is crucial, as it can be a determining factor in taste and aroma. The single-origin tea is further proof of its commitment to avoid blended teas, as the idea of multi-origin blends is strongly rejected. This is how Dilmah stands true to its promise of providing the finest quality of tea to its users and maintains its authentic value.

5. *Passionate Tea Maker*

   The quality of tea can be affected by a number of variables, from soil to climate and cultivation techniques. This makes standardization rather difficult to achieve and, thus tea producing is considered more of an art than science. This renders the passion and integrity of the tea grower and harvester quite important. In the case of Dilmah, the founder Merrill Fernando's strong passion for the art of tea growing and dedication to serving the

(Continued)

Box 6.1: *Continued*

tea-farming community also makes Dilmah different from its peers.

6. ***Ethical Business Practice***
Dilmah's founder Fernando has nurtured its philosophy of "business as a matter of human service" in running the company, thus putting special emphasis on ethics, integrity, and sustainability. Through the MJF Charitable Foundation, Dilmah actively gives back to the community by helping over 100,000 underprivileged Sri Lankans by 2015 — by working on the principle of social justice. The foundation runs a number of social and environmental projects, helping small entrepreneurs, rural villages, community welfare, kids' programs, culinary schools, and so on. Dilmah Conservation, in contrast, combines the foundation's work with environmental and wildlife conservation efforts.

7. ***Traditional Methods***
The traditional artisanal method of picking the finest tea leaves is pertinent to maintaining the quality of Dilmah teas. Any error in the method of tea processing and the impact is big on the tea's flavor and aroma. The traditional art of handpicking two leaves and a bud requires sincere practice and patience, something Dilmah strives to encourage in its community of tea growers. The crush tear curl (CTC) method, in contrast, offers a quicker and cheaper alternative but compromises tea quality and flavor.

8. ***Finest Quality***
Whether it is the promise of garden-fresh tea leaves or the unwavering commitment to single origin and unblended composition, Dilmah's focus on quality leaves no margin of error. The pursuit of the finest quality is adhered to at every step in the process, from handpicking tea to the artisanal style of preparing it for consumption.

(Continued)

Box 6.1: *Continued*

9. *Natural Goodness*

   The naturalness of tea makes it distinctive. From the appearance to aroma and taste, it is nature at play in making Dilmah's tea authentic and true to its natural goodness. By adhering to the artisanal style of production, Dilmah tea ensures natural freshness and aroma, which is evident in every cup of tea.

10. *Pioneer in the Tea Industry*

    This last factor contributes most to the authenticity of Dilmah, as it is a pioneer in bringing unblended single-origin teas to tea lovers back home and across the world and thereby, reinstating the authentic flavors of Ceylon tea globally. This turned out to be a paradigm shift in the way Dilmah emerged as a family-owned tea company, offering garden-fresh tea, originated directly from tea growers — unadulterated — on to consumers' tables. This pioneering effort is continued through innovation in the form of signature events, such as Dilmah Thé Culinaire, Dilmah Tea Sommelier, Chefs and the Teamaker, Tea in Five Senses, Mixologists and the Teamaker, and Real High Tea, and not to forget the Dilmah School of Tea, which imparts knowledge on artisanal aspects of tea to hospitality professionals and tea connoisseurs.

Source: Dilmah Ceylon Tea Company (2017b).

To create an authentic uniqueness, a company should be able to extend the brand internalization of DNA beyond the marketing department. What does a brand DNA constitute? It includes all the unique aspects of the brand that reflects from the common language of all employees within the company and not necessarily only those who face the customers (Barlow and Stewart, 2004). In fact, the brand DNA should animate all important processes in the company, ranging from leadership, recruitment, performance appraisal, and culture building. This is what we call codification (Kotler, Kartajaya and Hooi, 2017).

In this respect, the leadership of the founder has played an integral role in building Dilmah's codification. The undying commitment to the brand's various authenticities, as discussed earlier, is an initiative by Merrill J. Fernando. This is also outlined in his own words on the company's website: "My vision is to bring you tea of the highest quality. Tea that is fresh — rich in flavor and natural goodness — and at the same time to give workers and my country a fairer deal. I pledged to make my business a matter of human service" (Dilmah Ceylon Tea Company, 2017a).

This sense of commitment in running Dilmah is not only passed down to his two children but also inculcated in all the employees of the company. One way it is done is through a corporate culture, which bases itself on 12 unique principles. With the involvement of all parties in realizing such passion and commitment, a firm and strong corporate DNA is achieved, which helps it face external challenges. One of the most deviating temptations is the pressure to adapt to changing circumstances. This has led to many other players to blend teas from other origins. Although this is more competitive in price, it is less authentic. Dilmah's 30-year journey has stood the test of time to its unwavering commitment to maintaining the brand DNA of the company.

References

Bajaj, V (January 2010). A Sri Lankan underdog battles global tea giants. *New York Times*. http://www.nytimes.com/2010/01/09/business/global/09tea.html [14 February 2018].

Barlow, J and P Stewart (2004). *Branded Customer Service: The New Competitive Advantage*. San Fransisco: Berrett-Koehler Publisher, Inc.

Dilmah Ceylon Tea Company (2017a). *The Story Begins*. https://www.dilmahtea.com/dilmah-tea-company/founders-message.html [13 February 2018].

Dilmah Ceylon Tea Company (2017b). *Our Values*. https://www.dilmahtea.com/dilmah-tea-company/corporate-values.html [12 February 2018].

Gilmore, JH and BJ Pine II (2007). *Authenticity: What Consumers Really Want*. Boston: Harvard Business Review Press.

Herath, SK (January–June 2004). Tea industry in Sri Lanka and the role of Dilmah tea. *Delhi Business Review* 5(1), 1–15.

Hicks, MW (September 2015). Founder interview: Merryl J. Fernando of Dilmah tea. *Destinations of the World News*. http://www.dotwnews.com/interviews/founder-interview-merrill-j-fernando-of-dilmah-tea# [14 February 2018].

Hong Kong Trade Development Center (2017). *Sri Lanka: Market Profile.* http://emerging-markets-research.hktdc.com/business-news/article/Asia/Sri-Lanka-Market-Profile/mp/en/1/1X000000/1X09X08S.htm [13 February 2018].

Kotler, P, H Kartajaya and DH Hooi (2017). *Marketing for Competitiveness: Asia to the World.* Singapore: World Scientific.

Rosenfeld, C (February 2015). Tea in Sri Lanka: Travelers take sips steeped history. *CNN.* http://edition.cnn.com/travel/article/sri-lanka-tea-experiences/index.html [14 February 2018].

Sri Lanka Export Development Board (2014). *Industry Capability Report: Tea Sector.* http://www.srilankabusiness.com/pdf/industrycapabilityreport_tea_sector.pdf [13 February 2018].

Cathay pacific

Cathay Pacific is one of the largest international airlines in Asia, offering premium services to both business and leisure travelers. Having experienced rapid development since its establishment, more than 70 years ago, Cathay Pacific currently faces new challenges in the form of an expanding competitor base and shifting behavior of customers. To overcome these challenges and use them to its advantage, the airline has incorporated new strategies and tactics, with digital technology as the main enabler.

Cathay Pacific: Company at a Glance

Cathay Pacific, the flag carrier of Hong Kong, is headquartered in Hong Kong Airport. The airline was founded in 1946, and its major shareholders include Swire Pacific and Air China. The airline flies to over 206 destinations in 52 countries in Asia, North America, Australia, Europe, and Africa, with a fleet of nearly 200 aircrafts. The company employs nearly 19,900 people in Hong Kong while around 33,000 people work for the Cathay Pacific group globally, which also includes Cathay Dragon, the wholly owned subsidiary that flies regionally in Asia and caters mainly to Mainland China with 20 connected cities and AHK Air Hong Kong, an all-cargo carrier that offers regional freight services. The company is now in the process of making AHK Air Hong Kong a wholly-owned subsidiary (Cathay Pacific Fact Sheet, March 2018).

Cathay Pacific is also the majority shareholder in AHK Air Hong Kong Limited (Air Hong Kong), an all-cargo carrier providing scheduled services in Asia (Cathay Pacific Airways Limited, March 2017).

History and Growth

Cathay Pacific was founded in Hong Kong on September 24, 1946, by American Roy C. Farrell and Australian Sydney H. de Kantzow. Initially based in Shanghai, the two men eventually moved to Hong Kong and established the airline there (Cathay Pacific Airways Limited, 2018a). From this new base, the newly setup company gradually went on to build its business and eventually emerged as one of the leading players in the airline industry, especially in Asia. It began with passenger flights to Manila, Bangkok, Singapore, and Shanghai. The company swiftly expanded operations; in 1948, Swire, one of Hong Kong's leading trading companies and erstwhile known as Butterfield and Swire, bought nearly a 45% share in Cathay Pacific. Its leader John Kidston Swire became fully responsible for the company's management (Cathay Pacific Airways Limited, 2018a).

Eventually, Cathay Pacific registered a strong growth at an average rate of up to 20% a year between 1962 and 1967. The airline also began international operations by introducing flights to Osaka, Nagoya, and Fukuoka in Japan. By the 1970s, it was already utilizing computerized reservation systems and flight simulators. Its maiden Boeing 747–200 flight landed in Hong Kong in mid-1979, and by the year end, the airline had already applied for a permit to fly to London (Cathay Pacific Airways Limited, 2018a). As more B747's joined its fleet, it expanded its services to Europe and North America.

Cathay Pacific recorded a spectacular growth in the 1980s, which was a favorable period for the airline industry in general. In view of the global economic boom, especially vibrant in Asia, there were more and more flights carrying travelers, especially business travelers, tourists, and cargo shipments. The airline also expanded further to connect international locations, including London, Brisbane, Frankfurt, Vancouver, Amsterdam, Rome, San Francisco, Paris, Zurich, and Manchester during the 1980s. In 2000, Cathay Pacific started the new millennium with a whopping HK5 billion (around USD637 million) profit. However, moving forward, it experienced commercial challenges in the wake of the September 11 attacks, the Second Gulf War, and SARS. It launched a massive recovery attempt in the form of a "World's Biggest Welcome", a lucky draw contest offering 10,000 free in-bound tickets, and the "We Love Hong Kong" campaign, which helped Hong Kong in its recovery post the SARS outbreak (*The Sunday Times Sri Lanka*, 2002; Loh, 2004). That apart, Cathay Pacific also strengthened the links between Hong Kong and other global hubs with multiple daily services to London, Los Angeles, New York, and Sydney, along with increased frequencies to other major long-haul and regional destinations.

Cathay Pacific partnered with the global logistics company DHL to form a joint-venture in Air Hong Kong in 2002, thus expanding its capabilities in express overnight cargo deliveries. The collaboration helped Cathay Pacific expand the regional network of its delivery subsidiary in Asia and allowed DHL to take the competition head-on with its rivals, including FedEx and UPS BBC (2002). The partnership has been of strategic advantage for both the companies as DHL and Cathay Pacific continue to work together; in November 2017, Cathay Pacific also agreed to buy DHL's 40% shareholding in Air Hong Kong, thus making it a wholly-owned subsidiary. Under the agreement, the companies will continue to operate under a new block space agreement for an initial term of 15 years commencing on January 01, 2019 (Cathay Pacific Airways Limited, 2018b).

Cathay Pacific also established itself as a prominent airline to the Chinese Mainland starting 2003, when it resumed passenger services to Beijing. This was followed by passenger flights to Xiamen and freighter services into Shanghai (Cathay Pacific Airways Limited, 2018). The venture into the Chinese mainland with expanding connectivity strengthened Cathay Pacific's position in the regional aviation market. Moreover, Hong Kong also benefits from a location-based advantage, which is not enjoyed by many other cities or countries.

With several continuous efforts aimed at improving customer satisfaction, Cathay Pacific is recognized for setting industry standards for service. This is evident by the major awards it has bagged, including the "Airline of the Year" in the world's largest passenger poll conducted by

Skytrax in 2005. The airline received the same title in 2009 and 2014 (Skytrax, 2018).

As Cathay Pacific's passenger service division continues to grow and achieve recognition for its superior service quality, its cargo division also continues to step up its efforts in the company's consistent growth and expansion. In 2010, Cathay Pacific became the world's largest international cargo airline and the main hub, Hong Kong International Airport, the world's busiest airport in terms of cargo traffic (Denslow, 2011). As of today, the cargo division accounts for nearly 30% of the total revenue of Cathay Pacific Group (Cathay Pacific Airways Limited, 2018).

New Competition

Cathay Pacific mostly targets business travelers with its Preferred Account Program. It positions itself as an airline that offers superior services from the heart. With this in mind, one of the closest rivals of Cathay Pacific is Singapore Airlines, the flag carrier airline of Singapore with its hub in Singapore Changi Airport. Singapore Airlines is one of the world's most awarded airlines. It has always been a neck-to-neck rival of Cathay Pacific as the former also continues to earn recognition in customer review surveys by Skytrax; in 2018, Singapore Airlines was awarded the World's Best Airline by Skytrax with a five-star rating. The airline is ranked among the top 10 based on international passengers carried and among the top 15 based on revenue per kilometers (McCaffrey, 2014).

Other than Singapore Airlines, Cathay Pacific also has to fend off competition from gulf aviation players. Big brands such as Qatar Airways, Etihad Airways, and Emirates offer full-service flights, connecting several destinations in and out of Asia, for upper-segment travelers. The three Gulf mega-carriers have expanded rapidly in recent years. For instance, the Gulf airlines have collectively grown their seat capacity to the United States by nearly 1,500% since the finalization of the Open Skies agreement between the United States and their governments. The strong expansion, according to these Gulf carriers, is a result of increasing market demand supported by rising incomes in Asia and other parts of the world.

The current competitive scenario is becoming even more complex as Cathay Pacific deals with the emergence of new competitors that target the lower end of the market segment. There are two trends that encourage the emergence of the new competition. First, the economic slowdown in some countries has resulted in more travelers being sensitive to ticket prices and ultimately choosing cheaper airlines. The demand for business class has weakened, while budget air travel has boomed. Second, the rapid growth of direct flights from China to a raft of international destinations has done away with the need to stop in the city en route to a third destination. This is especially painful as China's outbound tourist market is already the biggest in the world by number of visitors (Juca, 2017).

These trends are pushing the rise of budget airlines around Asia and state-owned Mainland Chinese carriers, which have been flooding key routes with passenger seats and driving down fares. These threats can be tackled, to some extent, by diversifying into the flourishing budget air travel segment. For example, Singapore Airlines has succeeded in boosting operating profit from Silk Air and its no-frills carrier, Scoot, even when they contribute less than 30% to the total operating profit. That said, an over-dependence on low-cost carriers, if not taken care of smartly, could jeopardize the business of the main carrier (Juca, 2017).

New Strategy and Tactics

In an effort to counter this increasingly fierce competition, Cathay Pacific unveiled its new business strategy "Time to Win". The strategy focuses on the motto, "Life Well Travelled". It aims at aligning all business aspects toward the goal of enriching customers' lives with a superior travel experience. Four pillars — customer-centric, operational excellence, productivity, and value-focused and high-performance culture — anchor the strategy to connect and bring together the major work programs that will drive the change the company needs. "Time to Win" represents the most unconventional approach that Cathay Pacific has adopted in terms of strategic actions over the past 20 years. It focuses on its customers, improving its competitiveness and efficiency in all business aspects. The main enabler of these goals is digital technology (Cathay Pacific Airways Limited, February 2017).

Before the "Time-to-Win" strategy was launched, Cathay Pacific had already paid close attention to the use of digital technology to support its marketing communications. It was no half-hearted attempt as, early in 2015, the airline devoted more than 50% of its marketing campaign to digital platforms. The initiative "Life Well Travelled" included the use of social media and video, as well as advertising.

The airline also makes use of its "influencer community" — which includes both its fans and the famous personalities in the tourism and travel sector — to encourage travelers to share moments from their travel experience on social media platforms, including Facebook, Instagram, LinkedIn, and Twitter. YouTube is also used as a platform to share short videos. Using the tag, "#LifeWellTravelled", the campaign brings forth the memorable experiences of Cathay Pacific travelers (Loras, 2015). This is a new form of marketing communication that is expected to trigger "conversation" among the customers, a form of promotion that stands out from the regular advertising undertaken by the company. Kelly (2007) stated that one of the topics that can trigger conversations is personal stories, such as the campaign conducted by Cathay Pacific.

Through the use of digital technology, Cathay Pacific has also engaged its customers to help develop its products and services. The process of service improvement and product development is done by the company with the active participation of customers. In the concept of New Wave Marketing, this is called "co-creation" (Kotler, Kartajaya and Hooi, 2017).

A platform that allows co-creation between Cathay Pacific and its customers is Cathay Insight, an insight community of more than 10,000 customers. The Cathay Insight online community is a place where thousands of Cathay Pacific customers from 17 countries engage in conversations and help the airline "shape its products and services developed for the customers." Members routinely take part in engagement activities, providing feedback on their experiences with the airline. For example, the community has engaged in co-creation about in-flight experiences, catalyzed the introduction of new products, such as amenity kits, as well as given feedback on airport lounge design, marketing and advertising campaigns, and website navigation. The community records a strong retention of over 87% and a 47% response rate. According to the airline, the community has not only helped improve customer collaboration with stakeholders but also brought to light some of the business challenges faced by the airline (Vision Critical Communication, 2018).

With the launch of the new strategy, all previously launched New Wave initiatives — conversation and co-creation — have continued and with more serious and coordinated resource support. This is facilitated by organizational restructuring, which is done to ensure the focus on the four pillars of strategy. The core strategy remains the same, delivering on Cathay Pacific's brand promise "Life Well Travelled" for its customers.

References

BBC News (October 2002). DHL and Cathay in cargo venture. http://news.bbc.co.uk/2/hi/business/2311821.stm [24 March 2018].

Britton, R (May 2015). The big three: U.S. Airlines versus Persian Gulf Carriers. *Forbes.* https://www.forbes.com/sites/realspin/2015/05/12/the-big-three-u-s-airlines-versus-persian-gulf-carriers/#2808b9135aad [25 March 2018].

Cathay Pacific Airways Limited (February 2017). Introducing our new strategy. *CX World*, Issue 249.

Cathay Pacific Airways Limited (March 2017). *Annual Report 2016.* https://www.cathaypacific.com/content/dam/cx/about-us/investor-relations/interim-annual-reports/en/CX16_Final_en.pdf [24 March 2018].

Cathay Pacific Airways Limited (March 2018). Cathay Pacific Airways Limited Announces 2017 Annual Results. https://news.cathaypacific.com/cathay-pacific-airways-limited-announces-2017-annual-results-153103 [31 October 2018].

Cathay Pacific Airways Limited (2018b). *History.* https://www.cathaypacific.com/cx/en_ID/about-us/about-our-airline/history.html [24 March 2018].

Cathay Pacific Fact Sheet (March 2018). http://downloads.cathaypacific.com/cx/press/cxw/CX_Fact%20Sheet_en.pdf [31 October 2018].

Denslow, N (January 2011). Cathay Pacific, Hong Kong Airport become biggest for freight. *Bloomberg Businessweek.* https://web.archive.org/web/20110417033044/http://www.businessweek.com/news/2011-01-26/cathay-pacific-hong-kong-airport-become-biggest-for-freight.html [25 March 2018].

Juca, L (May 2017). Singapore Airlines and Cathay fight same headwinds. *Reuters.* https://www.reuters.com/article/uk-singapore-airlines-results-breakingvi/singapore-airlines-and-cathay-fight-same-headwinds-idUSKCN18F0UP [25 March 2018].

Kelly, L (2007). *Beyond Buzz: The Next Generation of Word-of-Mouth Marketing.* New York: AMACOM.

Kotler, P, H Kartajaya and DH Hooi (2017). *Marketing for Competitiveness: Asia to the World.* Singapore: World Scientific.

Loh, C (2004). *At the Epicentre: Hong Kong and the SARS Outbreak,* p. 88. Hong Kong: Hong Kong University Press.

Loras, S (February 2015). #LifeWellTravelled in first major digital push. *Clickz.* https://www.clickz.com/cathay-pacific-asks-what-is-lifewelltravelled-in-first-major-digital-push/27395/ [26 March 2018].

McCaffrey, C (2014). Airline spotlight: Singapore Airlines. *Flight Network.* https://www.flightnetwork.com/blog/spotlight-singapore-airlines/ [25 March 2018].

Skytrax (2018). *Airline of the Year Winners.* http://www.worldairlineawards.com/Awards/airline_year_winners.html [25 March 2018].

The Sunday Times Sri Lanka (February 2002). Cathay Pacific Airways launches "The World's Biggest Welcome." http://www.sundaytimes.lk/020217/bus6.html [24 March 2018].

Vision Critical Communication (2018). *Change Is in the Air: How International Airline Customers Shape Their Experience.* https://www.visioncritical.com/customer-stories/cathay-pacific/ [26 March 2018].

Blue Bird

Blue Bird is regarded as the leading player in the land transportation industry in Indonesia. Over time, the business has also branched out to include other forms of transportation services. However, the emergence and the growing popularity of technology companies, such as GO-JEK, Uber, and Grab, present new challenges for Blue Bird. With relatively cheaper tariffs and door-step service, these technology companies are making the competition tighter and more complex. Thus, the codification of the brand DNA has become one of the main tactics of Blue Bird in order to be able to show the uniqueness of its service while avoiding a price war.

Blue Bird's Business Profile

Blue Bird, the pioneering operator of the largest fleet of taxis in Indonesia, was founded on March 29, 2001. Twelve years after its establishment,

Blue Bird undertook a series of restructuring to continue its growth as a large business group, with 15 business entities focused on passenger and inland transport business activities. In addition to businesses such as bus rental, vehicle rental, and taxi service (regular and executive), Blue Bird runs related business activities that support its main activities, such as workshops and assembly facilities (Blue Bird, 2016).

Customer satisfaction has always been the top priority for the transportation giant, as evident from Blue Bird taxis being equipped with a system of taximeter, radio communications, and global positioning system (GPS) to provide a sense of security and comfort to the riders. Blue Bird classifies its business activities into two business groups: taxi and non-taxi businesses (Blue Bird, 2017).

Taxi Business

(a) Regular Taxi

Blue Bird provides regular taxi services under the brands "Blue Bird" and "Pusaka" in several cities in Indonesia, such as Jakarta, Bogor, Depok, Tangerang, Bekasi, Bandung, Banten, Batam, Semarang, Manado, Medan, Padang, Palembang, Pekanbaru, Surabaya, Makassar, and Bangka Belitung. The company also provides the regular taxi service under the brand "Lombok Taksi" in Lombok and "Bali Taxi" in Bali. As of the end of 2016, Blue Bird owns and operates the largest taxi fleet in Indonesia, with 24,873 units.

(b) Executive Taxi

Blue Bird operates its executive taxi business under the brand "Silver Bird" in Jakarta and Surabaya. The business targets the upper-class segment using a fleet of luxury vehicles with comfortable and spacious interior. Until the end of 2016, Blue Bird operated an executive taxi fleet of 1,114 units.

Non-taxi Business

(a) Limousine and Rental Cars

Blue Bird, through Pusaka Prima Transport, provides daily and long-term car rental services at 14 locations in Indonesia. These rental car services, along with drivers, are meant for individual and corporate customers. The company also offers vehicle rental service, with or without drivers, to corporations under long-term contracts. By the end of 2016, Blue Bird owned and operated 5,169 vehicles for rentals.

(b) Rental Bus

Through Big Bird Pusaka, the company offers bus rental services in nine locations in Indonesia. The services are generally intended for both domestic and international corporate customers, including international schools and multinational corporations. Until the end of 2016, Blue Bird owned and operated a fleet of 560 buses.

On October 29, 2014, Blue Bird conducted an Initial Public Offering (IPO) with the stock code "BIRD". The IPO was aimed to support Blue Bird's business development plan of maintaining its position as a market leader in the field of transportation services, particularly passenger transport services and land transportation services. Ferrying thousands of passengers every day, Blue Bird is considered a reliable and household name for taxi service in several major cities throughout Indonesia, both in business centers and at tourist destinations.

Disruption and New Competition

Over the years, Blue Bird has successfully maintained its position as a leading player in ground transportation, particularly for taxis. Due to its extensive network and excellent service, Blue Bird has become the ultimate choice for customers who want comfort and security. Yet this dominance has started to be threatened by external challenges in recent years, especially starting in 2016.

In 2016, macroeconomic conditions began to show improvements, both at home and abroad. The global economy continued to flourish in 2016, supported by strong growth in the economies of the United States and China. Indonesia's economy grew by 5.02% in 2016, a 4.88% improvement compared with 2015 (Amianti, 2017). This growth was supported by increasing household consumption, improved investment performance, and increased exports.

Since then, Indonesia's transportation industry, especially the land public transport industry, began to face disruptions due to the entry of a host of new-age transportation service providers. Technology companies such as Indonesia's GO-JEK and Malaysia's Grab and Uber that actually came into being several years earlier (e.g., GO-JEK was founded in 2010) began to gain wider acceptance in Indonesia, especially in big cities. A major reason why Indonesian consumers finally began to warm up to these "new kids on the block" was the cheaper rates offered by the companies as part of their market penetration strategy. As a result, Blue Bird felt the impact of the presence of these new competitors in the form of weakening business in the regular taxi and the executive segments (Blue Bird, 2017).

The emergence of these new competitors also caused a social upheaval in the community, especially between conventional and "online" taxi drivers. In March 2016, thousands of Indonesian taxi drivers brought parts of the capital, Jakarta, to a standstill in protest against the transport app providers. The ride-hailing apps such as Uber, Grab, and GO-JEK had made it difficult for the drivers to earn a living in this heavily congested city (*BBC News, 2016*). These protests caused a backlash, in that the motorcycle taxi (*ojek*) community also held mass-scale demonstrations, asking the government to recognize them (*The Jakarta Post, 2017*). The conflict finally encouraged the Indonesian government to intervene by creating new regulations for the app-based ride-hailing transportation players.

"Fighting Back" with Collaboration and Codification

Amidst this situation, instead of blaming each other, Blue Bird and GO-JEK decided to take a new initiative by launching a sharing platform referred to as Go-Blue Bird. This collaboration is a long-term commitment by Blue Bird and GO-JEK to innovate and give the best services to their communities, as well as to improve the well-being of drivers (Marzuki, 2017). Through this collaboration and by using the Go-Blue Bird platform, Blue Bird taxi drivers could acquire new passengers by utilizing the GO-JEK app and GO-JEK could offer an additional fleet of transportation to its users.

Blue Bird, however, was aware that the collaboration with an online transportation app alone was not enough to ensure the sustainability of its business in the future. Without a strong differentiation between Blue Bird taxis and app-based car drivers, consumers would consider "price" while determining their choices. If that happened, Blue Bird would be forced to enter a price war, which could eventually harm the company. Taking stock of the situation, Blue Bird soon realized that its service culture is indeed a source of strong differentiation that must be optimized to provide its customers with a convenient and safe transportation service. Unlike app-based car drivers, Blue Bird's taxi drivers are "employees recruited officially by the company", and their commitment to organizational culture is relatively stronger. A strong service culture, therefore, contributes to making Blue Bird's brand a different one from its new rivals.

A strong differentiation for Blue Bird can be cultivated by leveraging its authentic uniqueness in being able to internalize its brand DNA beyond the marketing department. A brand DNA is made up of the unique components of the brand that should provide for the common language used by all employees of the company and not only by the drivers who deal directly with customers. In fact, a brand DNA should animate all important processes in the company, ranging from leadership, recruitment, and performance appraisal to culture building (Barlow & Stewart, 2004). This is codification.

This "brand DNA codification" can be done through three interconnected layers (see Fig. 6.1). The first layer, consisting of symbols and styles, is considered the most tangible of the three and, hence, can be easily "codified." The next layers — "systems and leadership", the second layer, and "shared values and substances", the third layer, that are somewhat intangible and require longer time and harder effort — also have an increasingly fundamental role (Kotler, Kartajaya and Hooi, 2017). Here's how Blue Bird builds an authentic brand DNA by undertaking the codification process within the company.

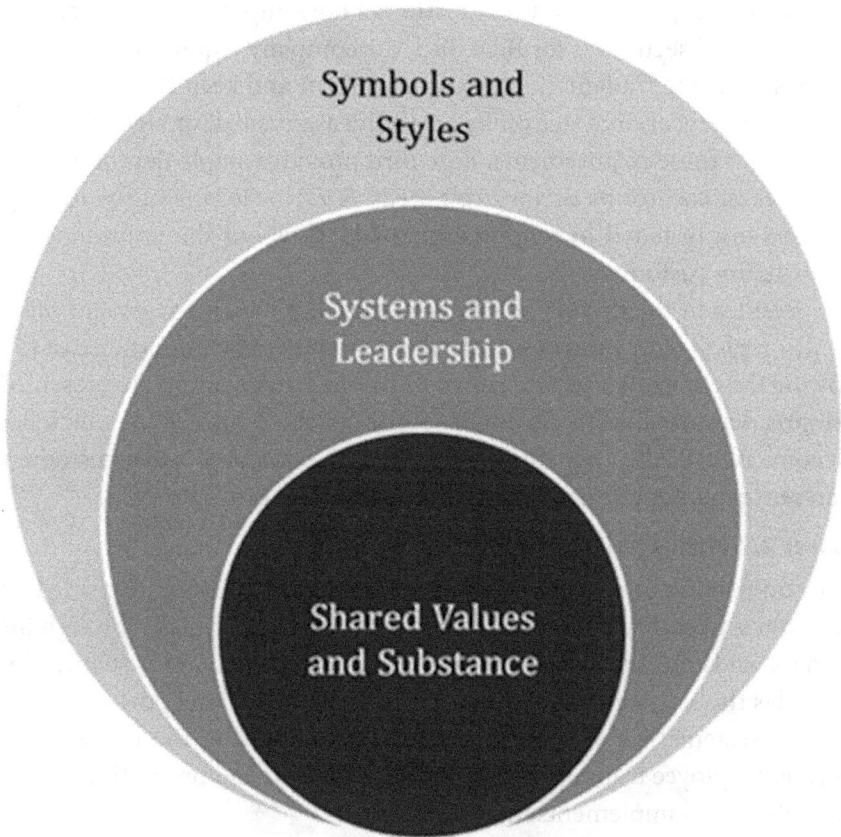

Figure 6.1: Onion Model of Codification.

Layer 1: Symbols and styles

Layer 1 deals with how the company "appears" to the stakeholders outside the organization and how employees utilize the various symbols and styles to reflect the brand DNA. The brand DNA should practically reflect all the human senses, including auditory sense (through music and jingles), visual sense (through space layout and color), and even smell (ensuring the proper scent). Through the placement of symbols and styles, which are in tune with the brand DNA, employees would be able to better understand and practise the expected behavior.

In ensuring proper communication of how important customer convenience and security is for Blue Bird, the company requires its drivers to always wear the trademark blue batik uniform and keep it clean, so that the passengers are not put off by any unpleasant smell or sight. In order to support these requirements, Blue Bird provides ample decent bathing facilities in each of its drivers' rest areas. Service slogans in the form of stickers are installed to reinforce the message about the importance of prioritizing customers.

Besides in the drivers' work areas, the Blue Bird management office is also replete with various slogans that emphasize the importance of following the company's service culture. Various visualizations are presented to spread awareness among employees about the Brand DNA, which has become Blue Bird's competitive advantage. The outcome is that customers can sense a unique service style while using Blue Bird services.

Layer 2: Systems and leadership

For codification to deliver optimum results, businesses should ensure that the efforts to codify the brand DNA characteristics permeate through the surface and into the various organizational processes and systems. This includes the way leadership exercises its decision-making powers.

By systems, we also mean systems encompassing the processes of hiring, employee training, performance appraisal, and promotion. Here's how Blue Bird implements it:

- *Recruitment*
  At Blue Bird, the HR recruitment process does consider not only the quantity but also the quality of prospects, which should be in accordance with the established HR standards, both technical and nontechnical. Drivers are recruited based on their competence and experience of driving a vehicle, as well as the suitability of their character with the service culture that exists in the company. In 2016, Blue Bird recruited 285 employees for organizational development purposes, as well as to replace outgoing employees (Blue Bird, 2017).
- *Training*
  Blue Bird has its own training centers, which routinely provide training to its employees, from managerial levels to drivers. Training is not only on technical competence but also on non-technical soft skills that are part of the service culture of the company.

- *Performance appraisal*
  Blue Bird uses mystery shopping to evaluate the services of its drivers, especially those who intensively interact with customers. Various media platforms — offline and online — are also utilized to collect customers' feedback on their experiences with Blue Bird services.

- *Compensation*
  Remuneration and welfare facilities are provided by the company in the form of basic salary, allowances, bonuses, health insurance, loans, educational scholarships, as well as opportunities for Hajj and Umrah. In addition to financial compensation, Blue Bird also recognizes drivers who show exceptional service to customers. One example is through appreciation published in regular, internal magazines.

Layer 3: Shared values and substances

The shared values and basic assumptions existing within an organization may appear intangible but have a deep impact on the conduct and interactions of the members. In the case of Blue Bird, the brand DNA codification that runs through the first and the second layers, over time, will result in the creation of service values, which become a de-facto soft-control system that dictates the behavior of all employees, especially those who interact with customers. Ultimately, Blue Bird's aim is to provide services that are complete with comfort and security for its customers. This becomes a joint commitment of all company employees.

The process of developing this codification takes a long time. However, the desired brand DNA codificaton can result in an authentic differentiation that is difficult to be imitated by competitors. In the new era that is full of disruptions, authenticity is needed, so that Blue Bird is not dragged into price wars, especially against new competitors who can offer lower rates.

References

Amianti, GD (February 2017). Indonesian economic growth accelerates to 5.02%. *The Jakarta Post*. http://www.thejakartapost.com/news/2017/02/06/indonesian-economic-growth-accelerates-to-5-02.html [27 March 2018].

Barlow, J and P Stewart (2004). *Branded Customer Service: The New Competitive Advantage*. San Fransisco: Berrett-Koehler Publisher, Inc.

BBC News (March 2016). Jakarta taxi drivers protest against Uber and Grab. http://www.bbc.com/news/world-asia-35868396 [27 March 2018].

Blue Bird (2016). *2015 Annual Report.* http://www.bluebirdgroup.com/wp-content/uploads/2015/10/Annual-Report-Blue-BIrd-2015-1.pdf [27 March 27, 2018].

Blue Bird (2017). *2016 Annual Report.* http://www.bluebirdgroup.com/wp-content/uploads/2015/10/AR-2016-PT-Blue-Bird-e-reporting1.pdf [27 March 2018].

The Jakarta Post (November 2017). Online Ojek drivers to protest, ask for regulation. http://www.thejakartapost.com/news/2017/11/22/online-ojek-drivers-to-protest-ask-for-regulation.html [27 March 2018].

Kotler, P, H Kartajaya and DH Hooi (2017). *Marketing for Competitiveness: Asia to the World.* Singapore: World Scientific.

Marzuki, Y (April 2017). Blue Bird, Go-Jek collaborate to launch Go-Blue Bird. *Digital News Asia.* https://www.digitalnewsasia.com/business/blue-bird-go-jek-collaborate-launch-go-blue-bird [27 March 2018].

CHAPTER 7

MARKETING VALUES FOR EXCELLENT EXECUTION

As noted previously, the third component of the marketing architecture, apart from "strategy" and "tactic", is "value", which consists of three sub-elements: brand, service, and process. In the horizontal era, brand, which is at the core of "value", has undergone a transformation to include a more human character. The other two sub-elements of "value", service and process, have also changed in the New Wave era: service has been redefined into "care" and process has become "collaboration".

As stated earlier, in the new era, marketing has become more horizontal. The relationship between brand and customers has become increasingly aligned. Therefore, we argue that the company would need to put more emphasis on the identity of a brand as a person, rather than as a product or organization. This approach would position brands like "human beings", not just as an institution "amidst" its customers. This is the era where brand is "character". With such a philosophy, companies can build brand leadership in this new era.

Service is the second element of marketing value. In practice, service is not merely related to the provision of aftersales support or a customer service helpline. It is a paradigm by which a company creates continuous value for its customers. Advances in technology and a continuously evolving business landscape have fundamentally shifted the concept of marketing. The question is whether the traditional paradigm of service, as practised in the Legacy Marketing era, still holds relevance? We advocate that human interactions remain a vital component of customer satisfaction, even in the digital age. In other words, human-to-human (H2H) interactions remain important to customers. We call this the paradox of today's era, when increasingly sophisticated technology is actually making customers more humane. As a consequence, the conventional concept of service must change into a model driven by care. Traditionally, a customer should always be treated like a king, whose wishes must be obeyed, regardless of whether or not it is in his or her best interest. As for the care-based concept, the customer is considered a friend and is positioned in parallel with the company.

Apart from service, the next aspect to consider in value creation is the "process", which is another important factor in marketing. The effectiveness and efficiency of the existing processes in a company — from the procurement of raw materials and production processes to the delivery of products or services to the users — determine the quality of the product, the cost incurred by the company, as well as the speed of product or service delivery. Ideally, companies ought to manage as many processes in the value chain as possible, so as to create high-quality products, keep costs low, and ensure timely delivery to customers.

Fortunately, the development of information technology provides companies with many, more effective ways to manage their supply chain. The Internet not only helps facilitate business transactions such as ordering, invoicing, payment, and procurement but can also improve coordination and collaboration, both within and across companies. This has led to the development of a new trend, in the form of collaborations in supply chain management, as a way forward for successful and sustainable business processes.

In short, the digital era has triggered the emergence of character, care, and collaboration as the more horizontal forms of marketing value. How are these concepts applied? All the four companies in this chapter — Gobi (Mongolia), Banyan Tree (Singapore), Amru Rice (Cambodia), and Myanmar Post and Telecommunication (Myanmar) — give practical insights on how marketing value in the New Wave context is delivered.

Gobi Mongolian Cashmere

Mongolia has the potential to be the cashmere capital of the world, where cashmere is considered one of the world's finest luxury fabrics. The pure cashmere fabric from Mongolia is increasingly preferred by global luxury goods and clothing companies as fast-fashion retailers incorporate relatively less expensive versions sourced from other countries. Mongolian businesses, using technology adopted from Japan, are aiming to leverage that potential. The challenge, however, lies in promoting the Mongolian cashmere's reputation in the world. Mongolian cashmere businesses have their work cut out, in building the home-grown cashmere brand in foreign markets, and not just limiting their role as a supplier of raw materials. Gobi is one such local industry player that has managed to build its brand and character.

The Mongolian Cashmere Industry

Cashmere is a luxury fiber obtained from the extremely fine undercoat of cashmere goats. It is considered one of the most expensive and luxurious fabric materials and known for its light, soft, and warm texture. It is mostly found in high altitude areas ("roofs" of the world), where bitter wind and winter temperatures inspire the growth of one of the world's finest fibers (Ng and Berger, 2017). One such ideal location for the breeding of cashmere goats is Mongolia. The unique Mongolian climate, which sees dramatic fluctuations in temperature throughout the year, rising about 40°C in summer and dropping below –40°C in winter, results in the natural growth of goats' beautiful downy undercoat (Gobi Mongolian Cashmere, 2018a).

The word "cashmere" is derived from a spelling of "Kashmir" — the northernmost state in India located in the Himalayan Mountains. The climate in Kashmir, where the fiber first originated, was ideal for the breeding of cashmere goats. These goats were exported to Mongolia, where nomadic herders began breeding them in the Mongolian rangelands, which have the ideal temperature and climatic conditions. The rising popularity and demand for cashmere wool have made cashmere goats a primary livestock for many Mongolian nomadic herders, who have steadily seen their flocks grow. Cashmere goats are not a specific breed but include any goat that has a unique, silky, and soft inner coat, which is six times finer than the human hair. This helps the goats survive the harsh, windy, and extreme climate of the region (World Intellectual Property Organization, 2012). In Australia, attempts to produce cashmere with Mongolian goats failed (Lawrence, 2009).

Today, Mongolia is known as the second-largest producer of raw cashmere, after China. Various estimates say that, whereas China produces 70% of cashmere wool, Mongolia accounts for around 20%. The remaining is produced in other regions, including Afghanistan, Iran, India, Pakistan, and Central Asia (Lawrence, 2009; Ng and Berger, 2017).

In the Mongolian Gobi Desert, the traditional nomadic herders — who represent one of the last nomadic cultures in the world — account for the majority of the Mongolian population. As much as 40% of the Mongolian population makes living through nomadic herding. A tradition that has been passed down from generations, nomadic herders breed livestock, one of which is cashmere goats. These are mainly bred for their cashmere wool. The rising demand for cashmere wool in the world has spiked interest in this nomadic community to increase their flock size of cashmere goats. This has led to a rapid increase in the production and the export of Mongolian cashmere wool. According to data from Mongolia International Capital Corp., raw and processed cashmere exports reached up to 9,000 tons in 2015, representing a CAGR of 36.3% since 2006 (Nikkei Asian Review, September 2017). Passed down from generation to generation, this knowledge of harvesting cashmere wool encompasses an intimate awareness of the local climate and environment, goat herding practices, and cashmere extraction techniques (World Intellectual Property Organization, 2012).

Gobi's Journey Towards Global Luxurious Brand

The Mongolian cashmere fiber started gaining popularity only in the 1980s. Until then, Mongolia was not seen as a major player in the global cashmere industry. The push towards commercialization of cashmere in Mongolia came when the Government of Mongolia established a cashmere factory in Ulaanbaatar in 1977. This was in view of the growing popularity of cashmere, which was seen as a way to boost the economy, provide jobs, and create additional incomes for its people. This factory was built with the help of the Japanese government, which provided technical assistance in its construction, and the project was supported by the United Nations Industrial Development Organisation (UNIDO). Today, Gobi operates four factories to process cashmere and camel wool for its textile and knitting products. This partnership brought in Japanese research and development (R&D), technology, modern equipment, and new management practices, all of which were a first for Mongolia at that time (World Intellectual Property Organization, 2012).

In order to effectively utilize this opportunity, 78 engineers from Mongolia were sent to Japan for training during 1979 to 1981 to learn the process of wool processing and machine operations. By 1981, the new 10-ha Gobi factory was up and running, and the company was officially opened for business.

Soon after, Gobi was able to produce quality products, which went on sale domestically and abroad, mostly in East European countries. This marked the first time a Mongolian company made its presence felt in Europe. Today, Gobi JSC is known as the largest vertically integrated cashmere and camel wool processing and garment manufacturing company in Mongolia (World Intellectual Property Organization, 2012). As the demand and acceptance grew, the Mongolian government saw a significant opportunity in tapping on the high value of cashmere by growing production of what is considered one of the finest, softest, and most luxurious woolen fabrics in the world. With the help of Japanese partners, the company quickly grew into one of the five largest cashmere producers in the world.

Starting in the early 1990s, the Mongolian economy witnessed a further transition in the wake of the collapse of the Soviet Union. With the government struggling to come out of recession following the Asian Financial Crisis, the prospects for the cashmere industry in Mongolia appeared even brighter as this industry became more important. Until the 1990s, Mongolia maintained close links with the Soviet Union, which also influenced how cashmere production and trade took place. Nomadic herders were appointed as state employees and received benefits such as pensions and herds were collectivized, which meant there was a quota on the number of animals one could manage. Cashmere wool and meat went mainly to Soviet markets, and the state-owned Gobi Cashmere was the monopoly processor (*The Economist*, 1999). Market reforms subsequently followed and private enterprise helped stimulate economic growth and cashmere production, which was seen as a driver of growth. This eventually resulted in the privatization of Gobi. In 1993, the Mongolian government decided to partially privatize Gobi. Finally, the Tavan Bogd Group, together with its Japanese partners, acquired 73.45% of the company in 2007. Shortly after taking over the majority of Gobi, the new Mongolian-Japanese owners implemented a 5-year plan to significantly upgrade the company's factory with modern, high-tech technology. This comprised the installation of automated knitting machines and new cleaning and shrinking machines, together with a new spinning equipment, which was sourced from a popular Italian company, Officine Gaudino (World Intellectual Property Organization, 2012).

From 2012 to 2014, Gobi became increasingly committed to penetrating foreign markets through sponsorships at international events, participation in global trade fairs, and expansion of new branch stores abroad, especially in Europe (Wikipedia, 2018). Through collaborations with foreign designers — especially in Japan — Gobi moved ahead with the launch of its own premium brands. One among them is "Yama", a new collection of clothing launched in 2016, which was manufactured from 100% Mongolian cashmere. These were obtained in an ethical manner from traditional methods and crafted through natural production processes (Gobi Mongolian Cashmere, 2018b) (Table 7.1).

From Commodity to Brand to Character

Economic liberalization was adopted by many countries that previously were under the influence of communism. Two such countries, Mongolia and China, represent the world's largest cashmere producers. For example, the new economic system brought along significant deregulations of state-owned industries. Gobi, was, for a long time, the only cashmere-producing company in Mongolia. Since the 1990s, 18 rival cashmere startups were established.

With the introduction of the market economy, the flock of goats herded by the nomads of Mongolia has risen considerably. However, this has also resulted in compromised quality. In an attempt to boost production, crossbreeding with coarser-haired Angora goats was adopted.

Table 7.1: Gobi's timeline.

Year	Events
1977	A treaty signed between the Mongolian and the Japanese governments to establish a cashmere and camel wool processing factory in Ulaanbaatar city.
1978	The foundation for the Gobi factory's plant was laid.
1979–1981	Nearly 78 engineers were sent to Japan for training on how cashmere and camel wool is processed, as well as operations of factory equipment.
1981	Gobi was opened officially after installing cashmere and camel wool processing machinery.
1986–1992	Sports facilities, hospitals, Gobi resort, kindergarten, and new employee apartments for 152 families were built.
1987–1989	Japanese SET-092 machine was installed.
1991	• Gobi factory received the first international quality certificate in Mongolia. • The International standard ISO-9000 was implemented. • 98% of the total manufactured products were exported.
1994	• ISO-9001 quality management system was implemented for the first time in Mongolia. • The first Japanese computerized knitting machines from Shima Seiki Company were installed.
1995–1996	With USD8 million investments, factories were expanded by importing Italian machinery and technologies.
1997	Gobi's second factory was established. It started producing woven textile products.
1998	• Gobi extended overseas sales and made cooperation contracts with customers from over 30 countries. • 45,000 cashmere products were exported to the United States for the first time.
1999	"5S" and a full system for quality control was implemented.
2000	The ISO-1004 international quality standard system for dyeing factory machines and technology were implemented.
2007	State-owned Gobi company was privatized.
2009	Technology upgrades were consistently made after privatization.
2010	• Gobi introduced printing technology on cashmere products for the first time in Mongolia. • It entered into a deal with Italian well-known designer *Saverio Palatella*.

(*Continued*)

Table 7.1: *(Continued)*

Year	Events
2011	• Gobi opened six new branded stores in Mongolia. • The production capacity of its factory doubled with the addition of 300 new employees. • Based on 100% cashmere fabric, a new luxury collection was launched that incorporates designs from Italian designer Saverio Palatella.
2012	• Gobi sponsored Chinggis Khan-2012 World Judo Championship. • Gobi sponsored the 2012 IJF Chinggis Khan Judo World Cup tournament. • Gobi displayed its national clothing collection at a theatrical show titled "Secret History of Mongolian Clothing" during an opening session of the UN General Assembly.
2013	Gobi participated successfully in IFF-JFF Panorama, Festival mode, Import Goods fair, and Cashmere World shows in Japan, Germany, Russia, Korea, and China.
2014	• New branch stores were opened in Brussels, Belgium, and Geneva, Switzerland — making a total of 47 overseas stores. • Gobi sponsored the Mongolian National Olympic Team in the Russian 2014 Winter Olympic Games in Sochi.
2015	• Gobi Corporation cooperated with Japanese No. 1 women's clothing manufacturer Alpine Co. Ltd. • 100% cashmere shawls, which are made of the 200-yarn count, were put on the market.
2016	Own premium and luxurious "Yama" brand with Italian design was launched.

Source: *Wikipedia (2018) and World Intellectual Property Organization (2012).*

As the male goat meat was no longer needed to feed the Russian troops in the 1990s, nomadic herders kept them alive, and used them for more crossbreeding. As a result, a coarser fiber of cashmere flooded the market. It was not easy to encourage Mongolian herders to focus on quality instead of quantity since they received payments based on volume (Mead, 1999).

With greater demand, cashmere production in China also increased from about 9,000 tons in 1990 to 12,000 tons in 1998, and the price of raw cashmere declined to less than a third of what it was in the early 1990s.

In order to avoid the reputation of being only "suppliers" of raw materials of cashemere wool, which does not fetch a good price, steps were to preserve and establish the reputation of Mongolia as the best cashmere producer in the world. To this end and to educate consumers about the different types of cashmere that they were buying, Gobi, with the help of the United Nations Agency for International Development, collaborated with three other Mongolian cashmere companies (Goyo, Altai Cashmere, and Mongol Nekhmel) to set up what is known as the Mongolian Fiber Mark Society. This is a non-profit organization, which is committed to developing the Mongolian cashmere industry's competitiveness and promoting Mongolian cashmere in the overseas market. It launched marketing activities aimed at enhancing the reputation of Mongolian cashmere in the world (World Intellectual Property Organization, 2012).

The society has worked hard to achieve this goal through the certification of what is titled: "Pure Mongolian Cashmere" and "Made with Mongolian Cashmere" (at least 50% pure Mongolian cashmere). These certifications enable companies such as Gobi to become more competitive and to improve exports, increase revenues, and enhance production methods.

The next step is to build the Gobi brand itself. Branding is necessary for the product to get out of the "commodity trap" (Kotler, 2003). Therefore, following the privatization of Gobi back in 2007, the new owners pursued a new brand image for Gobi, as a luxury cashmere fabric. Gobi came up with a comprehensive plan to invigorate the brand image by stressing on the pride that the cashmere has been produced in Mongolia.

The efforts to promote Gobi's reputation also continued at home. In 2008, Gobi set up a factory outlet next to its production complex in Ulaanbaatar. This outlet was designed by famous Japanese architect Keiichiro Sako and it stresses on the luxurious facets of Gobi's products. It allows customers to experience, touch, and feel some of the finest Mongolian cashmere. Along with popularizing its image as a luxury cashmere fabric brand, Gobi has also come up with new products and designs to appeal to younger and higher-income customer segments (World Intellectual Property Organization, 2012).

With an increasingly horizontal landscape business, brands are now facing a new era, which marks the end of the industrial age and the onset of a human era. This is motivating companies to imbibe more human characteristics and behave more like people. In view of the declining customer confidence in institutions, companies would need to put more emphasis on the identity of the brand as a person. This approach would position brands like human beings, not as an institution "amidst" its customers. This is what we term a transformation from "brand" to "character" (Kotler, Kartajaya and Hooi, 2017).

The effort to build a more horizontal and "characterized" brand is continued by Gobi through co-branding with renowned designers. The brand of the company is juxtaposed with the personal brand of these designers, which is expected to earn greater trust from customers. For example, in 2011, Gobi collaborated with Italian designer Saverio Palatella, famous for his knitwear designs, to create a new line of designs exclusively for the Gobi brand (Pyrkalo, 2013). That apart, Gobi also collaborated with various brands of foreign clothings that already have strong global reputations. With these various efforts, Gobi hopes to maintain a solid character and win the hearts of customers in this new era while also continuing to put Mongolia on the map as having the finest cashmere in the world. It also aims to encourage the reduction of pasture degardation in the rangelands.

In 2017, Gobi received about USD16 million in funding from the European Bank for Reconstruction and Development (EBRD) to support its expansion plans. Part of the deal also includes a technical cooperation (TC) project, which is geared toward developing a sustainable cashmere supply. The idea is to educate and train suppliers and cashmere goat herders in remote areas on how to improve the quality of the fiber and sustainability.

References

The Economist (August 1999). The cashmere crash. https://www.economist.com/node/232048 [29 March 2018].

Gobi Mongolian Cashmere (2018a). *In the Heartland of the Most Valuable Cashmere Fiber.* https://www.gobicashmere.com/pages/gobi [29 March 2018].

Gobi Mongolian Cashmere (2018b). *Yama: Rich Heritage of Mongolian Cashmere.* https://www.gobicashmere.com/pages/yama-cashmere [29 March 2018].

Kotler, P (2003). *Rethinking Marketing: Sustainable Marketing Enterprise in Asia.* Singapore: Prentice Hall.

Kotler, P, H Kartajaya and DH Hooi (2017). *Marketing for Competitiveness: Asia to the World.* Singapore: World Scientific.

Lawrence, D (2009). Mongolian cashmere: Softer than a baby's bottom. *The World Bank.* http://blogs.worldbank.org/psd/mongolian-cashmere-softer-than-a-baby-s-bottom [29 March 2018].

Mead, R (February 1999). The crisis in cashmere. *The New Yorker.* https://www.newyorker.com/magazine/1999/02/01/the-crisis-in-cashmere [31 March 2018].

Nikkei Asian Review (September 2017). *Pasture* Degradation Threatens Mongolia's Cashmere Industry. https://asia.nikkei.com/Economy/Pasture-degradation-threatens-Mongolia-s-cashmere-industry [31 October 2018].

Ng, D and J Berger (2017). The hidden cost of cashmere. *Forbes.* https://www.forbes.com/sites/insideasia/2017/02/16/cashmere-cost-environment/#210276682bc8 [29 March 2018].

Pyrkalo, S (August 2013). Mongolia's cashmere success. *European Bank for Reconstruction and Development.* http://www.ebrd.com/news/2013/mongolias-cashmere-fashion-success.html [29 March 2018].

Wikipedia (2018). *Gobi Cashmere.* https://en.wikipedia.org/wiki/Gobi_Cashmere [29 March 2018].

World Intellectual Property Organization (2012). *Protecting Tradition and Revitalizing a National Brand.* http://www.wipo.int/ipadvantage/en/details.jsp?id=3109 [29 March 2018].

Banyan Tree

Banyan Tree is an international hospitality brand headquartered in Singapore. Being a premium resort, hotel, and spa brand, Banyan Tree targets the luxury traveler segment looking for a romantic experience. The intermittent economic turbulence in Asia over the last two decades has only had a short-term impact on Banyan Tree and the tourism industry as a whole. Through the concept of care, Banyan Tree has been able to register growth, even in times of headwinds. However, the digital era presents its own unique challenges for the players in the hospitality industry. The emergence of disruptive new players who harness the power of digital platforms for rapid growth, has transformed the face of competition that exists today in several segments of the industry.

Tourism Industry in Asia: Growing Amidst Crises and Disruptions

The Asia-Pacific region was regarded as one of the fastest growing tourism regions in the world. Countries in the Asia-Pacific housed several globally renowned tourist destinations, and tourism was an important sector, with a major share in the region's gross domestic product (GDP) growth. Positive economic growth, political stability, and the emergence of aggressive players were some of the crucial factors behind the development of the tourism industry (Singh, 1997).

However, the Asian Financial Crisis of 1997 dealt a severe blow to almost all industries in Asia, including the tourism industry, and especially in Thailand, Indonesia, South Korea, Malaysia, Laos, Singapore, and the Philippines. The huge drop in some Asian currencies against the US dollar caused many companies to suffer big losses; some of the Asian companies were even forced to shut their business or undertake massive employee retrenchments. The tourism industry, in the countries most affected by the crisis, suffered a significant decline in terms of arrivals and earnings, after years of strong growth.

As Asia was still grappling with the aftermath of the financial crisis, the regional tourism industry was hit by another storm, severe acute respiratory syndrome (SARS), during 2003–2004. The outbreak of SARS had a wide negative impact on Asia. Even destinations not directly affected by SARS — such as Indonesia, Japan, Korea, the Philippines, and Thailand — recorded a significant drop in tourist arrivals between 10% and 50% (Wilks and Moore, 2004). This was followed by a devastating tsunami in December 2004, which caused widespread destruction and loss of life and property. During the early months of 2005, foreign tourist arrivals in affected areas, such as Phuket in Thailand, decreased significantly.

Fortunately, the impact of the turbulence and disasters faced by the travel and tourism industry between 1997 and 2005 was short lived. The industry soon bounced back with an improvement in foreign tourist arrival numbers. The resilience of the tourism industry in the face of adverse events and crises further sealed the industry's position as a backbone of economic growth for many countries in the region for the long term. However, the impact of the turbulence and disasters also went on to show its acute vulnerability to short-term shocks (Enz and Farhoomand, 2008).

With the onset of the digital era, the challenges faced by stakeholders in the tourism industry — especially travel agents and hoteliers — have become worse, owing to disruptions emerging from new types of competition and customer behavior. Internet companies such as Airbnb and CouchSurfing pose a real threat to the hospitality industry players in certain segments. The real evidence of such threats can be seen from the 2015 data, when one in three US leisure travelers stayed in some form of private accommodation (Quinby, 2016). The tourism industry is predicted to continue growing in the digital age, but the growth pattern may be different for different industry players. The emerging wave of aggregators and online-travel agents (OTAs) may take the place of most traditional actors. This is a monumental challenge that hoteliers, including Banyan Tree, are facing today.

Banyan Tree's Growth and Expansions

Banyan Tree Hotels and Resorts (BTHR) has become a leading player in the luxury resort and spa market in Asia. It also manages and has ownership interests in niche resorts and hotels. As of 31 December 2015, the group offers its customers a multifaceted travel and leisure experience through its 37 resorts and hotels, 68 spas, 81 galleries, and three golf courses (Banyan Tree Hotel and Resorts, 2016).

BTHR, a subsidiary of the Singapore-based Banyan Tree Holdings Limited, was established in 1992 by Ho Kwon Ping, the Chairman of Banyan Tree Holdings, Claire Chiang, his wife and Senior Vice President of the retail and merchandising arm, and Ho Kwon Cjan, his brother and Head Architect of the company (Enz and Farhoomand, 2008).

BTHR opened its first luxury resort in 1994 in Phuket, Thailand. Since then, the group quickly expanded its wings to other locations, as well as cementing its position as a respected player in the hospitality industry. The group also launched Angsana, a sister brand of Banyan Tree, in 2000. Angsana offers a contemporary experience to the younger family segments. As the Banyan Tree brand became more established, standalone Banyan Tree Spas were also set up as separate ventures in countries such as Singapore, Shanghai, India, and Dubai (Wirtz, 2010).

Banyan Tree's business expansion milestones can be seen in Table 7.2. The various international awards that Banyan Tree has received from various organizations, for service performance and its concern for the environment, also testify to the brand strength.

Table 7.2: Banyan tree's milestones.

Year	Events
1994	Banyan Tree Phuket — the Group's flagship resort — was established in Thailand. The resort includes the first Banyan Tree Spa and Banyan Tree Gallery.
1995	• Banyan Tree Vabbinfaru was opened in the Maldives. • Banyan Tree Bintan was opened in Indonesia.
1999	The first Angsana Spa — a more contemporary and affordable brand than Banyan Tree — was launched at Dusit Laguna.
2000	The Angsana Resort and Spa was launched with the opening of Angsana Bintan, Indonesia, followed by Angsana Great Barrier Reef, Australia.
2001	• The group opened the Spa Academy in Phuket. • Angsana Ihuru, Maldives, and Angsana Bangalore, India, were launched. • The Green Imperative Fund (GIF) was launched to further support community-based and environmental initiatives in the region.
2002	• Banyan Tree Seychelles was launched. • A city hotel was taken over from Westin Hotel Company and then rebranded as Banyan Tree Bangkok.
2005	• Banyan Tree opened its first resort in China, Banyan Tree Ringha in Yunnan. • Maison Souvannaphoum Hotel in Laos was opened. • The Group acquired Thai Wah Plaza, which houses Banyan Tree Bangkok in Thailand.
2006	• Banyan Tree Holdings Limited was listed on the Singapore Stock Exchange. • Banyan Tree opened new resorts in Lijiang, China. • Angsana Velavaru, Maldives, was opened. • The Group introduced Banyan Tree Private Collection, Asia's first asset-backed destination club, offering perpetual and transferable membership.
2007	• Two new resorts were launched — Banyan Tree Madivaru (Maldives) and Angsana Riads Collection (Morocco). • Two new Spa Academies were opened in Lijiang (China) and Bangkok (Thailand).
2008	• The group launched the Banyan Tree Indochina Hospitality Fund, a real estate development fund primarily focusing on the hospitality sector in Vietnam, Cambodia, and Laos. • Banyan Tree Sanya, China, was opened.

(Continued)

Table 7.2: *(Continued)*

Year	Events
2009	Banyan Tree opened new resorts in Mayakoba (Mexico), Hangzhou (China), Ungasan, Bali (Indonesia), and Al Wadi (UAE).
2010	Banyan Tree Cabo Marqués (Mexico), Banyan Tree Club and Spa Seoul (Korea), Banyan Tree Samui (Thailand), and Angsana Fuxian Lake (China) were launched.
2011	• The first Banyan Tree spa in Singapore — Banyan Tree Spa Marina Bay Sands was opened. • Banyan Tree opened new resorts in Macau (China). • Two new Angsana resorts were launched in Hangzhou (China) and Balaclava (Mauritius). • Sheraton Grande Laguna Phuket was rebranded as Angsana Laguna Phuket.
2012	Three resorts were launched — Banyan Tree Shanghai On The Bund (China), Banyan Tree Lăng Cô Central (Vietnam), and Angsana Lăng Cô, Central (Vietnam).
2013	Three resorts were opened in China — Banyan Tree Tianjin Riverside, Banyan Tree Chongqing Beibei, and Angsana Tengchong Hot Spring Village.
2014	• Banyan Tree celebrated its 20th anniversary. • The group opened a Banyan Tree resort in Yangshuo and an Angsana resort in Xi'an Linton, China. • The Group launched its third brand, Cassia.
2015	• The first Cassia hotel was launched in Phuket, Thailand. • The group launched its fourth brand, Dhawa, a casual and contemporary full-service hotel, targeting middle-class travelers.
2016	Banyan Tree restructured its workforce ahead of a "relatively prolonged" global downturn.

Source: Banyan Tree Hotels and Resorts (2016), Leong (2016), and Wirtz (2010).

Brand and Corporate Values

Banyan Tree's foray into the luxury resort sector was a response to a gap in the hotel industry supposedly left unserved by hospitality giants such as Hilton and Shangri-La. The company aimed to serve people who sought a more private and intimate experience from their stay. The gap probably resulted from a considerable price difference between the luxurious Aman Resorts and other resorts in the luxury resort market. The opportunity was seized by founders Ho and Chiang, who wanted to build a resort offering individual villas, architecture inspired by local culture and positioned as a private, romantic escapade for visitors. The idea clicked, and Banyan Tree took off. Although the travel and tourism industry in Asia suffered periodic crises, including the Asian Economic Crisis in 1997–1998, the September 11 attacks on the World Trade Center in 2001, SARS in 2003, and the tsunami on December 26, 2004, Banyan Tree did not lay off a single employee.

What is the secret of Banyan Tree's success, especially in the face of a difficult macro environment? In an interview, Ho Kwon Ping, the CEO of Banyan Tree Holdings Limited, stated that while establishing Banyan Tree, he was clear that Banyan Tree's brand building had to be one of the most important imperatives for this business. One issue that he was continuously preoccupied with, was how the company should "innovate the product without diluting the brand" and without losing the core values that defines Banyan Tree's corporate culture. Core values or value-based principles (VBPs) at Banyan Tree fundamentally are based on two principles: (1) Creating an intimate experience for customers and (2) caring for the natural and human environment. The practical implementation of these two principles is evident from Banyan Tree's CSR programs that not only aim to contribute positively to the environment and society but also intend to create a memorable experience for customers. Part of the company's CSR initiatives is designed to encourage environmental conservation and help ecological restoration. In its efforts to create greater awareness on environmental concerns, Banyan Tree solicits the involvement of interested guests in their research and environmental preservation work. For example, once the guests at Banyan Tree's Maldives resort took part in the company's coral transplantation program, free marine biology sessions were also organized for them to learn more about the amazing marine life and its conservation. Guests also got a chance to participate in the Green Sea Turtle Headstarting projects. The guests at the resort showed tremendous positive response and excitement toward the activities. The core values are also reflected in the conduct of hotel staff in taking care of guests, which is marked by sincere sensitivity and creativity. Banyan Tree has made an effort to empower its employees to provide care beyond company standards. For example, the house-keeping teams, while adhering to

general guidelines on the arrangement of rooms according to the premium resort's standards, are also given the freedom to decorate rooms
using their own creativity. They are also encouraged to treat guests as
friends and not shy away from impressing people with the uniqueness
of their respective characters. This concept is appropriately utilized at
Banyan Tree, which establishes itself as a romantic and intimate getaway
for guests (Wirtz, 2010). Even the frontlines at Banyan Tree are called
"caregivers" not "service providers".

Caring and Internalization of VBPs

To be able to have a team that acts as "caregivers", standard operating
procedures (SOPs) is not enough. Too much fixation on SOPs will make
employees seem stiff in providing services. Moreover, they cannot be
customized according to the uniqueness of each individual. Ho said that
what the company needed, more than exact standards, was a culture in
which everybody is friendly and helpful, and the most important part
of the culture is the values that must be internalized to all employees.
Banyan Tree itself has various techniques to instill its core values in its
employees. Below shows how Banyan Tree internalizes its core values to
its employees:

Engaging vision

Banyan Tree's vision is to build globally recognized brands with inspiring
exceptional experiences for its guests and to enhance both the physical
and the human environments in which it operates. In short, the founder
envisions Banyan Tree as an aspirational brand (Enz and Farhoomand,
2008). This kind of vision affirms that Banyan Tree aims not only to
provide a memorable experience to its customers but can also have a
positive impact on the environment and the local communities.

Staff recruitment

Banyan Tree strives to involve people living in the vicinity of its resorts
in its local community empowerment program. It often recruits qualified
local human resources. With a sizeable staff living around the resort, it
is likely to have a high concern for the local environment and social
issues. Furthermore, Banyan Tree resorts include a special gallery to
accommodate indigenous art and handicrafts produced by local artisans.

Service orientation

Orientation is generally conducted for new employees to get them familiarized with the corporate culture. All employees are taught the basic standards of five-star service delivery, from greeting and remembering the names of guests to anticipating their diverse needs. Some selected employees are also given a chance to personally enjoy the legendary Banyan Tree experience (Wirtz, 2010), so that they can understand what it feels like to be in the position of a guest.

To strengthen values related to environmental and community concerns, employees are actively involved in CSR programs. Some programs, especially those related to environmental conservation, require the involvement of both employees and hotel guests. In 2002, Banyan Tree launched a Green Imperative Fund (GIF) to formalize its activities in support of community-based and environmental initiatives.

Recognition and rewards

Banyan Tree invests generously in staff welfare. Recognition and rewards are bestowed upon employees for a level of care they provide to guests, reflecting Banyan Tree's values. The right recognition and rewards encourage employees to provide optimal services and also improve the sense of ownership among them. Employees can use Banyan Tree's air-conditioned buses to commute to and from work and also have access to various other facilities, such as a well-stocked canteen, medical services, and child care. Staff dorms come with attached bathrooms and are fitted with televisions, telephones, and refrigerators.

Care in the Digital Era

Banyan Tree has put perennial faith in the power of personal touches, as opposed to the sophistication of digital technology. This philosophy, in addition to other aspects, can be particularly seen in Banyan Tree Spa centers, which are located within Banyan Tree properties. The spa centers put special emphasis on "human touch" and rely less on advanced high-tech equipment. Visitors at the spa come in for an intimate, euphoric experience, which sets out to rejuvenate the body, mind, and soul, and are mainly targeted at couples looking for a private time.

Incorporating technology that is not customer-centric would indeed be a waste as customers do not derive any additional value from it. For example, hospitality businesses have spent millions to implement new technologies at their properties and put up kiosks with tablets in order to provide an enhanced digital experience through self-check-in. The usability of kiosks with tablets has indeed been proven at airports, where airlines have put them to serve flyers. In hotels, however, these kiosks remain mostly unused at many places. They have been"human" failing to anticipate that the guests might still prefer the more experience of being greeted by a staff and interacting with them during their check-in process. That said, advances in digital technology can indeed be used to strengthen the implementation of care within a hospitality business. If customer touch points can be accurately and exhaustively mapped, then hotels and resorts can identify the parts of the experience where digital technology can play an optimal role. The key is to be customer centric, that is, to focus on customer needs, rather than merely showing off technological sophistication. For example, in the tourism industry, a number of countries and local governments have developed applications for smartphones to help tourists plan a visit to preferred destinations, determine activity details, and choose food menu. In 2017, Virgin's hotel also launched an app called "Lucy" that allows guests to control room temperature, book room service, book spa treatments and even chat with hotel officials (Deloitte, 2017).

The digital revolution has given rise to new players in the hospitality industry. The availability of independent houses for booking by room aggregators, such as Airbnb and CouchSurfing, has proven to be a blow to some traditional hotels. Although, at present, a majority of the segment being served by such aggregators is not the same target market as Banyan Tree, it is not completely unlikely for the company to offer similar services with a more luxurious format in the future.

References

Banyan Tree Hotel and Resorts (2016). Banyan tree investor relations. http://investors.banyantree.com/Milestones.html [7 September 2017].
Deloitte (2017). *2017 Travel and Hospitality Industry Outlook*. Deloitte Center for Industry Insights. https://www2.deloitte.com/content/dam/Deloitte/us/Documents/consumer-business/us-cb-2017-travel-hospitality-industry-outlook.pdf [29 November 2018]

Enz, C and A Farhoomand (2008). *Banyan Tree: Sustainability of a Brand During Rapid Global Expansion*. Hongkong: Asia Case Research Centre.

Leong, G (February 2016). Workforce to be cut by 12%, including about 20 S'pore jobs; three top executives quit. *The Strait Times.* http://www.straitstimes.com/business/companies-markets/banyan-tree-to-slash-staff-ahead-of-coming-recession [7 September 2017].

Quinby, D (August 2016). The end of alternative accommodation: Airbnb is now the third-largest online accommodation seller worldwide. *Phocuswright.* http://www.phocuswright.com/Travel-Research/Research-Updates/2016/The-End-of-Alternative-Accommodation?cid=external_email [8 September 2017].

Singh, A (January 1997). Asia Pacific tourism industry: Current trends and future outlook. *Asia Pacific Journal of Tourism Research*, 2, 89–99. http://dx.doi.org/10.1080/10941669808721988

Wilks, J and S Moore (2004). *Tourism Risk Management for the Asia Pacific Region: An Authoritative Guide for Managing Crises and Disasters*, p. 9. APEC International Center for Sustainable Tourism. Gold Coast MC, Queensland: Asia Pacific Economic Cooperation.

Wirtz, J (2010). Banyan tree hotels & resorts. In *Services Marketing: People, Technology, Strategy*, C Lovelock and J Wirtz (eds.), 7th ed. New York: Prentice Hall.

Amru Rice Co., Ltd.

Amru Rice was registered by a young Cambodian businessman in 2011. Within a short span of time, the company became one of the champions in Cambodia's rice industry. However, as in other developing countries, the agricultural industry in Cambodia and, rice production in particular, continues to face some challenges, especially due to low production capacity and poor seed quality. Without effective and efficient production and distribution processes, the company's products won't stand a chance to compete in the global market. Technological advancements, however, have made it easier for companies like Amru Rice to collaborate with external parties so as to provide a greater value to the end-users. This case shows how Amru Rice has succeeded in implementing collaborations to bring great benefits to itself, as well as to farmers.

Cambodia's White Gold

Agriculture is a key economic sector in Cambodia, accounting for over 25% of the gross domestic product (GDP), along with industry (32%) and services (41%) (CIA World Factbook, 2017). On average, agricultural GDP growth in Cambodia has lagged behind the industrial and the service sectors, but it maintained an average annual rate of 4%–5% during the last decade. Among the various agricultural products, rice is the most important commodity in Cambodia (FAO, 2014). Nearly 50% of the Cambodian population is engaged in rice production. In 2015, up to 9.2 million tons of rice was harvested, the highest yield of any agricultural product, followed by manioc and corn (ResponsAbility, 2017).

Rice is also a staple food in Cambodia, with an average consumption of about 150 kg of rice per person annually. In a country where rice is fondly referred to as "white gold", many Cambodian farmers grow rice on their ancestral lands. They retain a part for their consumption and sell the surplus in the local markets to earn additional income (ResponsAbility, 2017). The production, processing, and marketing of rice are estimated to employ 3 million people or more than 20% of the country's working-age population (International Finance Corporation, 2015).

Cambodia's agricultural industry was dealt with massive setbacks during the civil war in the 1960s and the 1970s, which led to the suspension of rice exports. In 2009, the country began exporting rice. Since then rice production and exports have consistently gone up as a result of improved farming and irrigation techniques and lucrative farm-gate prices. Farmers too are benefiting from the rising trends; they are employing more professional production methods and organizing cooperatives for better management. A large part of the rice produced in Cambodia is exported to Thailand and Vietnam, where it is milled and either locally distributed or further exported to other countries as milled rice (International Finance Corporation, 2015). This also represents a huge untapped potential that Cambodian local millers and traders can benefit from, by investing and adding more value to the product, to expand direct exports and increase employment opportunities in the local market.

Major Challenges in the Rice Industry

As in other developing countries, the agricultural industry in Cambodia and, in particular, rice production continue to face some challenges. Research conducted by Singh *et al.* (2007) revealed a number of the upstream and downstream challenges faced by players in Cambodia's rice industry, and these are listed below:

- *Low-production capacity and poor seed quality*
  Lack of proper irrigation facilities and inadequate availability of fertilizers are two of the major constraints in increasing the rice production capacity in Cambodia. In terms of quality, a major chunk of the rice produced is still substandard, small and broken, and therefore, not suitable for export. The solution to this problem includes the provision of better seeds, so that a larger proportion of the rice produced in Cambodia can match export standards.

- *Inadequate rice milling technology and postharvest losses*
  In addition to limited capacity, rice milling technologies available to most producers are still outdated, which results in an inefficient conversion ratio. Also, postharvest losses are significant due to high administrative costs and a range of problems with processing, storage, transportation, and marketing.

- *Lack of marketing infrastructure and information*
  Cambodia's rice industry also takes a beating due to a weak marketing infrastructure. This not only undermines the rice quality in the export market but also makes it difficult for farmers to market their products to consumers, especially in rural areas. Due to this, farmers fail to have sufficient knowledge about marketing costs and financial services.

- *Trade constraint*
  The inability of Cambodian agricultural products to match international standards consistently poses a challenge to their competitiveness. This calls for a greater impetus on the adherence to global market standards in order to further successfully trade Cambodian agricultural products.

- *Limited technology and knowledge for value-added products*
  Any surplus quantity can be utilized in the creation of value-added products for domestic consumption, if not for exports. Value-added products in the case of rice could include rice noodles, rice bread, rice cookies, and rice juice. However, in Cambodia, this value-addition process is somewhat lacking due to the lack of knowledge and technical equipment required to process rice.

Amru Rice's Story

In the midst of such a challenging landscape, Amru Rice was registered by a young Cambodian businessman Saran Song on his 30th birthday in 2011. Prior to that, the entity was engaged in rice trading and, through eventual vertical integration, it set up its own semi-processing facilities. Moving upstream, it entered into contract farming with cooperatives in some provinces. It harvested its first rice from the contracted farmers in 2013, and since then, there has been no looking back.

The company today has a network of over 6,000 farmers and nearly 250 employees, producing a variety of long grain white rice and organic rice. Its manufacturing plants are certified by ISO, HACCP, and Good Manufacturing Practice (GMP), and the company intends to obtain certifications from BRC and the likes, to venture into retail. Within a short span of time, Amru Rice has risen to become one of the champions in Cambodia's rice industry. As of 2016, Amru Rice's total production of milled rice reached 80,000 tons per annum and that of rice paper and rice noodles increased to 1,000 tons per annum in 2016 (Amru Rice Co., Ltd., 2017a) (see Table 7.3 for detailed information on Amru Rice's milestones).

Along the line of its vision to become a "good corporate citizen", Amru Rice works with underprivileged farmers in the northern region of Cambodia. This stems from its objective to provide them with economic opportunities through business that is done ethically. Farmers working for Amru Rice are provided with technical training on cultivation, postharvest, and paddy collection techniques. Also, Amru Rice's main product is organic rice, which is more expensive than regular rice. This fetches higher margins, which are also passed down to the farmers. A focus on delivering the best-quality products to customers means acquiring organic certification for harvested rice, which requires the company to

Table 7.3: Amru Rice's milestones.

Year	Events
2011	• Set up a milling factory • Registered with the Ministry of Commerce as a rice processing and export company
2012	• Set up processing factories to clean and process milled and husked rice in Phnom Penh • Became one of the top five biggest rice exporters in Cambodia
2013	• Initiated the organic rice project with GIZ in Preah Vihear province using a contract farming business model with two cooperatives (200 household members) • Became one of the top two biggest rice exporters
2014	• Upgraded rice cleaning and processing lines to 15–20 tons per hour, produced 50,000 tons rice per year • Expanded the organic rice project in Preah Vihear with eight farmer cooperatives involving 1000 farmers • Received certification for organic rice grower, processor, and exporter from EcoCert • Maintained position as top two biggest rice exporters
2015	• Invested in rice milling plant in Battambang, with a production capacity of 30,000 tons paddy per year • Increased partnership with Agro Angkor Co. Ltd to do contract farming with 12 Agriculture Cooperatives in Preah Vihear • Received certification in Hazard Analysis and Critical Control Points (HACCP) from TUV Rheinland • Became the biggest rice exporter in Cambodia

Source: Amru Rice Co., Ltd. (2015) and Amru Rice Co., Ltd. (2017b)

work with farmers who do not use any pesticides and genetically modified organism (GMO) in their yields.

This has turned out to be a win-win for farmers, who already produced crops on chemical- and pesticide-free soils, benefit from organic rice harvests that earn higher margins (ResponsAbility, 2017).

Unlike several other players who prefer neighboring countries like Thailand and Vietnam, Amru Rice's main international market is Europe. The quality of its organic rice, which is in accordance with global market standards, allows the company to compete in markets like Poland, Romania, Russia, France, Latvia, Belgium, and Portugal. Amru Rice is certified by USDA and Ecocert. It also has collaborated with International

Finance Corporation (IFC) for a 3-year period to implement the developed Sustainable Rice Platform (SRP) standards and practices in its supply chain. The IFC will help train over 2,000 contract farmers, who work for Amru Rice in Kampong Cham Province, on SRP standards and practices (International Finance Corporation, 2017).

In a year's time after commencing the SRP standards and practices, in 2013, Amru's exported rice went dramatically up by 260% compared with the previous year, due to new emerging markets in Asia, especially in China and Malaysia, and market expansion in Europe for its premium fragrant jasmine rice. In 2015, Amru Rice became the biggest rice exporter from Cambodia.

As Amru Rice is cognizant of the fact that the quality of its products is key to staying competitive in the global market, it applies standard rules across all stages of production and distribution. From seed selection, field preparation, crops cultivation, rice sterilization, to exporting procedures, Amru Rice implements a rigorous process to maintain the nutritional quality and value of rice. Fig. 7.1 shows Amru Rice's complete production and distribution process.

Collaboration for Business Acceleration

Processes, whether related to production or distribution, are key determinants of how the product turns out and thus plays an important role in marketing. The effectiveness and efficiency of a production process — from raw material procurement to production to storage — affects the quality of the product, the cost incurred by the company in producing the product, and the delivery timelines. Quality, cost, and delivery (QCD) are the three keywords to measure the success of the company's existing processes. Companies ought to successfully manage the various processes in the value chain to achieve high-quality products, keep costs low and ensure timely delivery to customers.

The same holds true for Amru Rice as well. Without effective and efficient production and distribution processes, Amru's organic rice will not stand a strong chance to compete in the global market. The good news is that, in this horizontal era, the company does not have to handle everything alone. Technological advances have made it easier for companies to collaborate with external parties so as to provide greater value to the

Supplying seed
Each year AMRU's contract partners need 200-250 tonnes of seed.

Preparing field
Farming activities have to meet certification requirement.

Cultivating rice plants
The process from sowing to harvesting takes 5 to 6 months.

Harvesting
Harvesting usually takes two to three weeks' time.

Drying
Rice grains are dried and then transported to AMRU's regional Warehouse.

Milling
Residual moisture, if any, is removed from rice.

Storage
Dried rice is stored in AMRU's silos.

Refining
Rice is segregated based on its type and quality.

Transportation
Refined and cleaned rice is transported to AMRU's production facility.

CO_2 Treatment
Rice is sterilized from bugs using CO_2 treatment.

Exporting
Rice is loaded into containers and transported to the destination countries.

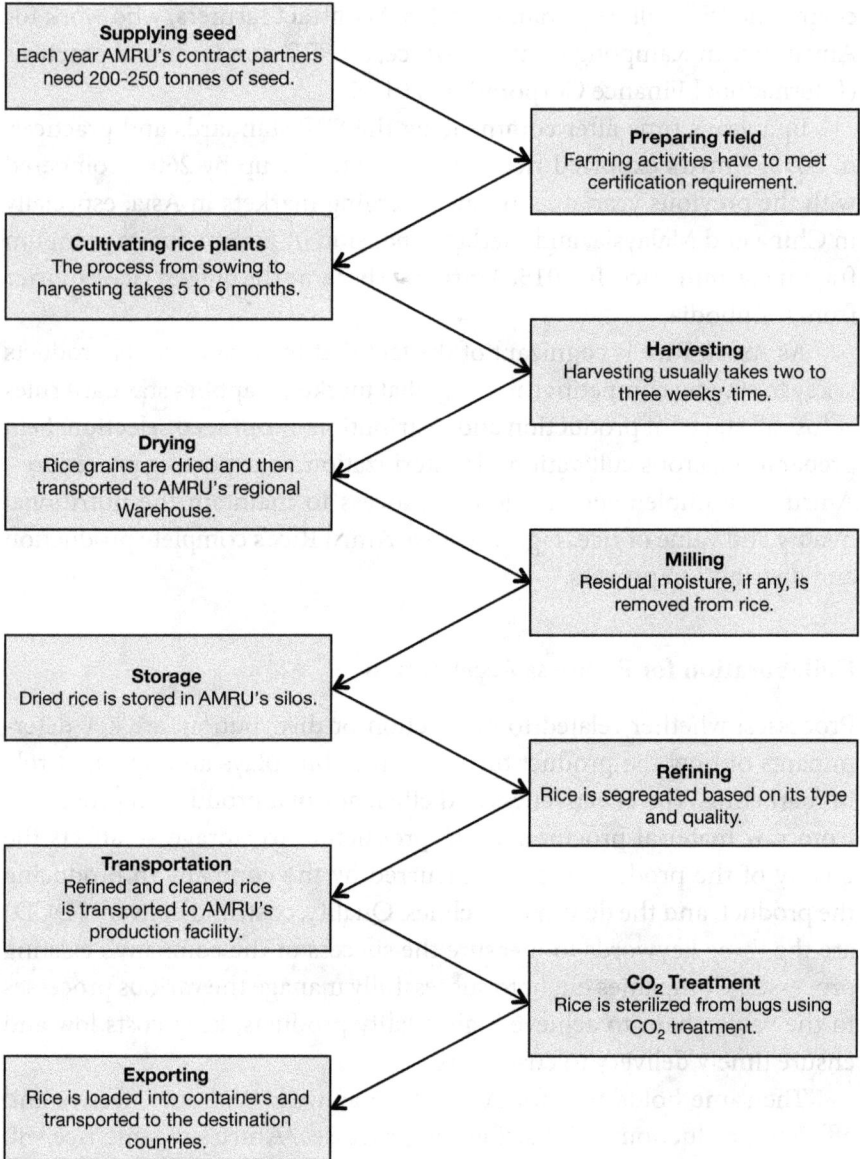

Figure 7.1: Amru's rice production and distribution process.
Source: Adapted from ResponsAbility (2017).

end users. A report on the future of value chain by the Global Commerce Initiative concluded that "an improved collaboration between all parties in the value chain will be essential in order to achieve a more efficient and effective value chain to better serve the needs of the consumer" (Global Commerce Initiative [GCI] and Capgemini, 2008).

Collaboration can be divided into two types: upstream and downstream (see Fig. 7a.2). Upstream collaboration typically occurs between a manufacturer and a supplier. It could be built in the form of mutual processes such as synchronized production scheduling and collaborative product development. Downstream collaboration, in contrast, takes place between companies and its channels of distribution, either wholesalers or retailers (Kotler, Kartajaya and Hooi, 2017).

A very good example of upstream collaboration can be seen in the case of Amru Rice. To ensure the availability of organic rice in sufficient quantity and guaranteed quality, Amru Rice does not rely solely on its own managed farmlands. Amru Rice has partnered with farmers communities in Cambodia. The project is centered in the Preah Vihear area and involves local agricultural cooperatives and about 3,000 farmer families.

Such collaborations bring great benefits to both the company and farmers. Amru Rice gets the benefits from a more consistent supply of

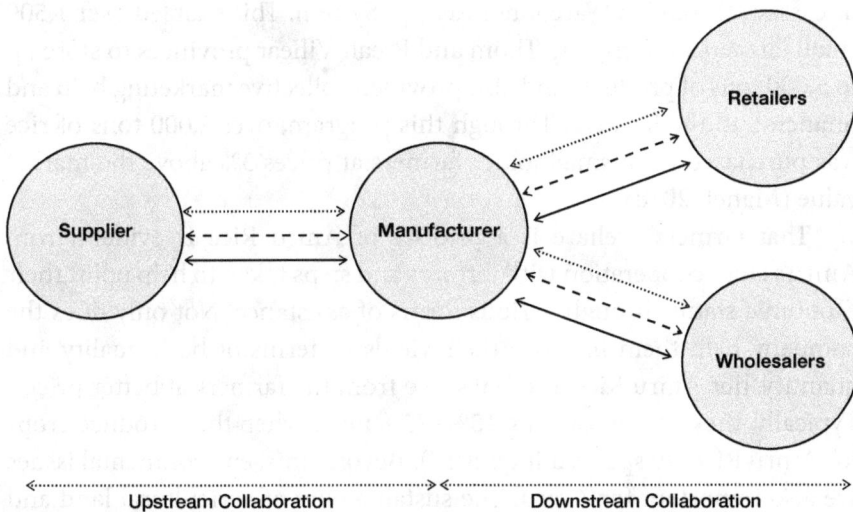

Figure 7.2: Types of collaboration.

organic rice that helps ensure a stable quantity and superior quality. This also enables the company to meet growing demands from both the domestic and overseas markets. The farmers, in turn, receive technical assistance and training from experts, arranged by Amru Rice and facilitated through a collaboration with its partner, ResponsAbility Investment AG. ResponsAbility's investment solutions include providing debt and equity financing, predominantly to non-listed firms in emerging and developing economies, and Amru Rice is one of its Asian partners.

In the training programs, farmers learn how to produce and properly use organic fertilizers. The support is provided through ResponsAbility's Technical Assistance unit, which offers financial guidance and logistical assistance and empowers farmers by helping them receive organic certification and making them more professional in their ways of working and improving their finances. Amru also extends direct monetary benefits to farmers. It provides free seedlings to disadvantaged farmers in the first year, and, in the following year, the farmers can obtain seedlings at 50% subsidized prices and pay the rest through their earnings from the first year. By the third year, most farmers can afford to finance the full costs themselves (ResponsAbility, 2017).

In another collaboration, Amru Rice teamed up with SNV Organisation in 2017, to help small-scale farmers store their yields of rice, cashews, or cassava through a Warehouse Receipt System. This enabled over 1,500 small farmers in Kampong Thom and Preah Vihear provinces to store up to 5,000 tons of products and also provided collective marketing help and financing to the farmers. Through this program, over 2,000 tons of rice was purchased from smallholder farmers at prices 3% above the market value (Manet, 2018).

That farmers' welfare is a priority of Amru Rice is evident from Amru's close cooperation with farmers and steps taken to help uplift their economic status through various forms of assistance. Not only does the company help them improve their yields in terms of both quality and quantity, but Amru Rice also buys rice from the farmers at better prices. Typically, they end up earning 15%–75% more when they produce crops for Amru Rice (ResponsAbility, 2017). Beyond this, environmental issues are also important for Amru. The sustainability of agricultural land and the surrounding village environment is safeguarded through the use of environment-friendly cropping methods.

With extensive upstream collaboration with farmers — through "carefully crafted" contract farming formats — and with the right partners for technological and logistical support, Amru Rice has not only improved its business performance substantially but has also put Cambodia's organic rice products on the global map. Moreover, it helped improve the livelihood of thousands of farmers and promote sustainable cultivation methods.

References

Amru Rice Co., Ltd. (2015). Company profile. http://www.amrurice.com.kh/company-profile/ [23 January 2018].

Amru Rice Co., Ltd. (2017a). Corporate profile. http://www.amrurice.com.kh/wp-content/uploads/2017/05/AMRU-CORPORATE-PROFILE-10012017_visitor-Last-updated.pdf [1 February 2018].

Amru Rice Co., Ltd. (2017b). Amru rice catalogue: Serving the finest cambodian rice. http://www.amrurice.com.kh/wp-content/uploads/2017/05/Amru-Rice-Catalogue.pdf [28 January 2018].

FAO (2014). Cambodia: Country fact sheet on food and agriculture policy trends. http://www.fao.org/docrep/field/009/i3761e/i3761e.pdf [28 January 2018].

Global Commerce Initiative (GCI) and Capgemini (2008). *2016 The Future Value Chain*. Paris:Global Commerce Initiative.

International Finance Corporation (2015). *Cambodia Rice: Export Potential and Strategies*. Phnom Penh: International Finance Corporation (World Bank Group).

International Finance Corporation (2017). IFC partners with AMRU Rice to promote sustainable rice production in Cambodia. https://ifcextapps.ifc.org/ifcext/pressroom/IFCPressRoom.nsf/0/BE48FC1647210D4285258145001A1AD7?OpenDocument [1 February 2018].

Kotler, P, H Kartajaya and DH Hooi (2017). *Marketing for Competitiveness: Asia to the World*. Singapore:World Scientific.

Manet, S (January 2018). Agricultural partnership hits its initial targets. *Khmer Times*. http://www.khmertimeskh.com/50104176/agricultural-partnership-hits-its-initial-targets/ [1 February 2018].

ResponsAbility (2017). Organic rice from Cambodia. https://www.responsability.com/sites/default/files/2017-04/Investment_Case_AMRU_Rice_Cambodia_EN.pdf [28 January 2018].

Singh, SP *et al.* (2007). The rice industry in Cambodia: Production, marketing systems and impediments to improvements. *Journal of Food Distribution Research*, 38(1), 141–147.http://dx.doi.org/10.1016/s0308-8146(99)00237-x

Myanma Posts and Telecommunications

The telecommunications industry in Myanmar has recorded a strong growth in recent years. In view of this, Myanma Posts and Telecommunications (MPT) — as a leading telecommunications company in Myanmar — is coming face to face with great opportunities, as well as challenges that are not easy to counter. The emergence of new competitors from overseas is one such challenge. This case study discusses how MPT is countering competition and improving the value of its products and services in the eyes of customers, especially through collaboration with various stakeholders in the digital ecosystem.

Myanmar's Telco Business Landscape

Today, Myanmar is one of the most vibrant telecommunication markets in Southeast Asia, with intensifying competition and expanding service options and consumer base. The telecom sector in the country underwent liberalization in 2013, and, since then, several foreign telecom companies have entered the market, expanding penetration from about 7% in 2013 to up to 54% in 2015. This represents one of the fastest-ever mobile penetration spikes. It is also much faster than comparable countries such as Thailand and the Philippines, which took 4 years to boost penetration to similar rates (Dujacquier, 2015).

In January 2017, there were at least 33 million active mobile subscriptions in Myanmar, which has an official population of 53 million (Digital in Asia, 2017). The trend of expanding mobile subscriber base is in line with increasing smartphone penetration; smartphone users now account for up to 70% of the country's mobile connections, higher than the Asia-Pacific average of 53% and even the European level of 68% (Peel, 2017). The Myanmar government looks to be fully committed to further liberalize the market and aims to tackle the remaining obstacles progressively. It is hoped that, by 2020, more than 90% of Myanmar's population will already have telephone access, up to 85% of them will enjoy internet access, and up to 50% of the population will be able to benefit from high-speed internet access (Dujacquier, 2015).

A new era for the telecommunications industry in Myanmar began in 2013, when the government started taking steps to open up the telecommunications market, issuing licenses to new service providers. Ooredoo, a Qatar-based telecom player, and the Norwegian state-controlled Telenor Group were the first foreign companies to enter the newly liberalized market, resulting in the reduction of consumer prices and a rapid growth in the number of subscribers, as well as the expansion of the country's infrastructure (Dujacquier, 2015). Ooredoo, which was earlier known as Qatar Telecom, is a state-controlled mobile company and the leading player controlling the local mobile market in Qatar. The group also controls several other major mobile operators in the Middle Eastern countries, including Oman (Nawras), Tunisia (Tunisiana), Palestine (Wataniya), Maldives (Ooredoo), and Iraq (Asiacell). In Asia, Ooredoo is primarily active in Indonesia (Indosat). Ooredoo has a cumulative customer base of over 100 million users (Ooredoo, 2018). In contrast, Telenor Group controls mobile operators across Scandinavia and Asia, with a customer base of about 172 million users (Telenor Group, 2018).

After the opening up of the Myanmar telecommunications industry for foreign players, the market grew rapidly. In November 2015, Ericsson named Myanmar the world's fourth fastest-growing mobile market (Trautwein, 2015). MyTel, Myanmar's fourth telecom operator, officially launched its services in the country in June 2018. The company backing MyTel is Telecom International Myanmar Company Limited — a joint venture between the Myanmar government-owned Star High Public Co. Ltd., a telecom company from Vietnam called Viettel, and a consortium comprising 11 Myanmar companies, MTNH (Gaung, 2018).

With an increasingly open market, competition in the industry is getting tighter. However, the biggest market share is still dominated by Myanma Post and Telecommunications (MPT), a state-owned enterprise under the supervision of the Ministry of Transport and Communications. With up to 23 million users, MPT is the leading telecommunications player in Myanmar, providing both fixed and mobile telecommunication services to people and enterprises in the country.

Myanma Posts and Telecommunications

Formerly known as The Posts and Telecommunications Corporation, MPT can be credited with pioneering the development of the telecommunications industry in Myanmar. The enterprise, which is based in Nay Pyi Taw, Myanmar, operates a nationwide infrastructure with the widest mobile network coverage of 96% throughout the country. It offers telephone services and maintains an expansive network of retail outlets and points of sale, which is in line with its aim to make telecommunications services more accessible in Myanmar (MPT, 2016a).

A new era for MPT began in 2014 when the firm signed a 10-year joint operation agreement with KDDI Summit Global Myanmar (KSGM), a joint-venture company established by Japan's KDDI Telco and Sumitomo Corporation. The agreement aimed to update MPT's telecommunications network and provide services to the Japanese standard. Having earned support from the Japanese government, the two Japanese companies eventually became MPT's foreign partners (Shin, 2014). Through this collaboration, MPT is committed to continue driving the development of the telecommunications sector and moving Myanmar forward.

Furthermore, the company is aware of how important digital literacy is to support customer growth and expansion. The company has launched what it calls "telecenters" to assist consumers in familiarizing themselves with various digital products and services. The company launched 40 telecenters in March 2018 and plans to triple the number to almost 150 by 2019. At these telecenters, MPT provides Wi-Fi and laptops and tablets for free use and has personnel who can help visitors on how to use the various value-added service (VASs) and several types of educational and entertainment content such as comics, novels, entertainment movies, English lessons, and healthcare information (MPT, 2018).

Collaboration for Value Enhancement

The digital era provides new ways to improve the value offering to customers. The development of internet technology provides companies with many newer, more convenient ways to manage their value chain. The Internet is not only rapidly transforming the way consumers perform their activities, including transactions such as ordering food, making payments, or procuring things, but also benefitting businesses with improved coordination and collaboration with internet technologies. This has allowed companies to pursue greater collaboration in value chain management, thus introducing more efficiency and sustainability in their business processes (Kotler, Kartajaya and Hooi, 2017). In view of this trend, MPT seems to realize the importance of collaboration with various government and private-sector stakeholders within Myanmar's digital ecosystem to deliver mobile and internet services to customers (see Fig. 7.3).

Various efforts are undertaken by MPT to develop quality products and services through both upstream and downstream collaborations. Upstream collaboration typically occurs between a company and a supplier (Kotler, Kartajaya and Hooi, 2017). Within the telecommunications industry, an important supply relates to infrastructure and support services. As a state-owned enterprise, MPT is well positioned to collaborate

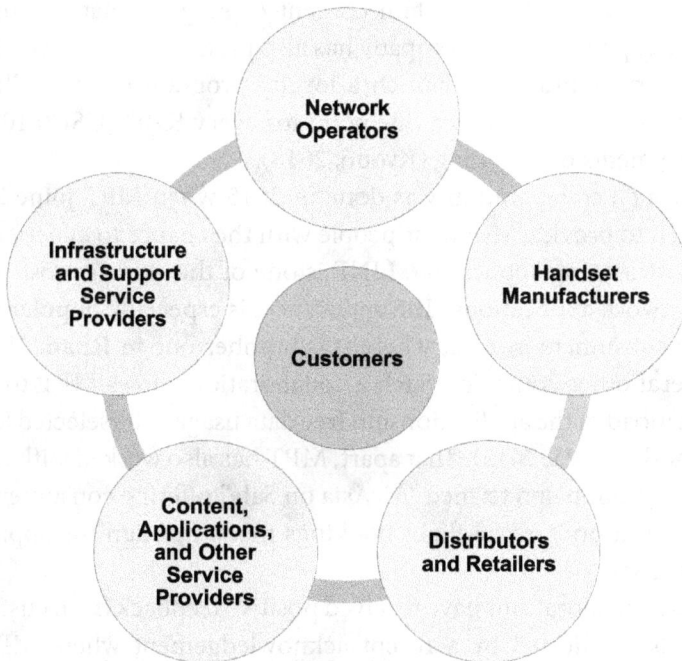

Figure 7.3:   Digital ecosystem.
Source: Kotler, Kartajaya and Hooi (2017).

with the Myanmar government in the provision of telco infrastructure to rural areas. This collaboration is also important for the Myanmar government because it is in line with its vision to reach mobile penetration targets of up to 90% by 2020.

MPT also intensively collaborates with handset manufacturers in the form of product bundling. MPT's main partners, in this case, are Huawei and Sony. Bundling with Sony is done for Sony Experia mobile handsets, while with Huawei, MPT offers bundled services for the Nova series. Moreover, MPT engages in co-branding with the Myanmar-based smart-phone maker MaxxCall to offer affordable smartphones to its customers (MPT, 2016b).

There is another form of collaboration done by MPT to increase the value it provides to customers. One of the stakeholders, in this case, includes content providers and application makers. Such collaboration allows MPT to provide greater benefits to customers, which eventually helps improve their loyalty toward the company. These benefits can be in the form of providing certain content or services that can improve customer experience. The company has also partnered with several prod-uct and service brands to launch a loyalty program for its millions of subscribers. Users could earn one point for every K200 (USD0.10) spent on fee payments or shopping (Kyodo, 2018).

One such collaboration was done in 2015 when MPT joined hands with LINE to provide Myanmar people with the chance to experience the popular messaging application. LINE is one of the world's most popular social network applications. The application is especially popular among younger consumers in Asia, where it is number one in Japan, Thailand, and several other countries. Such a collaboration allows MPT to offer a free download of the application and free data usage of its selected features for 2 months (MPT, 2015). That apart, MPT has also worked with AirAsia on a mobile campaign termed "AirAsia on Sale", offering consumers up to 20% discount on AirAsia flight bookings made through the application (MPT, 2016c).

These collaborations have received positive feedback from customers. This is also indicated by a recent acknowledgement where MPT was ranked as the most loved brand in Myanmar amongst 42 key brands in 2016, according to brand research by Millward Brown in Myanmar (MPT, 2016a).

References

Bloomberg (2018). Company overview of Myanma Posts and Telecommunications. https://www.bloomberg.com/research/stocks/private/snapshot.asp?privcapid=39653336 [4 August 2018].

Digital in Asia (January 2017). Myanmar 33 million mobile users, smartphone usage 80%. https://digitalinasia.com/2017/01/09/myanmar-33-million-mobile-users-smartphone-usage-80/ [1 August 2018].

D Dujacquier (September 2015). Advancing Myanmar's telecom infrastructure. *Myanmar Times.* https://www.mmtimes.com/opinion/16415-advancing-myanmar-s-telecom-infrastructure.html [1 August 2018].

Gaung, JS (June 2018). Military-backed Mytel becomes fourth telecom operator to launch services in Myanmar. *Deal Street Asia.* https://www.dealstreetasia.com/stories/myanmar-telco-mytel-launch-99492/ [4 August 2018].

Kotler, P, H Kartajaya and DH Hooi (2017). *Marketing for Competitiveness: Asia to the World.* Singapore: World Scientific.

Kyodo (June 2018). MPT mobile launches point reward programme. *Myanmar Times.* https://www.mmtimes.com/news/mpt-mobile-launches-point-reward-programme.html [7 August 2018].

MPT (2015). *MPT Announces Collaboration with Line.* http://mpt.com.mm/en/mpt-announces-collaboration-with-line/ [4 August 2018].

MPT (2016a). *Who Is MPT?* http://mpt.com.mm/en/about-home-en/who-is-mpt/ [1 August 2018].

MPT (2016b). *What Is Good with MPT Devices.* http://mpt.com.mm/en/home/mobile-services/devices/#1 [4 August 2018].

MPT (2016c). *AirAsia on Sale.* http://mpt.com.mm/en/airasia-sale-launch-en/ [4 August 2018].

MPT (2018). *MPT Expands Technology Information Centers Operations Across the Country to Fill the Digital Skills Gap.* http://mpt.com.mm/en/mpt-expands-technology-information-centers-operations-across-country-fill-digital-skills-gap/ [7 August 2018].

Ooredoo (2018). *About Ooredoo.* https://www.ooredoo.qa/portal/OoredooQatar/about-ooredoo [4 August 2018].

Peel, M (December 2017). Tech start-up tackles maternal mortality rates in Myanmar. *Financial Times.* https://www.ft.com/content/28217d56-8655-11e7-bf50-e1c239b45787 [1 August 2018].

Shin, A (2014). MPT promises a new era with KDDI. *Myanmar Times.* https://www.mmtimes.com/business/11072-mpt-promises-a-new-era-with-kddi.html [4 August 2018].

Telenor Group (2018). *Telenor Group at a Glance.* https://www.telenor.com/about-us/telenor-at-a-glance/ [4 August 2018].

Trautwein, C (November 2015). Myanmar named fourth fastest growing mobile market in the world by Ericsson. *Myanmar Times.* https://www.mmtimes.com/business/technology/17727-myanmar-named-fourth-fastest-growing-mobile-market-in-the-world-by-ericsson.html [1 August 2018].

Part III

Glorecalization Mindset

Asian companies, especially those that are going to expand their businesses beyond the local market, should adopt the 3C formula that we call the glorecalization mindset. In order to capture the minds and hearts of the increasingly digital customers, the formula must be implemented through a new, more horizontal wave of marketing.

In the 3C glorecalization formula, the first "C" stands for consistent global value. The value offered by a company to its customers consists of three New Wave elements: character (the new brand), care (the new service), and collaboration (the new process). It is important for marketers to integrate these three elements, while considering the high costs incurred in developing them.

The second "C" of the glorecalization mindset is a coordinated regional strategy. The New Wave Marketing strategy consists of communitization (the new segmentation), confirmation (the new targeting), and clarification (the new positioning). Asia has diverse cultural communities, and therefore, businesses that implement a coordinated regional strategy will best serve their customers. Three communities (subcultures) that cast a major influence on the dynamics of the Asian market are youth, women, and netizens.

The third "C" of the glorecalization approach is a customized local tactic. The New Wave tactic consists of codification (the new differentiation), New Wave marketing mix, and commercialization (the new selling).

Codification is about how you authentically differ yourself from your competitors. It has to be customized at the local level. Then, it should be translated into the New Wave Marketing mix and commercialization techniques that must be customized locally as well.

To summarize, there are three Cs that must be balanced by companies eyeing the market beyond their home — consistent global value, coordinated regional strategy, and customized local tactic. In the following chapters, you will read about successful Asian companies that have implemented the formula effectively and have made remarkable gains from these approaches, whether as a local champion, a regional player, or even as a multinational company.

CHAPTER 8

ASIA'S LOCAL CHAMPIONS

In any market, indigenous businesses can be among the toughest niche players. Multinationals today would be much less anxious about their peers as they would have — more or less — similar business models and hence adopt similar strategies. Big global businesses, with sophisticated systems and standardized products, also tend to struggle with cultural shocks and blocks when entering new, niche local markets. Smaller domestic players that are extremely agile in meeting the needs of the local customers are difficult to predict and therefore difficult to beat in the markets that they are entrenched.

What, then, are the winning strategies of these local champions that command the respect and loyalty of customers in markets where consumers are spoilt for choice by a wide range of products and services? How do successful local brands continue to do well in a globalized and highly competitive environment? In order to be local champions, relying on nationalist sentiments alone is certainly not a sustainable strategy. A better understanding of the local market should enable businesses to come out with products and services that can address the anxieties and desires of local consumers. This approach should aptly be supported by a strong marketing organization with local culture professionals. Moreover, the digital technology revolution that has swept across Asian countries also presents an opportunity for local players to develop low-budget, high-impact marketing strategies and tactics.

213

Although most of the local champions in Asia, especially from developing countries, emerged as strong players largely because of the monopoly they enjoyed owing to government regulations, the Asian market has since started to become increasingly open, resulting in tougher competition. In this scenario, the appropriate strategy, tactics, and values are critical for a local champion to maintain its dominance. The cases compiled in this chapter demonstrate the efforts of local champions, in the face of increased competition — competition from both regional and global companies due to the opening up of the domestic market. The cases also highlight how the companies' efforts help them develop a value offering that is able to appeal to a growing pool of digital consumers in their country.

UFC Group

Domestic players in various countries have a great opportunity to become local champions due to their deep understanding of their market conditions. The development of the domestic market can be a stepping stone for the companies in their endeavor to spread their wings abroad. UFC Group — with products that utilize the Mongolian natural resources — is known to be a company that has won the hearts of local consumers. That apart, its products are exported to many countries. The challenge, however, lies in the utilization of digital technology to optimize its achievements so far.

Mongolia: Economy and Technology Development

Mongolia is a landlocked sovereign state, with China as its neighbor to the south and Russia to the north. Economic activities in Mongolia have traditionally been based on agriculture and livestock. In recent years, foreign direct investment in extraction-based industries — which has significant deposits of copper, gold, coal, molybdenum, fluorspar, uranium, tin, and tungsten — has shifted the economic focus from agriculture and livestock to the extractive industrial sectors. In 2016, the extractive industries accounted for 20% of GDP and 86.2% of the total exports (EITI, 2017). As of 2017, the contribution of the agricultural sector in Mongolia's GDP stands at around 13.2% (Central Intelligence Agency, 2018).

In 2016, Mongolia was hit by an economic crisis. Economic growth slowed to 1% in 2016 amidst declining exports due to the weakening of the commodity market and slower growth in the key export market of China (The World Bank, 2017). Fortunately, the economy picked up in 2017, primarily on the back of positive developments in the mineral sector. The Asian Development Bank recorded economic growth of around 5.3% for Mongolia in the first half of 2017 (Asian Development Bank, 2017).

Meanwhile, the development of technology, especially information and communication technology, in Mongolia faces an unusual situation. Mongolia is one of the least densely populated countries in the world, and nearly half of the Mongolian population is in the capital Ulaanbaatar, which makes it the center of technological advances. Since its liberalization in the early 1990s, Mongolia's telecommunications sector has grown rapidly.

Mongolia has four major active telecom operators: MobiCom, Unitel, Skytel, and G-Mobile. They cover nearly 4.3 million Mongolian users in total, per 2014 estimates from the Communications Regulatory Commission of Mongolia (CRC). This figure, ironically, is higher than the population of Mongolia in 2014 — around 3 million. At the time, the records of the National Statistical Office of Mongolia indicate that hundreds of thousands of users own more than one SIM card or mobile phone (Oxford Business Group, 2018).

Meanwhile, internet penetration has not grown in line with the growth in the users of mobile phones in Mongolia. Based on the June 2016 data, internet users in the country reached 1,500,000 — 48% of the population (Internet World Stats, 2018). This indicates that there are still many Mongolians who use mobile phones without internet access. For operators, this seems to be an opportunity to promote smartphones and, consequently, data services, which in fact are becoming increasingly popular in Mongolia. The use of mobile and internet services is expected to continue to grow, and operators will likely keep on investing in new technologies in Mongolia (Oxford Business Group, 2018).

Apart from the private sector, which aggressively takes various initiatives, the government of Mongolia has also initiated various programs related to the development of e-governance and the digitalization of public services. As of now, there are facilities provided by the national data center, fiber optics network of provinces, state information exchange system, online complaint request center, and public service online machines. All these technologies lay the foundation for consumers to be better served through a greater availability of IT and digital technologies and one-window public services. The development of e-governance will allow citizens to get public services easily, regardless of time and distance. Moreover, digitalization of public services will bring transparency to the government system, help to eliminate bureaucracy and corruption, and save time and labor (Purevsuren, 2018).

Considering Mongolia's economic background and progressive technological developments, local industry players seem to be well positioned to take advantage of the positive trends. Among the local players who seem to be able to ride on these trends and demonstrate high competitiveness, especially in the domestic market, is the UFC Group.

UFC Group: Company History and Product Portfolio

The UFC Group was established in Mongolia as a state-owned enterprise. It started out under the name of Idesh Tejeeliin Kombinat, which roughly translates to Foodstuffs Combined. Eventually, in 1997, it was bought by some private owners and renamed "Uvs Hüns" (Uvs foods). With the expansion of its businesses, it began using its present name UFC Group in 2006. In 2011, the Mongolian Chamber of Commerce and Industry named the UFC Group as one of the top 10 companies in the country (LinkedIn, 2017).

The UFC Group operates six companies: UFC Trade (food and beverages), UFC Properties, UFC Construction Company, UFC Agriculture and Farming, UFC Hospital and Tourism, and UFC Construction and Engineering.

UFC produces and distributes a variety of 100% natural and ecologically pure products, including vodka, soft drinks, sea buckthorn juice, pure mineral water, and iodized salt. Other than beverages, the UFC group also produces breads and biscuits from natural ingredients. In 2009, the company received a certification for its laboratory by the ISO 9001 international standards. All its products, therefore, go through the certification process before arriving at stores for customers.

UFC's premium vodka brand is known as "Chinggis Silver". The Chinggis brand is today considered a highly regarded product not only in the domestic market but also internationally. It is exported to various markets, including Korea, Germany, Belgium, England, and Sweden. Another vodka brand of the group, "Moritoi Chinggis" (literally meaning "Chinggis Khan on a horse") received a "Grand Gold" designation from Brussels-based Monde Selection in both 2010 and 2011 (Table 8.1) (Wikipedia, 2018).

One more superior product from UFC is a natural juice processed from sea buckthorn oil. Sea buckthorn is a wild deciduous shrub that grows on the plains and reaches a height of 15,000 m above sea level. Being rich in nutrients such as vitamins A, B1, B2, C, E, and P; carotenoids; flavonoids; and phytosterols, sea buckthorn (Hippophae L.) fruits and leaves are highly nutritious and have great pharmaceutical value.

Table 8.1: UFC's milestones.

Year	Events
1942	UFC Group was founded under the name "Idesh Tejeeliin Kombinat" (literally means "foodstuffs combine") as a state-owned enterprise of the Mongolian People's Republic.
1997	Private owners bought out the company and renamed it "Uvs Hüns" (literally means "Uvs foods").
2005	The UFC Group purchased a majority interest in Uvs Hüns, while structuring in a new breed of entrepreneurial management who procured additional capital investment for expansion.
2006	The group began using its current name UFC Group and expanded geographically throughout Mongolia.
2009	The company received a certification for its laboratory by the ISO 9001 international standard.
2010–2011	"Moritoi Chinggis" (literally meaning "Chinggis Khan on a horse"), one of UFC's vodka brands, received a "Grand Gold" designation from Brussels-based Monde Selection.
2011	The Mongolian Chamber of Commerce and Industry named the UFC Group as one of Mongolia's top 10 companies.
2012	The company invested USD10.6 million in a new bottling processing factory with an objective to become the Number 1 vodka producer in Mongolia.

Source: Wikipedia (2018) and UFC Group's Linkedin (2017).

The Mongolian sea buckthorn has long been used as a traditional medicine. Today, sea buckthorn is used in about 200 industrial products, including cosmetics, life-saving drugs, and herbs to treat cancer, heart ailments, hepatic disorders, bums, and brain disorders. Due to its high levels of antioxidants, sea buckthorn oil is also extensively used as an anti-inflammatory, anti-bacterial, anti-radioactive, anti-ageing, and analgesic product, as well as for the promotion of tissue regeneration.

UFC's Local Actions

As a natural beverage maker, UFC — like any other player in the industry — is heavily reliant on the availability of raw materials to ensure business sustainability. As the demand for its products continues to increase, it is evident that the UFC Group cannot rely solely on its own plantations to meet its raw material needs. That said, a strong ownership of plantations would certainly serve as a competitive advantage in its bid to grow its business. The good news is, in this connectivity era, competitive advantage can also be built through collaboration with other stakeholders, such as governments, other companies, and suppliers.

In producing its flagship products, such as natural sea buckthorn juice and oil, UFC needs to ensure the supply of raw materials, which is not easily found. Hence, collaborating with the right suppliers is essential. Fortunately, the government of Mongolia puts special attention and places great value on plantations of such horticultural products. The cultivation of sea buckthorn in Mongolia has been on the rise, in view of the framework created within the national "sea buckthorn" and "Green Wall" programs. Prior to formalizing a national sea buckthorn production program, which began in 2009, around 80% of the 1,200 ha for horticulture cultivation was utilized in growing sea buckthorn. Following a ratification in March 2010, the cultivation area almost doubled to 2,210 ha. Even as the government supports a certain share of sea buckthorn plantations, the investment by the private sector, at both the personal and the enterprise levels, is growing. In 2011, the total area used for sea buckthorn cultivation reached 4,000 ha, which further expanded to 6,000 ha in early 2012 (Batmunkh, 2013).

Along with the government of Mongolia and UFC Group, which is a prominent industry player engaged in sea buckthorn production, some other players, including Uvs Seabuckthorn LLC, Entum LLC, Gangar Invest LLC, Khaan Jims LLC, and Tovkhon Jims LLC, are also involved in sea buckthorn cultivation and processing. Furthermore, there are numerous small and micro enterprises and households that grow sea buckthorn and produce sea buckthorn juice (Batmunkh, 2013).

In terms of partnerships, several players have come together to jointly engage in sea buckthorn cultivation in Mongolia. However, there have not been many successful collaborations on this front, partly due to the lack of a feedback mechanism in the supply chain and inactive sharing of the end results from the collaborative activities, among all the participants. The benefits hardly trickle down all the way. Limitations of modern cultivation and harvesting machinery technology also result in only 50%–70% of the crop being harvested. This indicates that the existing internal resources are not being used optimally.

In this era of connectivity, the UFC Group can effectively utilize information technology to aid its partnership process with other companies that are involved in sea buckthorn production. Provision of accurate information about the weather and technological developments on cropping and cultivation should lead to improvements. The exchange of information on market prices, availability of raw materials, and international demand will help sea buckthorn juice and oil producers maintain production capacity to match market demand. There is an immense benefit for almost all parties involved in the production process if there is greater sharing and optimization in the supply and demand curve.

On its part, the UFC Group is already aiming to capitalize on digital channels to increase market awareness, especially internationally, of its pure and natural products that are made from sea buckthorn. The company tries to communicate the various benefits and advantages of its product range. However, one limitation of its website is that the content is still presented in the local language; an English language translation should be offered to make the content more universally appealing.

The use of digital technology is also relevant for the domestic market, given the penetration of the Internet in Mongolia, which is predicted to increase. In particular, social media is a potential new channel to promote the products to consumers. As of June 2017, the number of Facebook users in Mongolia totaled nearly 1,500,000 or 49.1% of the total population (Internet World Stats, 2018). As local operators become increasingly aggressive in building information technology infrastructure and market their mobile data services, it is predicted that the penetration of smartphones and mobile services will also continue to increase. For local champions like the UFC Group, new opportunities should be utilized optimally.

References

Asian Development Bank (2017). *Mongolia: Economy.* https://www.adb.org/countries/mongolia/economy [8 March 2018].

Batmunkh, D (November 2013). Some ways to develop sea buckthorn cluster aimed at improving the National Competitiveness of Mongolia, ERINA Report, No. 114.

Central Intelligence Agency (2018). Mongolia. *The World Factbook.* https://www.cia.gov/library/publications/the-world-factbook/geos/mg.html [8 March 2018].

EITI (2017). *Mongolia 2016 EITI Report.* https://eiti.org/document/mongolia-2016-eiti-report [8 March 2018].

Internet World Stats (2018). *Asia Marketing Research, Internet Usage, Population Statistics and Facebook Subscribers.* https://www.internetworldstats.com/asia.htm [8 March 2018].

Linkedin (2017). *UFC Group.* https://www.linkedin.com/company/ufc-group [8 March 2018].

Oxford Business Group (2018). *Rapid Mobile Phone Uptake in Recent Years Has Set the Scene for Growth in Data Services for Mongolia's Telecoms Sector.* https://oxfordbusinessgroup.com/overview/rapid-mobile-phone-uptake-recent-years-has-set-scene-growth-data-services-mongolias-telecoms-sector [8 March 2018].

Purevsuren (January 2018). Mongolia to intensify digitalization of public services. *Voice of Mongolia.* http://vom.mn/index.php/en/p/38703 [8 March 2018].

Wikipedia (2018). *UFC Group.* https://en.wikipedia.org/wiki/UFC_Group [8 March 2018].

The World Bank (2017). *The World Bank in Mongolia.* http://www.worldbank.org/en/country/mongolia/overview [8 March 2018].

Myanmar National Airline

In this era of cut-throat competition, service firms may be able to survive and do well with innovative strategies relating to people, process, physical equipment, and structures and differentiate their services from their competitors. Myanmar National Airline is one such airline that can hold its ground even in uncertain times, which is marked by ever-rising competition.

Myanmar's Airline Industry

Myanmar's airline industry has experienced ups and downs over time. The capital city of Myanmar, Yangon, known as the financial hub of Myanmar, was a major trading center for Southeast Asia in the 1950s. However, civil aviation in the country went through a long period of decline in the 1960s (British Chamber of Commerce Myanmar, 2017). The industry showed signs of optimism again when the country finally had an elected government in 2011. Such a development and the opening up of the country resulted in increased foreign capital investments. Subsequently, several companies entered Myanmar's aviation market, enabling air travel to experience a boom in line with the country's economic growth and development (Nitta and Shiga, 2018).

Lately, the government has focused on rapidly developing the aviation sector in order to boost the economy and meet the growing demand. In order to make Myanmar a major aviation hub in Asia, it has developed a four-point strategy: liberalizing economic regulations, establishing new air links to international destinations, promoting national airlines, and improving infrastructure (British Chamber of Commerce Myanmar, 2017). Today, Myanmar has 3 international airports and 30 domestic airports, and international and domestic air traffic is increasing rapidly. Per the data from the Myanmar Department of Civil Aviation (DCA), the number of international passengers exploded between 2010 and 2016. In 2016, there were up to 6.65 million international air travelers in Myanmar, and the number is expected to rise to 30 million by 2030. The number of domestic travelers is on the rise too, up from 1.2 million in 2010 to 4.6 million in 2015 (ITA, 2017).

In this decade of high growth, domestic aviation market represents a huge potential. However, at the same time, the increasingly open market attracted a number of new players, causing overcapacity and presenting challenges for many players in the aviation industry. Currently, around seven airlines are competing in the domestic market, which consists of less than 3 million passengers. There was a company that suspended its operations in 2017, and further consolidation appears likely (CAPA, 2018).

Myanmar National Airlines: History and Progress

Myanmar National Airlines is the country's flag carrier with the most expansive network within the country. One of the oldest airlines in Asia, Myanmar National Airlines was established over 70 years ago, with Yangon International Airport as its main base. The airline flies to almost all major Asian destinations.

The airline began operations under the name "Union of Burma Airways" (UBA) back in 1948, when Myanmar (then Burma) gained independence from the British. Eventually, the name was changed to Burma Airways in 1972 and Myanmar Airways in 1989. The current name, Myanmar National Airlines, was adopted in 2014 after the brand makeover of the company (Myanmar National Airlines, 2018).

Before 1972, Myanmar National Airlines flew to 19 domestic destinations, using De Havilland Dove aircrafts. It still covers these 19 destinations, signaling the vast experience it has amassed over the decades. It was back in 1950 that UBA started flying to several international cities, including Bangkok (Thailand), Calcutta (now Kolkata, India), and Chittagong (Bangladesh). After the first half of the 1990s, it added several international destinations, including Singapore, Kathmandu (Nepal), Dhaka (Bangladesh), Hong Kong, and Jakarta (Indonesia).

Myanmar National Airlines suspended its international operations in 1993. It launched an upgraded domestic service in 2014 (Table 8.2), and in August 2015, it resumed its international operations with a flight to Singapore (Trautwein, 2015). The new Singapore route was one of the five Asia-Pacific routes that the airline planned to launch by 2016. Today, it is serving 28 domestic and 4 international routes, including Singapore, Hong Kong, Bangkok, and Chiang Mai (Airlinepros, 2018). Myanmar National Airlines also operates the largest and most modern fleet in the country, with 16 aircraft, including four Boeing 747s (Thu, 2018).

Future Challenges

Underfinanced and often unprofitable, Myanmar's airlines are currently facing intense competition from rivals inside and outside the country. The sector has several factors in its favor, such as the strong economic growth of the country, low fuel prices, and rising number of foreign

Table 8.2:   Myanmar National Airways' milestones.

Year	Events
1948	• Founded by the government as the Union of Burma Airways • Flew to 19 domestic points with De Havilland Dove aircraft
1950	Introduced the first international services with flights between Rangoon and Bangkok and Calcutta and Chittagong
1972	Changed its name to Burma Airways
1989	Renamed to Myanmar Airways with a new image and logo, while retaining its iconic UB two-letter airline code
1989–1993	Added more international destinations, including Singapore, Kathmandu, Bangkok, Dhaka, Hong Kong, and Jakarta
1993	Withdrew from international routes
2014	• Adopted the current name — Myanmar National Airways (MNA) — and underwent a brand makeover • Ordered six new ATR 72-600 planes from ATR to support its domestic expansion • Signed with GECAS to lease 10 Boeing 737-800 planes to facilitate its international expansion
2015	Celebrated the delivery of the airline's first Next-Generation 737-800 leased from GE Capital Aviation Services (GECAS)
17.8.2015	Relaunched foreign services with the first route to Singapore
4.12.2015	Second route to Yangon—Hong Kong
15.2.2016	Third route to Yangon—Bangkok (Thai)
4.11.2016	Fourth route to Yangon—Chaing Mai
4.6.2017	Added the Mandalay—Hongkong route
25.8.2018	Planned to launch a new route to Thailand as the airline opened reservations for the Yangon—Phuket route

Source: Myanmar National Airlines (2018) and ITA (2017).

tourists. However, airlines are not profitable due to the fierce competition. Myanmar has 10 carriers that connect almost the same destinations: the trio of large cities, Yangon, Mandalay, and Nay Pyi Taw, and a few other tourist locations such as Bagan and Heho. Moreover, many airlines are also operating below the passenger load factor of 60%–70% required to break even (Nitta and Shiga, 2018). This is partly attributed to the limited purchasing power of the middle class, as air travel is still considered much more expensive than bus or train travel.

Another problem in this highly capital-intensive airline industry is funding. More often than not, airlines are owned and established by one or two individual owners, who do not always have access to the capital market or bank loans and, thus, rely on their own funding. Fortunately, Myanmar National Airlines receives a loan from the government (Gilmore, 2016), and in the future, the airline aims to be a public company.

Myanmar National Airlines' Strategy

The basic concept in marketing is the marketing mix, which is composed of four Ps: product, price, place, and promotion. The selection of marketing mix strategies determines the success of a company. These strategies, however, require some modifications for service businesses as services are usually produced and consumed simultaneously, and the customers of service firms are actually a part of the service production process. Furthermore, as services are intangible, customers seek a tangible indication to help them appreciate the nature of a service experience. Myanmar National Airlines' marketing mix strategy helps it to succeed despite tough competition.

As a part of its strategy, Myanmar National Airlines began its brand makeover in 2015, promoting new routes and announcing additions to its fleet. At the structural level, the company, while remaining state-owned, operated as a "commercial entity under government control". It continuously upgrades its new technology, including setting up a new website for e-bookings and payments. The airline also offered tiered tickets in the form of business, premium economy, and economy class.

Also, Myanmar National Airlines' greater engagement in the international sector comes at an important juncture for the country. The Ministry of Hotels and Tourism expects 4.5–5 million tourists to come to Myanmar this year and 7.5 million by 2020, as previously reported by The Myanmar Times. Myanmar National Airlines provides competitive prices and collaborates with several online trip agencies for easy booking of tickets and promotions. Moreover, the airline is benefiting from the ongoing consolidation of Myanmar's aviation sector. In April 2018, the airline joined hands with another domestic airline, Mann Yadanarpon Airlines, to create a "Myanmar Sky Alliance". This commercial partnership aims to combine the two networks and collectively offers 13 domestic destinations (Ross, 2018).

References

Airlinepros (2018). Myanmar National Airlines. http://www.airlinepros.com/portfolio/myanmar-national-airlines/ [5 August 2018].

British Chamber of Commerce Myanmar (2017). *Myanmar Aviation Sector: Market Snapshot.* http://www.ukabc.org.uk/wp-content/uploads/2017/05/Myanmar-Aviation-April-2017.pdf [7 August 2018].

CAPA (2018). Myanmar Domestic aviation: Big growth potential but too many airlines. https://centreforaviation.com/analysis/reports/myanmar-domestic-aviation-big-growth-potential-but-too-many-airlines-406466 [5 August 2018].

Gilmore, S (2016). Myanmar's Airlines face pressure at home and abroad. *Myanmar Times.* https://www.mmtimes.com/business/19504-myanmar-s-airlines-face-pressure-at-home-and-abroad.html [5 August 2018].

International Trade Administration (2017). *Burma: Aerospace & Defense.* https://www.export.gov/apex/article2?id=Burma-Aerospace-Defense [6 August 2018].

Myanmar National Airlines (2018). *About MNA.*https://www.flymna.com/about#heritage [5 August 2018].

Nitta, Y and Y Shiga (July 2018). Myanmar's aviation industry stalls as third airline suspends operations. *Nikkei Asian Review.* https://asia.nikkei.com/Business/Business-Trends/Myanmar-s-aviation-industry-stalls-as-third-airline-suspends-operations [7 August 2018].

Ross, D (August 2018). Myanmar loses airlines. *TR Weekly.* http://www.ttrweekly.com/site/2018/08/myanmar-loses-airlines/ [20 August 2018].

Thu, EE (2018). Fuel Prices, Protectionism Hobble Myanmar Airline Industry. *Myanmar Times.* https://www.mmtimes.com/news/fuel-prices-protectionism-hobble-myanmar-airline-industry.html [5 August 2018].

Trautwein, C (August 2015). Myanmar National Airlines takes wing again in foreign skies. *Myanmar Times.* https://www.mmtimes.com/business/16038-myanmar-national-airways-takes-wing-again-in-foreign-skies.html [20 August 2018].

DataSoft Systems Bangladesh Limited

Technological advances create new opportunities for the sustainable growth of businesses. Bangladesh-based DataSoft Systems Bangladesh Limited is one such local champion that has successfully leveraged this trend by benchmarking against best practices in other countries. Through innovations, DataSoft has managed to develop products and services that meet global standards.

Company Overview

DataSoft Systems Bangladesh Limited has made its space in the Bangladeshi ICT industry as a platform for creativity and innovation. The Managing Director, Mahboob Zaman, a pioneer entrepreneur, has been the architect behind the success of the company, both in the local and the international markets. Through its involvement in the automation of the Chittagong Custom House and also in developing digital solutions to replace the manual system of microcredit programs, DataSoft has positioned itself as a key player in this industry.

Apart from developing mobile apps and virtual reality simulation, it developed automated banking services, land registrations, and port or logistic facilities (DataSoft, 2018b). Moreover, the company has been part of a major scientific discovery project in Bangladesh in which it collaborated with the Bangladesh Jute Research Institute (BJRI) to decode the genome sequence of jute. Apart from acknowledging successes, this case also discusses the challenges that DataSoft has been facing in order to position itself as the best in this sector.

Beginning of a New Voyage

On 8 August 2008, the Chittagong Custom House (CCH) tested "automation software" on a trial basis. This software was developed by Data-Soft Systems Bangladesh Limited, which supplied it using the Build Own Operate and Transfer (BOOT1) model. As a software development outsourcing company, DataSoft thus became a pioneer in the software industry of Bangladesh. At that time, many were suspicious about this automation strategy. There were several attempts to sabotage this effort, such as cutting fiber-optic cables and setting fires. The company also received threats from people who opposed it. According to Mahboob

Zaman, "It was a difficult time and people misunderstood automation". However, today it is a success story and people who once were opposed to it can see the benefits of automation. This automation brought remarkable changes in the cost and revenue structure of CCH. It saved both time and cost of their operations. Based on this, Mahboob Zaman mooted the idea of creating "Software as a service" (SaaS).

Mahboob Zaman is one of the pioneering entrepreneurs in the software industry of Bangladesh. He is a graduate in Statistics from Dhaka University and does not have any degree in IT. He never thought of building his career in the information and communications technology (ICT) sector or the software industry in particular. As a student of Statistics, he developed a taste for using software, which led to his curiosity and passion for software development and computer technology. As he recalled:

"There were only 3 computers in Bangladesh at that time. One was at the Bangladesh Institute of Development Studies (BIDS) at Adamjee Court, one at the Atomic Energy Commission, and the last one at the Bangladesh University of Engineering and Technology. We had an opportunity to visit BIDS once to see its computer. Computers, at that time, were very big in size. Software programs used to be written using punching cards and computers could read the programs once the cards were inserted. However, we were not allowed to enter into the computer room, but we were delighted to see the punching cards. Being a student of Statistics, I was fortunate to use big manual calculators. Students of Physics and Chemistry at that time used to refer us modern."

In 1997, Mahboob Zaman thought of forming a software company. He met one of his teachers Mr. Abdullah in the United States, who was the only Bangladeshi working for IBM as a Vice President. Per his suggestion, Mahboob Zaman requested Dr. Zafar Iqbal of Shahjalal University of Science and Technology to work with him. Professor Iqbal was already known to the people in the IT sector, but it was also evident to him that one needs to have more knowledge about the sector to be a leader in the industry. Accordingly, he thought of going to Bangalore, India, the hub of IT companies at that time, to understand the best practices in the sector. He contacted M. L. Ravi, the president of the Computer Society of India, Bangalore Chapter. In the meantime, he also listed 23 different topics for discussion, related to success and failure stories, setting up different types of companies, certification process, universities to visit, and seminars to attend.

The tour lasted for 2 days, and they utilized every moment of the trip. The team, including Dr. Muhammed Zafar Iqbal, visited the Indian Institute of Management (IIM), Indian Institute of Technology (IIT), and two other universities. They also visited the site of Infosys as part of the trip. At Infosys, they met N. R. Narayana Murthy, the co-founder of Infosys. Narayana Murthy listened to them with keen interest, gave suggestions to begin the new venture, and also explained the whole system of Infosys to them. It was evident that Infosys concentrated on its key activities — software development — and outsourced the rest of the activities. It helped them to remain focused and to put 100% of the effort into this area.

N. R. Narayana Murthy also invited Mahboob Zaman and Dr. Iqbal to observe a real business video conferencing between Infosys, represented by key personnel from different departments, and one of its foreign clients. Mahboob Zaman and Dr. Iqbal closely observed the business norms, etiquettes, and so on, which were adopted in the meeting. They also noticed that, when the meeting started, it was already the end of the day at Infosys, but it was the beginning of the day at the client's office. Mahboob Zaman commented:

"This was the main reason why I entered into the industry. I think this is a business which is related to human life. It is needed in every sphere of our lifestyle and it is the only business that we can cover globally for 24 hours."

DataSoft: A Journey for Change

Mahboob Zaman and Dr. Muhammed Zafar Iqbal returned from the India trip with countless ideas. They not only understood the essential building blocks of setting up an IT company but also accepted that there is no substitute for professionalism and a good corporate culture.

These were some key findings from their India trip:

- First, every educational institution they visited was teaching according to the industry requirements (Java, C++, HTML, etc.). All the roads led to IT.

- Second, behind the success of many companies, big or small, there was a direct or indirect contribution by the non-resident Indians (NRIs) who were either transferring technology or technological know-how or were engaged in the marketing of products and services.

- Third, access to finance is very important for companies to succeed. In India, banks and non-banking financial institutions, as well as business houses, funded a number of projects. If an idea was good, it immediately received the financial support from several institutions.

After returning from India, Mahboob Zaman and Dr. Muhammed Zafar Iqbal decided that they cannot depend on computer science graduates only, to successfully launch a business in the ICT or IT sector. Graduates from different other disciplines should also be included in the team. According to Mahboob Zaman:

"… a person with a better understanding of logic and mathematics should be given a chance. Hiring people from only a computer science background will limit the scope for expansion."

Therefore, they hired graduates with Science, Applied Science, and Engineering backgrounds as well. This was not the conventional way of hiring people in this sector, but they took a risk. To them, it was a critical parameter for their success, which allowed them to engage people from non-computer sciences to do programming.

In 1998, DataSoft published a newspaper advertisement to recruit programmers, stating that:

"This ad is for those people who are eager to take up challenges, people who are enthusiastic and who want to become a world-class programmer. Successful candidates will be provided training for six months along with allowance."

This offer was very attractive and eventually received a huge response because, at that time, it was a new idea in Bangladesh. The typical IT training providers such as the National Institute of Information and Technology (NIIT) and APTECH used to charge fees for such training, but DataSoft provided the training for free and also offered allowances. Around 1,200 people applied, 376 candidates took the written exam, and the shortlisted candidates were interviewed. In the end, 25 were selected for the job and DataSoft's journey began.

DataSoft's Products and Services

DataSoft began with a new slogan, "We want to make your computer meaningful." This is because a computer without software is simply a box, and software gives life to computers. To DataSoft, software facilitates activities of a business. Therefore, the company conducted a research study to identify business sectors that were interested in investing in technology to improve their businesses. Based on this research, DataSoft started with six generic types of solutions for the garments industries, hospitals, libraries, and for the members of the Parliament.

Based on the books written by Dr. Muhammed Zafar Iqbal *Biggyaner Eksho Mojar Khela* (A Hundred Interesting Science Games) and a few others, the company also went with developing gaming solutions. The solutions were standardized so that they could be used for different organizations. DataSoft also customized these solutions for different businesses, depending on their needs. In fact, in some cases, an entirely new system was developed through the customization process. The efforts in developing new software continued further. Today, DataSoft has several world-class standard solutions on offer (see Table 8.3).

Accreditations and Award

Accredited as a CMMI Level 3 company since 2009, DataSoft has always been ahead of its game in comparison with other local firms. On 24 April 2014, DataSoft started its journey as a CMMI Level 5 company, and with that, it introduced a new era in the IT industry of the nation. It is the first software company in Bangladesh to be documented as a CMMI Level

Table 8.3:   DataSoft's products and services.

Products	Services
Financial ecosystem solutions	Software development solutions
Port and logistic solutions	System management and implementation
Virtual reality	Education and training
Marketplace	Data advisory services
Mobile application	Infrastructure as a service
ERP-Smart enterprise	

Source: DataSoft (2018b, 2018c).

5 software development company. Only around 377 companies across the world have been recognized as CMMI Level 5 companies (DataSoft, 2018a).

DataSoft is also a recipient of the Superbrands award in Bangladesh. The company has a successful track record in delivering the most innovative and cost-effective technical services to customers in both commercial and government sectors. It uses a continuous training and human resource development approach to remain competitive in the industry and to serve its clients better.

One of Datasoft's strengths is its quality management framework. It uses an 11-step framework in ensuring the quality of its products: requirement development, technical solution, product integration, verification, validation, organizational process focus, organizational process definition, organizational training, integrated project management, risk management, and decision analysis and resolution.

Synthesis of its Success

According to Mahboob Zaman, since Bangladesh was a late-comer in the IT industry — India started in the early 1980s — it cannot adopt the same strategies used by the early entrants. For example, in India, big business organizations such as Tata Motors Limited, Aditya Birla Group, and Reliance Industries Limited have strategic business units (SBUs) in the IT sector. In contrast, big business organizations in Bangladesh usually do not operate in the IT sector; small IT companies, run by young individuals, work on focused IT projects such as games and mobile apps.

The number of freelancers in the IT industry is rapidly growing in Bangladesh. The Bangladesh government is also encouraging such entrepreneurial ventures in the IT sector. As such, there could be significant changes in the Bangladesh economy, if technological know-how of freelancers could be sharpened using necessary technologies. However, only having a qualified workforce is not enough; products and services developed by these professionals must pass some standards. Especially if a company wants to enter into the global market, it needs to have international certifications on standards, such as ISO certifications and process implementations like CMMI Level 3 appraisal.

As one of the local champions in the IT industry of Bangladesh, DataSoft is sufficiently qualified to make a serious foray into the regional market in Asia. The challenge of developing quality products and services is not too much of a problem as DataSoft's quality management meets global standards. The main obstacles are related to brand management. As is true for players from other developing countries, DataSoft must take its brand building and customer management efforts to the next level to compete with other players in Asia, especially from developed countries, where the IT industry is more advanced.

The company is already on its way to make its mark in Asia, and it is eyeing the markets outside the home country. For example, DataSoft has developed a USD450 IoT-enabled device to alert households in Mecca, Saudi Arabia, when the water level in their portable tanks hits 10%, indicating a change or refill is in order (Islam, 2018). The company has also signed an agreement with a Japan-based company Smart Life to provide IoT-enabled household solutions for purposes such as regulating power usage, preventing gas leakage and water wastage, and controlling room temperature in over 10,000 apartments. With its strides into the software development sector in Asia, DataSoft aims to not only position itself as a regional brand but also help put Bangladesh on the map as a country playing a role in advancing the digital revolution in Asia.

Note: This case is contributed by Syed Ferhat Anwar, A. K. Enamul Haque, and Fahmina Chowdhury from Insight Institute of Learning, Bangladesh. Some updates and additions of information have been made to match the topic of the book.

References

Anwar, SF, AKE Haque and F Chowdhury (2014). *DataSoft System Bangladesh Ltd.* Dhaka: Insight Institute of Learning.

Datasoft (2018a). *About Us.* http://datasoft-bd.com/about-datasoft/ [1 August 2018].

Datasoft (2018b). *Products.* http://datasoft-bd.com/products/ [31 July 2018].

Datasoft (2018c). *Services.* http://datasoft-bd.com/services/ [1 August 2018].

Islam, MZ (July 2018). Giant stride by local tech firm. *The Daily Star.* https://www.thedailystar.net/business/giant-stride-local-tech-firm-1612807 [1 August 2018].

Fauji Fertilizer Company Limited

Agriculture is considered the backbone of several economies in the world, and Pakistan is one such economy. Despite being an agricultural economy, it faces considerable challenges in the form of low agricultural production, food insecurity, and inefficient management in the agriculture sector, which is full of complexities. This negatively affects the overall economy. One factor aiding the agricultural sector in Pakistan is the contribution from fertilizer companies. Consistent innovations in fertilizer companies are required to balance supply and demand. Fauji Fertilizer Company Limited is one of the largest fertilizer production companies in Pakistan. It aims to provide solutions to existing problems, which has helped it become a top local player in the fertilizer industry in Pakistan.

Pakistan: Economy and Agriculture

Agriculture plays a crucial role in the economies of many least developing countries (LDCs) like Pakistan. Pakistan is one of the 10 major wheat producers in the world, with an average of 24 million tons output per season. The contribution of agriculture to Pakistan's gross domestic product (GDP) is 26% (Farooq *et al.*, 2013). The significance of agriculture to the economy can be seen from three perspectives:

- It provides food to the population of the country.

- It is a means of foreign exchange earnings.

- It stimulates and supports related domestic industries and expansion into the international market.

Pakistan's population is rapidly growing, thus increasing the demand for food every year. Food and shelter are some of the important needs of any economy; therefore, these should have consistent annual growth, just like the increase in population.

Fauji Fertilizer: History and Milestones

Fauji Fertilizer Company Limited (FFC) was incorporated in 1978 as a joint venture between Fauji Foundation and Haldor Topsoe. Its head office is located at Mall Road in Rawalpindi Cantonment. FFC has two plants, one of which is located at Goth Machhi and the other at Mirpur Mathelo. The company began its operations with an annual production capacity of 570,000 metric tons.

Today, it is the largest producer of urea in Pakistan. It has been supplying 54 million tons to the farming community since its inception (Fauji Fertilizer Company Limited, 2018a). FFC also owns the largest urea manufacturing facility of Pakistan, which consists of three ammonia or urea units. FFC has played an integral role in the industrial and agricultural progress in Pakistan, by providing quality fertilizers and allied services to its customers (Table 8.4).

Fauji's Customer-Oriented Strategy

In 1978, FFC set up a marketing group to take care of its fertilizer marketing operations, including planning, sales, distribution, agricultural

Table 8.4: Fauji Fertilizer Company Limited.

Year	Events
1978	The company was established.
1982	FFC commenced commercial production of urea with an annual capacity of 570,000 metric tons.
1993	Production capacity was enhanced by establishing a second plant with an annual capacity of 635,000 metric tons of urea.
2002	FFC acquired ex Pak Saudi Fertilizers Limited (PSFL) Urea Plant.
2013	FFC formally implemented SAP Business Planning and Consolidation, becoming the first to have such an implementation in Pakistan.
2016	FFC raised its production benchmark with an ever-highest urea production of 2,523,000 tons, due to restored gas supply and operational efficiencies.
2018	FFC and Hub Power Company (Hubco) joined hands with a Chinese state-owned firm for setting up a 330-MW coal-fired power project to overcome a power shortfall in Pakistan by utilizing domestic coal.

Source: Abacus Consulting (2013), Fauji Fertilizer Company Limited (2018c), and *The Express Tribune* (2018).

services, field warehousing, advertising, sales and promotion, market research, finance, and administration. As it began commercial production of urea, the marketing group assisted with the marketing of the product under the brand name "Sona". Eventually, apart from Sona urea, it also marketed other fertilizer products, including nitrogenous, phosphatic, and potassic fertilizers. The company has stepped up its operations with several targeted marketing activities by identifying 13 sales regions and creating 63 sales districts, which are further supported by a strong dealer network and expansive warehousing (Fauji Fertilizer Company Limited, 2018b).

The company also helps market products of its sister manufacturing companies, including Fauji Fertilizer Bin Qasim Ltd., such as 550 Kt of Sona urea granular and 750 Kt of Sona DAP. When these products were introduced, the market was flooded with the products from other urea producers, including Engro, Dawood Hercules, and the National Fertilizer Corporation. Among these, Engro and Babber Sher urea had positioned themselves as premium brands in Sindh and northern Punjab, respectively. The intensifying competition in the market resulted in the creation of a huge surplus of urea in the domestic market, thus posing a challenge at the very start of the journey. FFC, however, managed to turn the challenge into an opportunity by creating its own distinctive market share through its product. Since then, Sona has cemented its position as the No. 1 urea fertilizer brand in Pakistan.

FFC's success in Pakistan can be attributed to its customer-oriented strategy. It believes in offering a range of service-backed programs along with its products. In doing so, FFC offers efficient and effective support services to back up its product range, with a special focus on improving farmer education through practical and innovative agricultural techniques. Thus, FFC not only serves as a fertilizer company but also plays an increasingly vital role in the agricultural development of Pakistan by providing premium-quality fertilizers and education to farmers in order to improve their yields, incomes, and livelihoods.

Fauji Fertilizer's Local Tactics

Competition is an evitable part of the business world. Competitors can enter the market at any time and in different ways. The right set of innovation and marketing strategies must be carried out by a company in order to win or maintain its top position. FFC has succeeded in implementing this approach and emerged as a market leader. The company is fast to recognize the potential and the problems of the market and bring in innovative solutions with an aim to deal with such challenges.

On 4 November 2013, FFC became the first company to implement SAP in Pakistan (Abacus Consulting, 2013). The company decided to implement SAP to enhance its capacity and sustain market leadership, as well as venture into more challenging areas at various locations. SAP — known as systems, application, and products in data processing — provides the end-to-end connectivity for all the business processes and activities of the company (Dawn, 2009). It serves to significantly improve efficiency by streamlining the operations of FFC, which currently controls over 60% share of the urea manufacturing and marketing sector in the country.

Although Pakistan is considered an agribusiness country, its agricultural potential is far less exploited. The performance of agriculture remains low due to poor technology, weak management, lack of investment in production, and pests and livestock disease problems and financial issues, which affects the agricultural economy. The country's food system is insecure, and there is a food shortage. Considering its huge potential, Pakistan has set up Vision 2025, which is aimed at lowering the wide gap in yield and productivity between the national average and a significantly higher performance benchmark set by advanced agricultural economies, which are able to utilize more sophisticated farming techniques.

In a bid to help Pakistan realize its Vision 2025 of improving agricultural contribution toward the GDP, FFC has embraced digital technologies, including real-time analytics. FFC has successfully deployed the SAP S/4HANA next-generation business suite (*ProPakistani Newspaper*, 2018). SAP S/4HANA is an entirely new generation of SAP Business Suite that is characterized by simplifications, massively increased efficiency, and helpful features, such as planning and simulation options in many conventional transactions. SAP S/4HANA signals a move away from the transactional system that merely records data to give the end users active decision support in real time, which is based on data from both internal and external sources (SAP, 2015).

References

Abacus Consulting (2013). *Abacus Implements First SAP Business Planning & Consolidation Solution at Fauji Fertilizer Company Limited.* http://abacus-global.com/?q=mediacenter/news/Abacus%20Implements%20First%20SAP%20Business%20at%20Fauji%20Fertilizer [14 August 2018].

Dawn (2009). FFC adopts SAP to raise productivity. *Dawn.* https://www.dawn.com/news/500724 [14 August 2018].

Farooq, MU, *et al.* (2013). Key factor affecting GDP in Pakistan over the period 1975–2011. *Journal of Economics and Sustainable Development,* 4(1), 142–149. ISSN: 2222-1700 (Paper) ISSN 2222-2855 (Online).

Fauji Fertilizer Company Limited (2018a). *About Us.* http://www.ffc.com.pk/ [14 August 2018].

Fauji Fertilizer Company Limited (2018b). *Marketing Group.* http://www.ffc.com.pk/marketing-group/ [14 August 2018].

Fauji Fertilizer Company Limited (2018c). *Our Manufacturing Plants.* http://www.ffc.com.pk/manufacturing-plants/ [14 August 2018].

ProPakistani Newspaper (2018). Fauji Fertilizer Company modernizes its business management system. https://propakistani.pk/2018/01/26/fauji-fertilizer-company-modernizes-business-management-system/[14 August 2018].

SAP (2015). What is SAP S/4HANA? https://news.sap.com/2015/03/what-is-sap-s4hana-13-questions-answered/ [14 August 2018].

The Express Tribune (March 2018). Hubco, Fauji Fertilizer to set up coal-fired power plant. https://tribune.com.pk/story/1661205/2-joint-venture-hubco-fauji-fertilizer-set-coal-fired-power-plant/ [14 August 2018].

CHAPTER 9

ASIA'S REGIONAL PLAYERS: ASIA VISION, LOCAL ACTION

With its population size and economic growth, Asia has become one of the biggest potential market for companies from various industries. The region has been dubbed the global economic engine. Growth in Asia will be driven by rising middle-class wealth and supported by governments around the region that are implementing structural reforms and strengthening macro-economic policy frameworks.

However, Asia is not an easy market to conquer, especially for global players, who mostly hail from the West and who may not have a deep understanding of the region. No wonder then that some multinational companies have had to leave.

Local champions from Asia that have built solid business foundations in their country of origin are well positioned to leverage the opportunity to enter the broader regional markets. These are the companies with a great vision in Asia, perhaps eventually for the world. However, with the emergence of regionalization, the global value that the customer receives should not be entirely standardized. There should be a coordinated regional strategy, as each region has different characteristics. At the same time, Asian companies should adapt their tactics effectively in accordance with local preferences.

This chapter presents the case of some Asian companies that have successfully expanded their businesses outside their domestic market; they are ACLEDA Bank (Cambodia), Axiata (Malaysia), Universal Robina Corporation (Philippines), and Vinamilk (Vietnam). These businesses have managed to successfully integrate strategies at the regional level with the marketing tactics at the local level. In the context of the digital era, this chapter also covers initiatives of these businesses in crafting marketing programs that are more horizontal in nature.

ACLEDA Bank

Originally founded in January 1993, ACLEDA Bank is now one of Cambodia's largest domestic commercial banks in terms of total assets. This local champion is also beginning to spread its wings in the regional market, especially to some of the neighboring countries in Southeast Asia. The advancement of digital technology — both in Cambodia and in Southeast Asia — has provided new opportunities to ACLEDA Bank to improve its service quality and security. In this case, readers will find how ACLEDA's domestic success story in integrating online and offline strategies gave it a strong advantage to penetrate the regional market.

ACLEDA Bank at a Glance

In the aftermath of the global financial crisis, leading Asian banks have emerged as more resilient, registering strong performance and, in some cases, even surpassing the average growth rate in the global banking sector. Across Asia, we witness the rise of "local champions", which are reporting strong gains from their product portfolios that include retail and investment banking, credit, and insurance. In view of emerging players and already stiff competition, consolidation in the banking sector is expected to be more pronounced, especially in ASEAN. This is on the back of the ASEAN Economic Community (AEC), which promotes the free flow of goods and services in the region. The ASEAN Banking Integration Framework allows banks meeting certain criteria ("Qualified ASEAN Banks" or QABs) to have greater access to other ASEAN markets and more flexibility in operating there. After being able to operate across borders, banks can take advantage of economies of scale to reduce costs and increase efficiency (EY, 2015).

One such local champion is ACLEDA Bank, which is fast spreading its wings in the regional market. ACLEDA Bank Plc. is a public limited company, formed under the Banking and Financial Institutions Law of the Kingdom of Cambodia. Originally founded in January 1993, the bank began as a national NGO to develop and provide credit to micro and small enterprises. The expansion of its network to cover all of Cambodia's provinces and towns and its ability to operate at a profit to ensure its sustainability led both its board and international partners to conclude that it should be transformed into a commercial bank. ACLEDA Bank is now one of Cambodia's largest domestic commercial banks in terms of total assets (see Table 9.1 for detailed information about ACLEDA's organizational transformation).

Regional Expansion

Having cemented its position in the domestic market, ACLEDA Bank began expanding to some of the neighboring countries in Southeast Asia. In 2008, the bank expanded its business to Laos, becoming the first Cambodian bank to operate within the country. It chose Laos as the first location of its regional branch due to the country's economic situation and cultural similarity.

That said, ACLEDA Bank's expansion to the neighboring country did not come easy; the bank faced its own set of challenges in dealing with a new, intensely competitive market. Laos' banking sector has evolved considerably over the past 5 years, growing rapidly on the back of a liberal — although progressively constraining — regulatory landscape. The banking industry has 42 banking institutions — both private and state owned — out of which five are domestic and the remaining are foreign, with nearly 500 service units and over 1,000 ATMs. Microfinance institutions are also expanding their presence in the country, with over 142 licensed microfinance institutions. In spite of this, ACLEDA Bank Lao Ltd. managed to maintain its position as a market leader in terms of retail banking, number of offices, and small business lending to Laotian entrepreneurs in remote areas, which cover 15 provinces and cities,

Table 9.1:   ACLEDA's milestones.

Year	Events
1993	Established as a national NGO for micro and small enterprises development and credit.
1997	Began its plans for transformation into a licensed microfinance institution.
1998–1999	Focused on meeting the criteria set by the National Bank of Cambodia (NBC) to qualify for the specialized bank license.
2000	Received a specialized banking license from the National Bank of Cambodia that transformed it into ACLEDA Bank Ltd.
2002	• Saw an increase in the number of depositors from 3636 to 19,070. • Became the leading supplier of retail banking services in Cambodia.
2003	Licensed as a commercial bank after having tripled its capital to USD13 million, and was renamed as ACLEDA Bank Plc.
2008	Opened a new office in its neighboring country, Lao PDR.
2009	Established ACLEDA Training Centre to provide training in microfinance services.
2010	Launched "ACLEDA Unity", its mobile phone banking service, which offered financial services in both Khmer and English languages.
2013	Expanded into Myanmar with a paid-up capital of USD10 million.
2014	• Nominated as a World Economic Forum Global Growth Companies candidate • Became a member of the World Economic Forum.
2017	Extended to 261 branches, which are located in all provinces and towns in Cambodia.

Source: ACLEDA Bank (2017b) and Asian Institute of Finance (2015).

among the 18 provinces and cities of the Lao PDR (ACLEDA Bank Lao Ltd., 2017).

The expansion undertaken by ACLEDA Bank in Laos is aimed at improving its position in the country. Based on the 2016 annual report, ACLEDA Bank Lao Ltd. had registered income growth of 29% for the fourth consecutive year. Over the year, its lending grew by 70 and deposits by 1%, while its assets increased by 11%. The increase in loans stemmed mainly from small enterprises (ACLEDA Bank Lao Ltd., 2017).

To strengthen its performance in Laos, ACLEDA Bank Lao had prepared several strategic plans. The foremost priority is to expand its services in retail banking across the country, targeting small business enterprises with customized financial services solutions. The bank is also aiming to bolster its service culture and provide more sophisticated services to its customers by emulating the best practices of the parent unit. Innovation in financial services is also high on its agenda to tap customers' evolving needs that arise from greater wealth accumulation.

In 2013, ACLEDA Bank opened its first branch in Myanmar, following the lifting of international sanctions on the country in early 2012 (Becker, 2013). A country that was marked by extensive socialist control, with international sanctions placed against it throughout the past two decades, Myanmar has started implementing significant reforms that have led the country to its current growth. As an indication of the growth potential, ACLEDA MFI Myanmar has already opened six new offices, with one branch and four subbranches located in the Yangon Region and one branch located in the Bago Region (ACLEDA Bank, 2017a).

By the end of March 2015, authorization was received by ACLEDA Bank from the Microfinance Business Supervisory Committee of Myanmar to operate in 45 townships in the Yangon Region and 28 townships in the Bago Region. In these areas, the community of micro-entrepreneurs has become the bank's main target market. They can be served by the bank's micro-business loans and department. As of 2016, ACLEDA MFI, the subsidiary operating as a microfinance institution in Myanmar, has registered a strong performance in credit, with more than 48,500 active borrowers at the year-end. To further support development, its head office in Yangon and all its branches use the in-house systems developed by ACLEDA Bank Cambodia (ACLEDA MFI Myanmar Co. Ltd., 2017).

In Myanmar, ACLEDA Bank has to deal with competition from both local and foreign players. There are 4 state-owned banks, 24 private banks, 13 foreign bank branches, 48 representative bank offices, and 170 licensed microfinance institutions. These include 5 INGOs, 24 NGOs, 29 foreign companies, 4 partnership firms, and 107 local companies. How does ACLEDA Bank stand its ground against such intense competition? One differentiation between ACLEDA Bank and its local and regional rivals is targeting low-income people as its customers. ACLEDA Bank CEO, In Channy, once said,

"We are targeting the low-income community and generating business activity in the local community rather than existing large corporations. We are believers in the model of starting at the grass roots level, bringing them up and [then] they become larger customers." (Becker, 2013)

Digitalization in Cambodia and Asia

The development of digital technology has radically changed the global business landscape. Some major banks in developed Asian countries are struggling due to new and upcoming challenges in the form of mobile money, peer-to-peer lending, as well as online-only banks. Given the growing Internet and mobile penetration in the country, the trend is also catching up in Cambodia. Data collected by USAID and the Asia Foundation in September 2016 show that Cambodia's phone market is saturated, with over 96% of Cambodians owning their phone and more than 99% being reachable through some sort of phones (Phong *et al.*, 2016). The emergence of cashless transactions facilitated by providers such as home-grown early mover Wing, e-Money (Metfone), and foreign-owned SmartLuy (Malaysia), True Money (Thailand) is stirring up the increasingly crowded e-payments market in Cambodia. This poses new challenges to conventional banking institutions.

Despite the high mobile phone penetration in Cambodia — as in other developing Asian counterparts, including Laos and Myanmar — Internet use has substantial room for growth. In 2015, only 31.8% of the population in Cambodia were Internet users, whereas 12.6% in Myanmar and 14.3% in Laos were Internet users. The data is consistent with the use of Internet, which is still relatively low compared with the other regional counterparts (GSMA Intelligence, 2015).

Nevertheless, in line with the commitment of governments in Asia to continue improving ICT infrastructure, Internet penetration is expected to increase in the future. For example, data from 2016 show that nearly half of Cambodians (48%) claim to have access to the Internet, up 16% from a year earlier. Studies also found that, in 2016, the Internet became the most important channel through which Cambodians access information (30%) — surpassing TV (29%) and almost doubling the radio (15%) — and this is expected to continue gaining annual market share (Phong *et al.,* 2016). This could come as an opportunity or a challenge for banking players in Cambodia and in Asia, such as ACLEDA Bank.

Online and Offline Strategy

To seize the opportunities in Asia, EY, a global leader in assurance, tax, transaction, and advisory services suggested that the players in the banking industry need to:

- Invest in digital channels to meet customer needs — but not at the expense of personal interaction with customers. Banks must find the right balance between self-service and the provision of "human touch" to sell higher-value products and services. In the case of ACLEDA, short-message-service (SMS), which does not require advanced mobile technology, can be used to improve mobile service for its micro clients.

- Invest in technology-driven models — not only to reduce costs and drive efficiencies but also to respond to new entrants from the fin-tech sector who are using technology to provide faster and cheaper solutions to customers. Some banks in Asia collaborate with telco companies to offer new services to customers.

ACLEDA Bank seems to have already taken note of the suggestions stated above. In a bid to extend its contribution to the development of the national economy as well as to capitalize on technology advancement to improve the quality of its services and security, ACLEDA Bank launched ACLEDA Unity in 2010.

The objective of ACLEDA Unity is to provide financial services to Cambodians, irrespective of what mobile network they subscribe to and where they are located. Customers can access services related to day-to-day banking transactions, such as balance inquiry, mini-statements, fund transfer, bill payments, top-up, as well as card-less ATM cash withdrawal, through their mobile phones. This removes the necessity to visit a branch, which operates for only a fixed number of hours. The cardless money withdrawal is facilitated through the mobile number, M-PIN, and OTP for added security. The basic premise of ACLEDA Unity was to provide

ACLEDA's customers with virtually anytime–anywhere access to banking services.

In its early phase, ACLEDA Unity served only the existing ACLEDA Bank customers by providing them with additional services through their mobile phones. But starting 2012, ACLEDA extended its mobile financial services to new untapped consumer segments, with solutions developed in further collaboration with Fiserv, called Mobiliti Reach. This allows ACLEDA Bank to cater to customers who are not the bank's customers or account holders. The idea was to extend the services to customers who did not have access to conventional banking services.

During the launch of this newer version of ACLEDA Unity, Mr. In Channy, President and Chief Executive Officer of ACLEDA, explained the rationale:

"We started our mobile journey in 2010 by offering our customers a compelling set of mobile banking, alerting and payment capabilities. We soon realized that there was significant growth potential for mobile financial services among the many Cambodian consumers who do not have bank accounts. The extension of services to these consumers via ACLEDA Unity and Mobiliti Reach is enabling us to become the leading financial services provider amongst textile workers, farmers in remote rural areas and anyone else in Cambodia." (Business Wire, 2012)

This new form of ACLEDA Unity services helped the bank reach out to those customer segments who could not be serviced through traditional banking channels. These unbanked consumers had little information or ability to save or borrow money, which prevented them from participating in the formal economy. Through Mobiliti Reach, ACLEDA Unity offered total banking functionality through mobile wallets, P2P payments, bill payments, alert notifications, and integrated customer care access. This mass-market segment, in turn, appeared to establish a new revenue-generating stream for ACLEDA Bank. Through the mobile channel, it has helped ACLEDA emerge as a winner in its pursuit to provide a secure, hi-tech banking service to Cambodians.

Despite significant technology deployment in its banking services, ACLEDA Bank is aware of the fact that, in the digital age of today, the human dimension is still coveted by the customers. An offline approach involving face-to-face interactions remains necessary to build a deeper intimacy with the customers. Therefore, in order to win the hearts of a community at the bottom of the pyramid, ACLEDA Bank utilizes more horizontal, New Wave approaches. The company is not positioned above the customers but parallel to them. Its corporate sales staff is trained to act as consultants who can advise customers on how to leverage on funds obtained. As a result of this two-way communication, customers can derive a greater value from the company's services. This is an example of the co-creation process, where transparency of information is a key to building relationships with customers as active partners. In that context, ACLEDA Bank CEO once stated:

"We ask customers to share with us and we share with them too and when they tell us the truth we give them access to financial services. We tell them right from the beginning how transparent we are and we lend, based on information — other banks lend based on collateral. That's how we are different." (Becker, 2013)

ACLEDA Bank's success in integrating its online and offline strategies lends it a strong advantage to expand its penetration in other Asian regions. After Laos and Myanmar, ACLEDA has indeed planned to expand its operations to Thailand and China. With each new market posing a new set of challenges, the bank must constantly innovate to find the right formula by leveraging on digital technology advances and delivering a personal touch in service.

References

ACLEDA Bank (2017a). *2016 Annual Report.* https://www.acledabank.com.kh/kh/eng/bp_annualreport [19 January 2018].

ACLEDA Bank (2017b). *Brief Overview.* https://www.acledabank.com.kh/kh/eng/ff_overview [21 January 2018].

ACLEDA Bank Lao Ltd. (2017). *2016 Annual Report.* http://www.acledabank.com.la/la/assets/pdf_zip/ACLEDA_AnnRept2016.pdf [21 January 2018].

ACLEDA MFI Myanmar Co. Ltd. (2017). *2016–2017 Annual Report.* http://www.acledamfi.com.mm/mm/eng/pr_annualreport [21 January 2018].

Asian Institute of Finance (2015). *A Case Study on ACLEDA Bank Plc.: Making Commercial Microfinance Work in Cambodia.* Kuala Lumpur: Asian Institute of Finance.

Becker, SA (March 2013). ACLEDA opens in Myanmar, expands in Laos. *The Phnom Penh Post*. http://www.phnompenhpost.com/post-plus/acleda-opens-myanmar-expands-laos [21 January 2018].

Business Wire (2012). *ACLEDA Bank Plc. Extends Mobile Financial Services to New Segments with Mobiliti Reach from Fiserv*. https://www.businesswire.com/news/home/20121028005020/en/ACLEDA-Bank-Plc.-Extends-Mobile-Financial-Services [21 January 2018].

EY (2015). *Banking in Asia Pacific: Size Matters and Digital Drives Competition*. Asia Pacific: EYGM Limited.

GSMA Intelligence (2015). *The Mobile Economy: Asia Pacific 2015*. London: GSM Association.

Phong, K, L Srou and J Solá (2016). *Mobile Phones and Internet Use in Cambodia 2016*. 2 113 https://asiafoundation.org/wp-content/uploads/2016/12/Mobile-Phones-and-Internet-Use-in-Cambodia-2016.pdf [21 January 2018].

Axiata

Axiata is known as a leading telecommunications company in Asia, servicing a subscriber base of over 320 million in 10 countries. It has controlling interests in six mobile operators under the brand names of "Celcom" in Malaysia, "XL" in Indonesia, "Dialog" in Sri Lanka, "Robi" in Bangladesh, "Smart" in Cambodia, and "Ncell" in Nepal and with strategic interests in "Idea" in India and "M1" in Singapore. As a telecommunications operator, the company is among the top three providers in several regions. This case shows that at a time when telecom companies may seem to be struggling with devising and executing core business strategies to take full advantage of digitalization, Axiata appears well positioned to benefit from its strong regional operations.

Malaysia Telecommunications Industry

The telecommunications sector in Malaysia is controlled by the Malaysian Communications and Multimedia Commission (MCMC), a regulatory body formed with the enactment of the Multimedia Commission Act (1998). The sector has witnessed strong growth over the past two decades due to the adoption of a number of regulatory measures, particularly the privatization of the national telecommunications entity in 1987 and a liberalization of the market. The national entity, which was eventually renamed as Telekom Malaysia in 1990, remains the most dominant provider of fixed telephone services today. In the cellular service sector, however, multiple licenses were issued between 1990 and 2000, and several industry players existed in the market, before eventually consolidating into three by 2007. These three major players were Celcom, owned by Axiata; Digi, and Maxis.

Celcom Axiata Berhad is the oldest mobile telecommunications provider in Malaysia. As of Q1 2017, Celcom, a member of the Axiata group of companies, has about 10.6 million subscribers in Malaysia. Digi, a Malaysia-focused cellular operator, is a part of global telecommunications provider Telenor Group and has about 12.3 million subscribers in Malaysia. Maxis, an integrated communication services provider, has a subscriber base of over 10.67 million, as of Q1 2017.

According to the World Economic Forum's Global Information Technology Report 2016, Malaysia leads the emerging and developing Asian economies by moving one spot up to the 31st position, largely due to the government's firm commitment to fulfilling the digital agenda. The Networked Readiness Index indicates that Malaysia has a value of 4.9 at 32nd position (2015), compared with Singapore, the country on the top, which has a value of 6.

With approximately two-thirds of its 31 million population accessing the Internet, Malaysian consumers are active users of social media and chat applications. According to the WEF report, individual Internet usage has grown considerably, as Malaysia moved 10 spots up, to 47th position, in 2016, and most notably in the adoption of mobile broadband, which has reached almost 60%. With improved networks, greater Internet access, multimedia service-enabled devices, and an application development ecosystem, the use of digital media has increased.

Businesses in Malaysia are also taking full advantage of consumers' rapid mobile and internet adoption; they can interact with consumers online and, in some cases, can even reoptimize their business models and organizational structures. An increase in the international Internet bandwidth (currently ranked 81st), combined with a drop in broadband prices (110th), is likely to give a boost to Malaysia's digital economy

(WEF Report), which — per the Malaysian government's plans — should contribute to 20% of the GDP by 2020.

Axiata — Advancing Asia

Axiata was incorporated in Malaysia in 1992 as Telekom Malaysia International (TMI), which operated as a division of Telekom Malaysia Berhad. TMI eventually underwent a demerger exercise, from Telekom Malaysia, and changed its name to Axiata Group Berhad in March 2009.

Axiata's tagline rings true in line with the company's expansion efforts in the region over the past decade. Today, Axiata is known as a leading telecommunications company in Asia, amassing a subscriber base of over 320 million people in 10 countries (Axiata Annual Report, 2016). The company has controlling interests in six mobile operators under the brand names of Celcom in Malaysia, XL in Indonesia, Dialog in Sri Lanka, Robi in Bangladesh, Smart in Cambodia, and Ncell in Nepal and with strategic interests in Idea in India and M1 in Singapore. Axiata employs over 25,000 people across Asia. Table 9.2 lists some of the major operating and associate companies of Axiata in Asia.

Table 9.2: Axiata's regional presence in Asia.

Company	Country	Year of Establishment	Nature of Business	Number of Subscribers
Celcom	Malaysia	2008	Mobile	10.6 million
XL Axiata	Indonesia	2005	Mobile, multimedia, telecommunications	46.5 million
Dialog	Sri Lanka	1995	Communication services, telecom, infrastructure, media, and digital	11.8 million
Robi	Bangladesh	1996	Mobile telecom operator	33.8 million
Smart	Cambodia	2013	Mobile	8.1 million
Ncell	Nepal	2016	Mobile telecom operator	14.9 million
IDEA[a]	India	2008	Mobile services	192.1 million
M1[a]	Singapore	2005	Mobile and fixed-line phone services	2.18 million

[a]Associate/affiliate companies.
Source: Axiata.com.

In 2012, the company established Axiata Digital to target the rapidly growing Internet-based businesses and get closer to its 2020 vision of being the New Generation Digital Champion. It beefed up its efforts by launching a host of digital brands in the areas of mobile money, mobile advertising, e-commerce, entertainment, and education. It established edotco as the first regional integrated telecommunications infrastructure services company in Asia, to cater to the tower services sector.

Through its regional mobile and telecommunications subsidiaries, Axiata has deployed a range of technologies in the region, from GSM, GPRS, EDGE, 3G, HSPA+, WiFi, 4G LTE, to LTE-ADVANCED. Axiata's Celcom was the first player to launch 3G service in Malaysia in 2005. Indonesia (46.5 million) and Bangladesh (33.8 million) are Axiata's largest markets in terms of subscriber base. In Indonesia, through XL, 91% of the population is covered by 3G and 53% by 4G. While in Bangladesh, Robi has 29% of the population covered by 3.5G and 99% of the population is covered by 2G.

In its home market, Celcom covers 76% of the population by 4G and 90% by 3G. Dialog 3G is well positioned in Sri Lanka where 85% of the population is covered. The newly acquired Ncell has around 15 million subscribers, with almost 30% covered by 3G.

Creating a Regional Champion

Chronicling its journey since incorporation, Axiata identifies two distinct periods — Phase 1 (2008–2010) and Phase 2 (2011–2015), which mark Axiata's transformation from becoming an independent company in Malaysia to emerging as a regional champion. The third phase, dubbed Axiata 3.0, kick started in 2016, with Axiata eyeing the ultimate vision to become a Digital Champion by 2020.

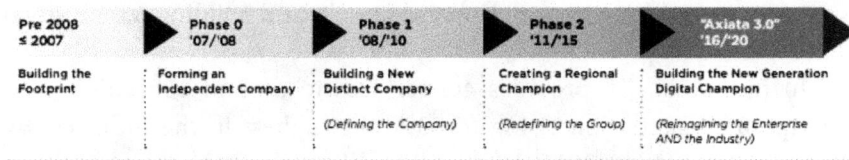

Pre 2008 ≤ 2007	Phase 0 '07/'08	Phase 1 '08/'10	Phase 2 '11/'15	"Axiata 3.0" '16/'20
Building the Footprint	Forming an Independent Company	Building a New Distinct Company	Creating a Regional Champion	Building the New Generation Digital Champion
		(Defining the Company)	*(Redefining the Group)*	*(Reimagining the Enterprise AND the Industry)*

Figure 9.1: Axiata's journey.

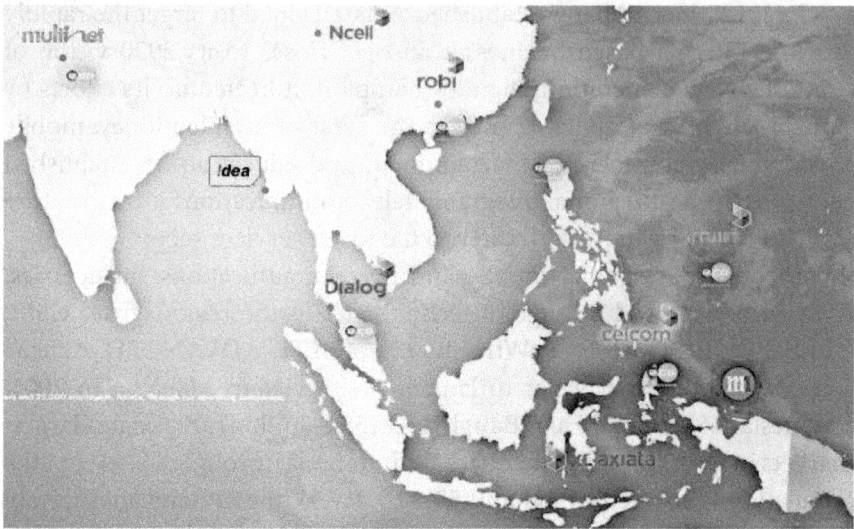

Figure 9.2: Axiata's Regional Expansion
Source: Axiata.com.

Axiata's Journey

Axiata's regional expansion has been fundamental to its redefinition as a group by creating a footprint across 10 countries and capturing hundreds of millions of customers in the region. In Indonesia, Axiata's 6% subsidiary company XL has positioned itself among the top telecommunications provider. It has over 20 years of experience in catering to the Indonesian consumers' unique needs. XL can be credited for bringing mobile services to ordinary Indonesians with the introduction of its budget "IDR1/second" program in 2007. In view of the Indonesian customers' evolving mobile usage habits that are driven by high data demand, XL is looking to stay ahead of the competition. It aims to improve the 4G adoption rates by enhancing coverage, modernizing distribution through forging partnerships with traditional channels, and building online video content and data promotions.

In Indonesia, XL provides 4G services to around 100 cities, with smartphone penetration rising to 63%, the highest in the industry. By the end of December 2016, XL had 29 million smartphone subscribers, representing an increase of 64% (YoY) (Axiata Annual Report, 2016). XL was also the first telecommunications operator in Indonesia to commercially launch 4.5G on the 1800 MHz spectrum in April 2017. This covers the major tier-one cities, including Jabodetabek, Bandung, Surabaya, and Denpasar.

Another prominent Axiata's operating company, Dialog, is Sri Lanka's largest foreign direct investor, with investments of up to USD2 billion. The company has been voted the Telecom Service Provider of the Year in Sri Lanka for several years. Catering to around 11.8 million subscribers, Dialog maintains a strong presence in the country through its fully owned subsidiaries, Dialog Broadband Networks (Private) Ltd. (DBN) and Dialog Television (Private) Ltd. (DTV). DBN is Sri Lanka's second largest fixed telecommunications service provider, while DTV offers a direct-to-home (DTH) digital satellite pay-TV service and is the market leader in Sri Lanka's Pay TV sector.

In order to attract young app developers, Dialog operates its own application program interface (API) Ideamart. A Global Mobile Award winner for "Best Technology Enabler" at the 2015 Mobile World Congress, Ideamart helps professional and amateur applications' developers, as well as small and medium entrepreneurs and tech startups, to build apps using simple-to-use web interfaces and share their innovations with mobile consumers across Sri Lanka. The ecosystem currently includes up to 1.5 million Sri Lankan mobile consumers and 5,000 developers and content providers.

In Bangladesh, Robi is a joint venture entity wherein Axiata holds 68.7% controlling stake, Bharti 25%, while the remaining 6.3% is held by Japan's NTT DoCoMo. Bangladesh's second largest mobile operator, Robi was the first player to introduce GPRS and 3.5G in the country. With a special focus on rural and semi-urban areas, Robi has invested heavily in its infrastructure capabilities. Following a merger with Airtel, Robi is looking to not only benefit from the network integration but also leverage Airtel brand's strength as the telco brand of choice for the youth market in Bangladesh.

Smart Axiata was Cambodia's first mobile operator to provide 4G services since 2016. Its extensive network covers more than 98% of the Cambodian population. Smart Axiata is also aiming to evolve into a digital lifestyle brand. With the launch of SmartPay, a new payment app solution for purchases, the company provides monetization opportunities to the local app developer community. Smart Axiata is also the only authorized distributor of Apple iPhones in Cambodia, which further boosts its brand strength. The company is also known for its CSR initiatives in the country, with the launch of a number of programs, such as the SmartEdu Scholarship Program that is in partnership with the Ministry of Education. It has launched programs in the field of ICT literacy and digital startups. For its involvement in the national literacy program, Smart Axiata was awarded the Telecom Asia Best Community Project in 2016. In 2017, the company earned the Cambodia Mobile Service Provider of the Year by Frost & Sullivan.

Axiata is looking to transform into a digital, regional company and has even undergone some management reboot in 2016 to become a more agile organization and manage its digital companies more efficiently. It beefed up its efforts by investing in high-speed fiber Internet connection services, which provide a much faster data speed to private and business end users. The following section takes a closer look at Axiata's digital endeavors.

Catering to the Digital Customer

Although telecom players are largely responsible for enhancing consumers' mobile and Internet experiences, their own efforts in targeting digital customers in the markets where they sell their products and services, seem to fall short. Dr Roman Friedrich and coauthors, in their report *Becoming a Digital Telecom,* noted "it is especially ironic that the industry that provides the backbone to digitization — telecommunications — has been slow to digitize its internal operations or to benefit from this evolution".

Despite supporting much of the network infrastructure for fixed and mobile Internet and spending billions of dollars in meeting the exploding data demand, telcos in Asia and elsewhere have largely been slow to adopt digitalization. In capitalizing this seemingly missed opportunity, telecom operators need to bring in the changes and restrategize by developing new digital capabilities. A McKinsey study with 80 global telecoms also confirms a strong correlation between profit margin and advanced digital capabilities.

One of the areas where digital capabilities are increasingly being put to use by telcos is the introduction of self-service in customer management. Telecommunications providers in Asia and elsewhere have developed and launched self-care applications for their mobile customers. These apps help customers manage their accounts, upgrade or top-up plans, or purchase products and services such as talk-time or broadband data without visiting a store. This is the easiest way telecom companies can digitize their end-user experience, boosting convenience and delivering an actual value to the customer through digitalization. Axiata's operating companies in the region, including XL (My XL), Smart (SmartNAS), Dialog (Dialog SelfCare), and Robi (My Robi), operate such self-care apps. Although self-care platforms are popular and could impress a digital user, they can also help in collecting feedback, positive or negative, from customers on app stores. A negative feedback calls for marketers to take note of and promptly resolve issues faced by the customers, ideally through personal intervention.

XL — Revamp, rise, reinvent

XL adopted the 3R strategy in 2015 to build a more profitable and sustainable company. The focus was on building a more data-centric business by improving the coverage and the quality of its network.

In recognizing digitalization as the way forward, XL in Indonesia focuses on three aspects of the process. First, optimizing its ability to analyze customer data to carefully and correctly determine the unique needs and wants of customers. Second, transforming complex business processes to adopt more efficient execution and operations. Finally, developing the digital services infrastructure, with a digital work culture as the foundation. By identifying unique customer needs and optimizing billing processes, XL's mobile payment solution (XL Tunai) allows the customer to pay for BPJS Kesehatan (Indonesia national medical health insurance), electricity bills, credit cards, and so on. Together with its partners, XL launched an app Xmart Village, which is aimed at developing under-served rural areas with the use of digital technology, especially targeting tourism. Moreover, the company is undertaking local initiatives. For example, it created the first public library equipped with virtual reality (VR) devices, so that children in villages can gain access to books through the digital media.

Eyeing fin-tech

Dialog is a major telecommunication player in Sri Lanka. In order to keep up with evolving customer requirements, Dialog has launched several brands to serve the digital customer; one such brand is eZ Cash. As the country's top online payment service, with almost 50% share of Sri Lanka's mobile market, eZ Cash was launched in 2012 and has so far accumulated over 2 million subscribers. Dialog's Women Portal in Sri Lanka aims to "safeguard, uplift and encourage women". Dialog also runs a shopping website (WoW.lk), Doc.lk by Digital Health (Pvt) Ltd, and the country's leading digital education service Guru.lk operated by Headstart (Pvt) Ltd. The company is now stretching its wings to the finance sector by acquiring a listed financial firm Colombo Trust Finance PLC (CTF). The acquisition allows the company to enter the mainstream financial service sector by combining its digital connectivity strengths with financial technology (fin-tech).

Axiata's digital services arm, Axiata Digital Services Sdn Bhd (ADS), decided to set up a joint venture with Malaysian money service provider Merchantrade Asia in 2017. The venture aims to offer digital financial services and solutions.

ICT-enabled agriculture

In Bangladesh, the Axiata group company Robi is working toward the cause of pushing the use of ICT in the agricultural sector, which is a core economic sector in the country. The company launched Mobile Krishe, an app that helps farmers with information on modern farming methods, such as weather forecasting, production and cultivation advice, disease and insects and price information, and achieve higher yields on their crop. Considering the low-literacy level among rural farmers, making technology available and accessible to farmers is a major challenge. The company is exploring the potential use of ICT in enabling payments of government subsidies to farmers directly through the mobile platform.

Robi has also partnered with the GSMA mWomen Innovation Fund to create a mobile learning service for rural young girls. It acts as a mobile platform to deliver English lessons through voice and SMS to help users become more employable in industries, such as garment manufacturing. Robi's Digital Smart Buses project employs six buses and provides basic ICT training to 240,000 young women across 64 districts in the country.

A New Growth Era

Asia is on the cusp of a digital revolution. At a time when telecom companies seem to be struggling with devising and executing core business strategies in the digitalization age, Axiata appears well positioned to benefit from its strong regional presence and relentless focus on this ever-expanding digital connectivity. The company is among the top three providers in several regions. That said, the company also seems to know that it is not the time to bask in glory; competition is cut-throat, and customers are unsparing and highly demanding. They want better speed in their connections, greater convenience when buying or using telecom products, and more relevant services meeting their unique needs. They also seek a smooth, personalized experience from an operator that provides the biggest bang for their buck! Innovation is at the heart of any initiative aimed at accomplishing this feat, whether in partnerships with Uber (as in the case of Robi) or being the frontrunner in launching 5G services (as in the case of Dialog) in South Asia.

Although Axiata remains strong in its home market, competition from Digi and Maxis has created some pressure to jumpstart product innovation. In a recent review, Celcom Axiata Berhad's CEO Michael Kuehner said that the focus on improving the network took precedence over releasing half-baked products to customers. The performance of network-dictated customer experience and data usage in Malaysia has gone up from 3.5 GB per customer in Q2 2016 to 6.2 GB in 2017. The focus on regional markets is paying off well as Axiata reports double-digit growth in several countries.

References

Anand, A, D Begonha and G Caldo (December 2015). *Lessons from Digital Telcos: Five Initiatives to Improve Business Performance.* McKinsey & Company. https://www.mckinsey.com/industries/telecommunications/our-insights/lessons-from-digital-telcos-five-initiatives-to-improve-business-performance [29 November 2018].

Annual Report (2016). *Axiata.com*. http://axiata.listedcompany.com/misc/ar2016.pdf. [19 September 2017].

Axiata National Contribution Report 2016. Axiata.com.

Cellular News (4 October 2017). Asia's Best-in-Class Companies Celebrated at the 2017 Frost & Sullivan Asia-Pacific Best Practices Awards.

Karamjit, S (18 September 2017). Celcom trying to create a startup culture to regain its mojo. *Digital News Asia*. https://www.digitalnewsasia.com/mobility/celcom-trying-create-startup-culture-regain-its-mojo [19 September 2017].

The Star (3 February 2017). *Indonesian unit XL seen as a Drag on Axiata Group Performance*. http://www.thestar.com.my/business/business-news/2017/02/03/analysts-unimpressed-with-xl-results/#seh3cD5GlddPqBpk.99 [27 September 2017].

Wataru, Y (9 August 2016). Malaysia's Axiata pushing into Asia's telecom frontiers. *Nikkei*. https://asia.nikkei.com/Business/AC/Malaysia-s-Axiata-pushing-into-Asia-s-telecom-frontiers [11 September 2017].

Universal Robina Corporation (URC)

Universal Robina Corporation (URC) is a Filipino company that has been successful in creating a strong foothold in several ASEAN markets, with its products spanning various consumer food categories. It has full-scale operations in eight countries outside the Philippines, and its products are exported to markets across the world. In the consumer food business, the company faces intense competition from local and regional players that try to vie aggressively for market share across all categories. This case will show how URC has strengthened its position in the regional market with the help of its middle-class and millennial consumers.

Philippine's First MNC

Universal Robina Corporation (URC) is one of the largest branded food product companies in the Philippines, with the distinction of being called the country's first "Philippines Multinational". URC offers a wide range of brands of snacks, candies, chocolates, and instant drinks. Moreover, URC operates a business group that specializes in the production and marketing of agricultural products and commodities. This indicates how

URC already benefit from vertical integration that increases its business strength.

URC was founded in 1954 when John Gokongwei, Jr established Universal Corn Products, Inc., a corn starch manufacturing plant in Pasig. Today, URC has established a strong presence in ASEAN (Thailand, Malaysia, Singapore, Indonesia, Vietnam) and in Asia (China and Hong Kong). It has further expanded its reach to the Oceania region the acquisition of Griffin's Food Limited, the number one snacks food company in New Zealand, and Snack Brands Australia (SBA), the second largest salty snacks player in Australia.

Despite venturing into Oceania, Asia continues to represent a market with huge potential for URC, and hence the company has taken some bold moves to expand in the region. URC's President and Chief Executive Officer, Lance Gokongwei has said:

"URC has always looked to the future, and it has always set its eyes on becoming a major player in Asia. We saw that in order to establish significant growth, we would need to expand operations overseas. There is a large addressable market in ASEAN with the number of middle income consumers expanding. It is a huge opportunity for URC to build brands across the region." (Department of Trade and Industry of Philippines, 2015)

Based on the company's milestones, the growth and development of URC, spanned over four eras, is described in Table 9.3.

Based on the product categories it serves, URC's business portfolio can be divided into three groups: Branded Consumer Foods Group (BCFG), Agro-Industrial Group (AIG), and Commodity Foods Group (CFG) (Universal Robina Corporation, 2017a).

Branded Consumer Foods Group

URC's BCFG business is further classified into two divisions, BCF Philippines, which caters to the domestic market, and BCF International, a fully owned subsidiary that handles the business in the ASEAN and Oceania markets. BCFG manufactures a variety of food items, from beverages to instant noodles, salty snacks to bakery and confectionary. BCFG has registered strong growth on the back of a strategic expansion in ASEAN, consistent innovations in products and attractive marketing campaigns. The company's expansion also includes strategic joint-ventures and

Table 9.3: The four eras of Universal Robina Corporation.

Age of Manufacturing	**1950** Started as a corn starch manufacturer (agro-industrial)
Age of Brands	**1960** Entered the branded consumer food business and launched brands such as Blend 45, Chippy, and Potato Chips
Age of Domestic Expansion	**1970** • Ventured into the flour milling business • Entered the hog business **1980** • Entered the sugar milling and refinery business • Launched Cloud 9 and Piattos
Age of Globalization	**2000** • Launched *Jack 'n Jill* as the umbrella brand for snack foods • Expanded its markets in Indonesia and Vietnam, after Hong Kong, Malaysia, Singapore, China, and Thailand • Introduced *C2* to the Philippines and Vietnam **2010** • Launched *Great Taste* White and Mang Juan • Entered a JV with Calbee and Danone and acquired Griffin's Foods Ltd. • Started operating a URC factory in Myanmar and Biomass Cogeneration plant in the Philippines • Launched Griffin's in Asia **2016** • Acquired Snack Brands Australia **2017** • Entered into a beverage JV with Hong Kong's Vitasoy

Source: Universal Rubina Corporation (2017a, b).

partnerships formed with several renowned international consumer food companies, including ConAgra of the United States, Nissin Foods and Calbee of Japan, and Danone of France.

URC has built three significant mainstream brands — *Jack 'n Jill*, *Great Taste*, and *C2*. The company has also expanded its portfolio to include premium brands through acquisitions of Griffin's Foods (e.g., Griffin's and Nice & Natural) and SBA (e.g., Kettle, Thins, CC's, Cheezels, and Natural) and through strategic joint ventures with ConAgra Foods (Hunt's), Nissin Foods (Nissin and Payless), Danone (Blue), and Calbee

(*Jack 'n Jill* Calbee). (see Table 9.4 for detailed information about BCFG's product categories).

Agro-Industrial Group

AIG focuses on providing clean, safe, and quality farm products to Filipino households. With URC AIG, the company aims to be known as a provider of "total agri-solutions" and a partner in farm management. AIG is engaged in the production of animal feeds, glucose and soya products, hogs and poultry farming, as well as animal health products. Robina Farm Hogs is involved in a variety of raw materials, primarily imported breeding stocks such as pigs. It also sells value-added segments (carcasses and fresh meat cuts). The products are guaranteed as "no antibiotic and no hormone" to ensure healthy and safe consumption. Retailing is done for meat products in-house as well as for poultry; Robina Farms commercial table eggs are certified by the Good Animal Husbandry Practices (GAHP) and are also halal certified.

Table 9.4: BCFG's product categories.

Mainstream Brands	***Jack 'n Jill***: The umbrella brand of snack food products that are well recognized in ASEAN ***Great Taste***: A ready-to-drink coffee brand that makes the modern coffee-drinking experience accessible to many; first and leader in the "creamy" subsegment ***C2***: A healthy ready-to-drink tea that comes from naturally brewed tea leaves
Premium Brands	**Griffins**: High-quality sweet biscuits with more than 150 years of heritage **Nice & Naturals:** A wide range of healthy wrapped snacks **Thins:** The original thin cut chip **Kettles:** The pioneer hard bite or premium chip **Cheezels:**. A dominant cheese ring product **Natural:** A new challenger in crinkle cut **CCs:**. The original corn chip
Brands from Joint Ventures	**Hunt's**: Ready-to-eat canned beans and easy-to-cook tomato-based products **Nissin:** Famous cup and pouch noodles **Payless:** Value-for-money instant noodles **B'lue:** Unique water plus drink ***Jack 'n Jill* Calbee**: Innovative range of Japanese salty snacks

The farms employ infrared debeaking technology to help minimize chicks' mortality and increase egg production. Various commercial feeds that the company provides are corn grains, soya beans and meals, feed-wheat grains, wheat bran, wheat pollard, soya seeds, rice bran, copra meal, and fish meal.

Commodity Foods Group

This business group is divided into two major categories, namely URC Sugar and URC Renewables. URC Sugar is involved in sugar milling and refining, whereas URC Renewables is engaged in the production of fuel-grade anhydrous ethanol, suitable for gasoline blending and biomass-fired power cogeneration (CoGen). URC Sugar operates six mills and three refineries across the country, whereas URC Renewables operates an ethanol distillery plant — the first such plant in Southeast Asia to utilize a spent wash incineration boiler that helps to ensure environmentally safe and hazard-free operations.

Competing with Local and Global Players

URC faces intense competition from local and regional players in the consumer food business. Competitors continue to vie aggressively for market share across all categories, especially snacks and coffee. URC competes principally with Switzerland's Nestlé and Indonesia's PT Mayora Indah in the coffee segment and Liwayway Marketing of the Philippines and Mondelez of the United States in the snack segment (Venzon, 2016).

Liwayway Holdings Company Limited, famous as Oishi, is a snack company based in the Philippines. The company was established in 1974 when the first snacks — Oishi Prawn Crackers and Kirei Yummy Flakes — were manufactured using Japanese technology. In 1993, Oishi eventually ventured into China, marking its first international expansion with the Shanghaojia brand (Oishi, 2017). At present, the Liwayway Group is present in eight countries: Philippines, China, Vietnam, Myanmar, Thailand, Indonesia, Cambodia, and India.

Another strong challenger in the snacks category is Mondelez Philippines. Mondelez Philippines is part of Mondelez International, a new company established following the split of Kraft Foods Limited in October 2012. Mondelez is a strong player that usually holds one of the top two positions in the Asia-Pacific markets across several categories, including biscuits and chocolates. It has popular brands — such as Oreo cookies and Cadbury chocolates, Halls candy, and Tiger energy biscuits — in its portfolio. The Asia-Pacific market contributes up to 15% of Mondelez's business, with more than 75% of the total being generated from food categories, including biscuits, chocolates, gum, and candies (The Philippines Star, 2013). To sustain its growth in the Philippines market, Mondelez Philippines has introduced several new products — such as Eden Mayo, Eden Sandwich Spread, Oreo Coconut Delight, and the Tang Citrus flavors namely Calamansi, Dalandan, and Honey Lemon — to cater distinctly to the Filipino market (Remo, 2015).

The instant coffee category faces no less intense competition. Many Filipinos, both in the urban and in the rural areas, frequently consume coffee every day. Coffee is, in fact, sold more than any other fast-moving consumer goods (FMCG) in the country (Loresco, 2013). In this category, URC faces stiff competition from the likes of internationally renowned coffee brand Nestlé and an Indonesian consumer food company PT Mayora Indah.

Nestlé has been in the Philippines for over 100 years. Although Nestlé's products were already available in the Philippines as far back as 1895, it was not until 1911 that the Nestlé and Anglo-Swiss Condensed Milk Company was established in the country, with its first sales office in Calle Renta, Binondo. Its product range has since expanded to include coffee, milk, beverages, non-dairy creamer, food, infant nutrition, ice cream and chilled dairy, breakfast cereals, confectionery, and pet care. In the instant coffee category, Nestlé's Nescafe brand is one of the dominant players.

Meanwhile, Mayora Indah is one of the market leaders in Indonesia in the instant coffee category. The company is known for its innovative products, which are launched in the form of various flavored coffees, such as Torabika Ginger Milk, Torabika Duo Full Cream Milk, Torabika Moka, and Torabika 3 in One, Torabika Diet, Torabika Cappuccino. The latest Torabika Creamy, with a separate sugar sachet, helps consumers adjust the sugar in their coffee. Moreover, there is also another coffee brand that offers a range of products, such as Kopiko Brown Coffee, Kopiko White Coffee, and Kopiko White Mocca (Mayora, 2017).

After establishing a firm grip on the domestic market, Mayora is aggressively expanding abroad in ASEAN and in global markets. In the Philippines, Mayora started its journey back in 1994. A noteworthy success came in 2006, with the launch of Kopiko 3-in-1 Black Coffee, which was followed by new launches such as the Kopiko Kopiccino and Kopiko L.A. Coffee in the coming years (The Freeman, 2014).

Conquering Asian Consumers

URC takes pride in being known as the Philippines' first "Pan ASEAN Multinational" company. Over the years, the company has been successful in creating a strong foothold in several ASEAN markets, with its products spanning various consumer food categories. The company's strength lies in advanced manufacturing capabilities and a wide distribution network, supported by rigorous innovation, in offering products that meet consumers' tastes and preferences. Today, URC has full-scale operations in eight countries outside the Philippines, and its products are exported to markets across the world, including the United States, Europe, Japan, Korea, the Middle East, as well as African countries such as Ghana and Nigeria.

The onset of the ASEAN Economic Community (AEC), which was finalized in 2015, has given further impetus to URC's drive to strengthen its position in the Southeast Asian market. The AEC is envisioned to be a single market and production base for the 10-member ASEAN community with an estimated consumer base of 600 million people. The integration would result in duty-free importation and inevitably create conditions for tougher competition among businesses from member countries. While keeping close eyes on AEC and following the socio-economic developments in the region, URC intends to expand its operations in emerging markets such as Myanmar, Laos, and Cambodia. This is evident from the fact that URC expanded its business presence in Myanmar in 2016. The company has established a stronger distribution system with its new partner, which has four branches across the country (Universal Robina Corporation, 2017a).

The expansion efforts in ASEAN and strategic investments are paying off; URC now commands a leading market position in the biscuits and wafers product categories in Thailand. Its *C2* ready-to-drink tea is the market leader in Vietnam. It has also built three strong regional brands: *Jack 'n Jill* snack foods, *C2* ready-to-drink tea, and *Great Taste* coffee (Department of Trade and Industry of Philippines, 2015).

Beyond Southeast Asia, China and Hong Kong also hold strong potential for URC. The company also expanded its presence in the Asia-Pacific by acquiring New Zealand's leading snacks food manufacturer, Griffin Foods, for about NZD700 million (P24 billion) in 2016. Sales in 2016 from Griffin in New Zealand were flatter than those in the previous year, due to lower volumes that resulted from premium pricing. In order to further strengthen its position in Asia, URC intends to improve customer engagement. To that end, URC has decided to pay special attention to two key customer segments, both in the local and Asian markets: the middle-class consumers and the millennial consumers.

Why is the increasing middle-class consumers an important segment for URC? It is because consumers with growing purchasing power are becoming more aspirational, and this is also reflected in their spending. This segment is on its way to eventually trade up for premium offerings, making it a potential target for URC's premium brands. The company, meanwhile, is pursuing relentless innovation by launching new brands or entering untapped segments within the snack foods and non-alcoholic beverage categories. This includes premium offerings of its snacks items, such as the indulgent chocolate and crème biscuits from Griffin's, premium salty snacks from SBA and Calbee, functional and on-the-go beverages in Vietnam, as well as targeted launches under the *Jack 'n Jill* mega brand across ASEAN markets (Universal Robina Corporation, 2017b).

The company is also closely eyeing millennial consumers both in the domestic and in the regional markets. In Southeast Asia alone, about 40% of citizens are under 30 years of age — a huge market (Kearney, 2015) for any player. These consumers are also unique as they are digitally savvy. The world is increasingly recognizing the far-reaching impact this millennial generation is casting on society, especially with the proliferation of digital technology and social media, which allows them to widely express their opinions.

URC, therefore, has started to complement its marketing activities with various digital initiatives. One of them is the utilization of mobile applications to provide a more comprehensive experience for *Jack 'n Jill* customers in the Philippines. With the slogan "Magical moments anytime anywhere", customers can make their day brighter by watching the fun and positive videos from John Lloyd Cruz, its brand endorser. They also get exclusive access to announcements about special events, promotions, and new products. The app is also packed with exciting games and activities, such as Magic Match, Magic Beats, and Magic in a Pack. In view of the growing number and rising importance of the millennial consumer segment, such digital campaigns are likely to become commonplace by companies, including URC, for the domestic and the regional markets.

References

Department of Trade and Industry of Philippines (2015). *Business Beyond Borders*. Manila: Department of Trade and Industry of Philippines.

The Freeman (August 2014). Kopiko lLaunches nNew vVariant, rReveals fFour cCelebrity eEndorsers. *The Philippines Star*. http://www.philstar.com/cebu-business/2014/08/06/1354448/kopiko-launches-new-variant-reveals-four-celebrity-endorsers [(last accessed 5 January 5,2018]).Universal Robina sales muted by tougher competition.

Kearney, AT (2015). *The ASEAN Digital Revolution*. http://www.southeast-asia.atkearney.com/innovation/asean-innovation/asean-digital-revolution/full-report/-/asset_publisher/VHe1Q1yQRpCb/content/the-asean-digital-revolution/10192 [5 January 2018].

Loresco, S (September 2013). Top brands targeted by phishing SCAMS: Source: Mcafee Top 10 Brands Filipinos Buy. *Rappler*. https://www.rappler.com/business/features/38191-top-10-brands-filipino-consumers-choose-to-buy [5 January 2018.

Mayora (2017). *Products*. http://www.mayoraindah.co.id/mayora-products/coffee/ 5 January 2018].

Oishi (2017). *About Us*. https://www.oishi.com.ph/about-us/ [5 January 2018].

The Philippines Star (July 2013). Kraft Foods Phl nNow kKnown as Mondelez Phl. *The Philippines Star*. 97 3787 http://www.philstar.com/business/2013/07/03/960867/kraft-foods-phl-now-known-mondelez-phl [(last accessed 5 January 5, 2018]).

Remo, AR (March 2015). Mondelez eyes faster sales growth in PH. *Inquirer*. http://business.inquirer.net/188738/mondelez-eyes-faster-sales-growth-in-ph [January 2015].

Universal Robina Corporation (2017a). *Annual Report 2016*. Quezon City: Universal Robina Corporation.

Universal Robina Corporation (2017b). *Kantar: Great Taste Is PH's 2nd Most Chosen Beverage Brand*. http://www2.urc.com.ph/article/kantar-great-taste-is-ph-apos-s-2nd-most-chosen-beverage-brand [5 January 2018].

Venzon, C (May 2016). Universal Robina sales muted by tougher competition. *Nikkei Asian Review.* https://asia.nikkei.com/Business/AC/Universal-Robina-sales-muted-by-tougher-competition?page=1 [5 January 2018].

Vinamilk

Domination in the domestic market provides a company with a strong initial capital that can be utilized to expand its wings to a wider market, especially in areas with similar consumer characteristics. In Vietnam's dairy industry, Vinamilk's position as a local champion is well recognized. Nevertheless, the desire to win the hearts of customers in Asia — as part of its immediate territory — demanded that Vinamilk continues its procurement innovation to secure its position.

Vietnam's Largest Dairy Company

Established in 1976, Vinamilk was previously referred to as Southern Coffee-Dairy Company, which functioned as a subsidiary of the Food General Directorate. Since then, the company has expanded its presence through acquiring dozens of dairies and a vast portfolio of F&B products, from milk, juices, and cereals to ice-cream and cheese. Its vision is to become a world-grade brand in the food and beverage industry, where people put their trust in its nutrient-rich and healthy products.

In 2010, Vinamilk became the first company from Vietnam to be included in the *Forbes* Asia's 200 "Best Under a Billion" list, which includes the 200 top-performing small- and mid-sized companies with annual revenues under USD1 billion (*Forbes*, August 2010). In 2017, Vinamilk became the largest dairy company in Vietnam and topped the 2017 list of 40 most valuable Vietnamese company brands. This is the second consecutive year in which the Vietnamese milk giant had topped the list, with a brand value of more than USD1.7 billion (*Nhan Dan*, July 2017).

The company's principal business activities include processing, producing, and trading of fresh milk, packed milk, powdered milk, nutrition powder, yoghurt, condensed milk, soy milk, beverages, and other dairy products. Growing dairy cows is also an important part of its business as fresh milk is used as a raw material to produce dairy products. The company's products are not just known in Vietnam but are also exported to other countries, especially other ASEAN countries and the United States (see Table 9.5 for more details on the company's milestones).

Table 9.5:   Vinamilk's milestones.

Year	Events
1976	Was established based on three dairy factories from the old regime
1978	Became United Enterprises of Milk Coffee Cookies and Candies
1993	Renamed to Vietnam Dairy Company
1995	Inaugurated the first dairy factory in Hanoi.
2003	Legally changed its name to Vietnam Dairy Products Joint Stock Company (Vinamilk), following its IPO in the Ho Chi Minh Stock Exchange
2006	Inaugurated the first dairy farm in Tuyen Quang
2010	• Invested in a New Zealand-based whole milk powder producing company with a capacity of 32,000 tons/years • Invested in the United States and opened more factories in several countries • Registered export revenues of 15% of total revenue
2012	Inaugurated the Danang Dairy Factory, Lamson Dairy Factory, Vietnam Beverages Factory, with modern production lines originating from the United States, Denmark, Germany, Italy, and the Netherlands
2013	Inaugurated the super dairy factory in Binh Duong (one of the most modern factories in the world, which is 100% automated and located in a 20-ha area).
2016	• Launched its brand in Myanmar, Thailand, and expanded operations in ASEAN • Introduced condensed milk and creamer, under the Driftwood brand name, to the US market
2017	Topped the 2017 list of 40 most valuable Vietnamese company brands, released by *Forbes* Vietnam

Source: *Nhan Dan* (July 2017), Vinamilk (2015a), and Wikipedia (2017).

Growth Amidst Fierce Competition

Vinamilk's journey to success was not devoid of roadblocks; some management teams that steadily supported Vinamilk decided to make an exit in 2009 and joined a new rival TH Milk. The new competitor had big ambitions for the market and acted swiftly; for example, it imported 28,000 cows in the country for fresh milk production. Vinamilk responded by setting up a large dairy plant with an investment of USD120 million, as well as boosting sourcing from overseas (*Forbes*, September 2010).

Vinamilk continued to face competition from companies like Friesland, which have become more aggressive in their regional expansion through increasing investments in dairy farms and factories and more aggressive advertisement campaigns. Some other global players, such as Nestlé, Abbott, and Mead Johnson, also must not be underestimated. Moreover, over the past several years, newer players such as Moc Chau and Ba Vi have emerged in the liquid and yoghurt market segments, resulting in greater competition.

Vinamilk, however, aimed to remain strong, owing to one of its competitive advantages in the form of a wide range of products. Starting with only two product categories and a few featured products, Vinamilk has expanded its product line to 10 categories (liquid milk, yogurt, powdered milk, nutrition powder, oat–cocoa, condensed milk, ice cream, cheese, soya milk, and beverages) and with more than 250 SKUs to meet the market's diverse demand (Vinamilk, 2017).

This diverse product range helps the company meet the demands of a wide array of customers, and it is also adept at gauging its customers' evolving preferences and tastes. In view of the changing lifestyles in favor of healthy products, Vinamilk has also come up with new value-added and healthier products, such as a product with collagen and powdered milk with extra nutritional content.

Aside from its product leadership, the company is also popular for the vast availability of its products, which is another of Vinamilk's competitive strengths. As of December 2015, it had 243 exclusive distributors nationwide, far more than its closest competitors Friesland and Nestlé. These intermediaries directly serve more than 212,000 retailers. Vinamilk products are also present in 1,609 small and big supermarkets and more than 575 convenience stores throughout the country. A strong network of distribution channels helps Vinamilk swiftly and easily penetrate the market with its new products (Vinamilk, 2016).

Vinamilk's success in keeping the pulse on Vietnam's dairy market is evident from the market share growth in 2016 from 2012, across several major product categories: liquid milk rose from 45.9% to 54.5%; infant formula milk rose from 21.7% to 25.1% in six major cities and it owned 40.6% of the national market in 2016; drinking yogurt increased from 24.4% to 33.9%; and condensed milk rose from 79.4% to 79.7% (Vinamilk, 2017).

Product Development and Market Expansion

Notwithstanding its strong position in the domestic market, Vinamilk still focuses on product innovation as a part of its business strategy to meet the new needs of consumers. In recognition of the emerging opportunities, Vinamilk made a surprise entry into a whole new segment in 2011 — fruits and vegetable juices. This helped the company to diversify into an entirely new market with high-growth potential, as consumers adopt healthier lifestyles and can afford to spend more on healthy food products (Vinamilk, 2012). Shortly after its launch, this new product line gained recognition in the market. A critical factor that contributed to this success can be attributed to Vinamilk's existing brand presence and an extensive distribution network.

Following the success of its juice range, in February 2012, the company launched fruit juices for children, a first-of-its-kind product in Vietnam. The underdeveloped market turned out to have huge potential and was effectively tapped on. The new fruit and vegetable juice business is nevertheless rife with competition from international companies, such as Coca Cola with its *Minute Maid* line and PepsiCo with its *Tropicana Twister* (Fawzi & Sproule, 2012). It may be too early to evaluate the success of Vinamilk's new product range, but the company manages to hold a sizeable market share in Vietnam, due to its familiarity with the market and its strong brand recognition.

Besides continuous product development, Vinamilk also makes quite aggressive market expansion. In April 2013, the company started operating two modern dairy plants in the southern province of Binh Duong. In its first phase, the first factory was estimated to produce over 400 million liters of milk per year, and this was expected to double in the second phase. The second factory was expected to produce around 54,000 tons of powdered milk, that is, four times the current output (Nikkei Asian Review, 2016).

In January 2014, Vinamilk was granted an investment certificate to build a joint venture business in the name of Angkor Dairy Products Co. Ltd. in Cambodia. The business objective was to build a dairy manufacturing factory to serve the Cambodian market (Vinamilk, 2015b). In 2014, the company set up a subsidiary in Poland to tap the European market. It also opened a branch in Russia at the beginning of 2016, pushing ahead with its move into Russia and the former Soviet Union, after Vietnam signed a free trade pact with the Eurasian Economic Union in 2015 (Nikkei Asian Review, 2016). In another development, Vinamilk acquired all of Angkor Dairy Products in 2017 (Nikkei Asian Review, 2017), and now it has been reportedly eyeing China's dairy market (Vietnam Plus, 2017). China is a big dairy market that is estimated to be worth nearly USD30 billion, and Vinamilk has signed an MoU to supply its products to the Chinese market.

Vietnam's and Asia's Digital Consumers

Vietnam, akin to its other emerging Asian counterparts, is a mobile and Internet-friendly nation. That also makes it incredibly easy to connect to the Internet at public places, regardless of where you are. The Internet revolution in Vietnam began not too long ago, and this has helped the country benefit from the late-adopter advantage, in terms of relatively inexpensive hardware availability and affordable Internet accessibility.

With nearly 36% of the population owning a smartphone, the country is seeing high mobile usage and Internet penetration, as well as increasing popularity of social media usage. Young millennials in the country, especially working professionals and business persons, actively use smartphones to check e-mails, browse the Internet, watch YouTube, and connect with others on social media. For 80% of the smartphone users, visiting social networks is considered the primary activity (Davis, 2016). The rising phenomenon of digitalization is, therefore, turning the tables by placing greater power in the hands of consumers than brands. The

Internet and social media usage allows customers to share their product or service experience with tens of thousands in their online networks.

In terms of technology adoption, Vinamilk is in a leading position by implementing dairy farming and food processing technologies in its production units. By utilizing some of the latest techniques and tools, Vinamilk continues to develop new product formulations.

The emergence of digital consumers is a phenomenon-changing dynamic in almost all industries. Establishing and maintaining customer relationships using online platforms is one initiative that needs to be taken to strengthen the company's presence in emerging communities.

On its part, Vinamilk has already tapped on the social media for its marketing. As of January 2018, Vinamilk's Facebook page has been liked by more than 581,000 people. The YouTube channel has nearly 504,000 subscribers. Since the brand is predominantly targeting the domestic market, its content on social media is still in the local language.

If Vinamilk is looking to build brand strength and character amidst the regional digital consumers, it needs to make more effort in providing universal content, probably in the global language, English. Moreover, Vinamilk introduced an E-Shop to sell its products online in 2016 (*VNExpress*, 2016). The company added another sales channel to its expansive network by launching the e-commerce website giacmosuaviet.com.vn, which is gaining popularity and is also offered as a mobile app, to sell a wide range of its products that can be paid for electronically.

The company utilizes digital technology advances to apply the horizontal principles of New Wave marketing. Product innovation, which has conventionally been Vinamilk's strength, can be further capitalized through co-creation. This encourages the involvement of consumers in the product development process. Digital platforms can greatly assist in the execution of co-creation because of the flexibility it provides to consumers in sharing inputs on ideas and improvements, any time and from anywhere.

Vinamilk's large customer base can also be leveraged as an alternative channel of distribution. Through communal activation, Vinamilk will be able to build greater loyalty among the existing consumers while stepping up the acquisition of new consumers. These are some of the possibilities that can be explored by Vinamilk to strengthen its position in the local market and to increase its penetration in the region.

The development of digital technology, which is sweeping the world and Asia, is going to fundamentally change the face of competition in the future. As Vinamilk continues to pave its way to expand and capture a larger share of both domestic and regional demand, it will face numerous challenges from increasing competition due to digitalization. However, if it continues to play its cards right, Vinamilk's technological adaptability and product diversity will help keep its business booming, despite the numerous roadblocks it has to overcome.

References

Davis, B (February 2016). Growing smartphone ownership in Vietnam opens door for mobile marketers. *Forbes*. https://www.forbes.com/sites/davisbrett/2016/02/18/growing-smartphone-ownership-in-vietnam-opens-door-for-mobile-marketers/#4e03a11f34ed [19 January 2018].

Fawzi, D and K Sproule (2012). *Vinamilk: Fruit Juice for Kids in Vietnam. Case Collection*. Singapore: Singapore Management University.

Forbes (August 2010). *Asia's 200 Best Under a Billion*. https://www.forbes.com/lists/2010/24/asia-under-billion-10_Vietnam-Dairy-Products-%28Vinamilk%29_TF84.html [18 January 2018].

Forbes (September 2010). *Udder Success*. https://www.forbes.com/global/2010/0913/best-under-billion-10-vinamilk-vietnam-dairy-udder-success.html#3f1b9e9e7543 [18 January 2018].

Dan Nhan (July 2017). Vinamilk tops Forbes list of 40 most Valuable Vietnamese brands. http://en.nhandan.com.vn/business/item/5318602-vinamilk-tops-forbes-list-of-40-most-valuable-vietnamese-brands.html [18 January 2018].

Nikkei Asian Review (February 2016). Vinamilk revenue up 14% in 2015 on strong overseas business. *Nikkei Asian Review*. http://asia.nikkei.com/Business/AC/Vinamilk-revenue-up-14-in-2015-on-strong-overseas-business [18 January 2018].

Vietnam Plus (December 2017). Vietnam's dairy giants export milk to China. *Vietnam Plus*. https://en.vietnamplus.vn/vietnams-dairy-giants-export-milk-to-china/123902.vnp [22 January 2018].

Vinamilk (2012). *2011 Annual Report*. https://www.vinamilk.com.vn/static/uploads/bc_thuong_nien/1412564524-5a8b33a7ce272c21f33291faf10e78aa4372fb85c3320e4f1f0c891da8b43ac3.pdf [18 January 2018].

Vinamilk (2015a). *Vinamilk Story*. https://www.vinamilk.com.vn/en/lich-su-phat-trien [18 January 2018].

Vinamilk (2015b). *2014 Annual Report.* https://www.vinamilk.com.vn/static/uploads/bc_thuong_nien/1426843683-7fd7119f0c2d2e9bd538f170cf960824f6fb16f7e94da5af5361b851a598634a-en.pdf [18 January 2018].

Vinamilk (2016). *2015 Annual Report.* https://www.vinamilk.com.vn/static/uploads/bc_thuong_nien/1463564750-564913525bcfdc84fcad83da839f2d6dc773b1020ce26bb54f12255adcc9a66e.pdf [18 January 2018].

Vinamilk (2017). *2016 Annual Report.* https://www.vinamilk.com.vn/static/uploads/bc_thuong_nien/1491555026-8200b97437fc4416662f04431290995f23e8b83ea13bb8fb4a9fc1498893d1c2.pdf [18 January 2018].

VnExpress (October 2016). Dairy giant Vinamilk launches online shopping site. *VnExpress.* https://e.vnexpress.net/news/business/dairy-giant-vinamilk-launches-online-shopping-site-3478893.html [22 January 2018.

Wikipedia (2017). *Vinamilk.* https://en.wikipedia.org/wiki/Vinamilk [18 January 2018].

CHAPTER 10

ASIA'S MULTINATIONAL COMPANIES: GLOBAL VALUE, REGIONAL STRATEGY, LOCAL TACTIC

Not many companies are truly global; most companies are usually strong only in some regions in the world. The regional scale that provides profitable opportunities makes regional markets attractive. However, even large companies with popular brands, abundant resources, decades of experience, and world-class management teams may still find it challenging to grow in markets and geographies far away from their homes.

However, some Asian companies decide to venture out of their comfort zones and spread their wings in the international market. As they succeed in building a strong business foundation locally and regionally, some businesses take big risks in launching their products and services to customers outside of Asia. It has not been smooth sailing for all. The dynamics of the global market with its ups and downs have forced some of these Asian companies to give up and return to their home turf. A few though have managed to survive and even grow into global players that are recognized worldwide.

This chapter discusses some Asian companies that have managed to maintain and develop their presence in the global market. Four companies have been selected from different Asian countries — Korea's Samsung Electronics, India's Infosys, China's Huawei, and Japan's Kao — to demonstrate an overview of the implementation of concepts discussed in this book. By analyzing the values they offer, the strategies and tactics used, we aim to learn how the "glorecalization mindset" has been realized, especially in winning the hearts and minds of global consumers who embrace a digital lifestyle.

Samsung Electronics

Samsung Electronics is a multinational consumer electronics company based in Suwon, South Korea. Today, the multibillion-dollar company Samsung, along with its subsidiaries, is known as a leading brand for consumer electronics and home appliances worldwide. Some of its products routinely capture the highest market share in the world, with Samsung mobile phones being the best-selling handphones in the world. All these achievements of the company cannot be separated from its neatly coordinated strategy at the regional level — especially at the level of Asia and ASEAN — and supported by localized tactics in each country.

Company Growth and Global Expansion

Samsung Electronics is a South Korean multinational electronics company headquartered in Suwon, South Korea. Samsung Electronics, a flagship company of the Samsung Group, accounts for nearly 15% of South Korea's economy. The company, which was established as a home appliance manufacturer back in 1969, has become a leader in the infotainment business — information, telecommunication, audio and video. It also deals in healthcare, environment and energy products. Samsung's success on a global scale — as the largest smartphone manufacturer in the world — has made it symbolic of South Korea's economic transformation, from one of the world's poorest countries after World War II to a prospering developed economy in Asia today (Ullah, 2017).

Samsung Electronics' three business divisions — Consumer Electronics (CE), IT & Mobile Communications (IM), and Device Solutions (DS) — serve as the main pillars for generating synergy and delivering products and services with unrivalled quality to its worldwide customers (see Figure 10.1 for information on Samsung Electronics' business divisions). The CE division is further segmented into Visual Display, Digital Appliances, and Health and Medical Equipment businesses. The IT & Mobile Communications division comprises Mobile Communications and Networks businesses, while the Device Solutions division consists of Memory, System LSI, and Foundry businesses.

Since the launch of its first mobile phone in 1988 in South Korea, the company has come a long way and created a stronghold in the smartphone market by acquiring a major market share (20.8%) globally (Samsung Electronics, 2017a). This success, however, did not come easy as, back in 1990, Motorola ruled the market while Samsung was just taking fledgeling steps (Michell, 2010). Until the mid-1990s, Samsung's mobile phone division also struggled with poor quality and inferior products.

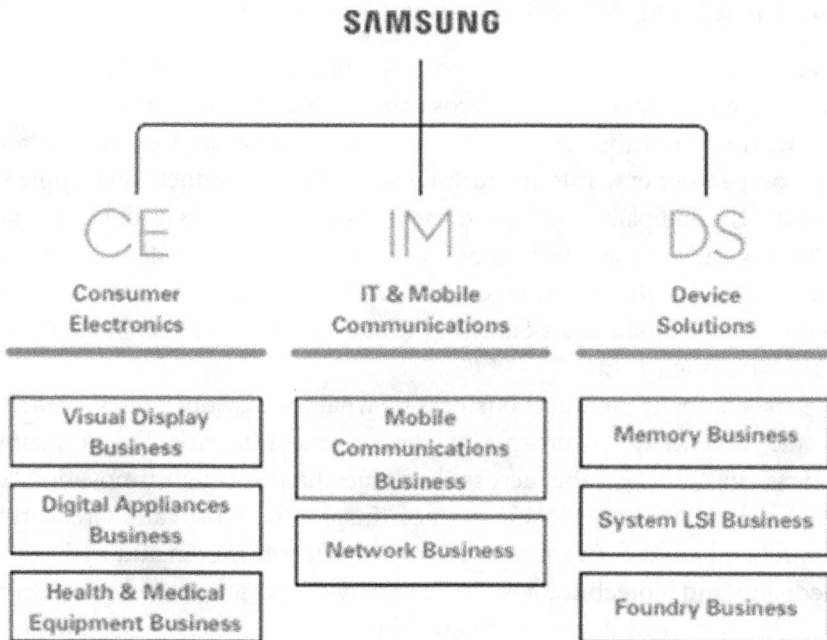

Figure 10.1: Samsung Electronics' Business Divisions
Source: Samsung Electronics (2017a).

Samsung shifted its focus to component manufacturing for a brief period between 1995 and 2007 but eventually zoomed in on consumer products again. The company brought a diverse range of mobile phones to the market, catering to a broad range of consumers. In 2007, it officially toppled Motorola to become the world's second-largest mobile phone manufacturer, and in 2012, it became the world's largest mobile phone manufacturer, overtaking Nokia (Ihlwan, 2007). In the first quarter of 2012, the company sold 93.5 million units compared with Nokia's 82.7 million units (Lunden, 2012). Since then, it has been almost a decade of intense rivalry between Samsung and Apple, with the Samsung Galaxy range being a direct rival to the Apple iPhone (IDC, 2018).

As of 2016, Samsung Electronics operates 220 worldwide hubs, including 15 regional head offices, 38 production bases, 53 sales bases, 34 research and development centers, 7 design centers, and 73 other offices. The company has operations in 79 countries and has 308,745 employees and 2,468 suppliers (Samsung Electronics, 2017a).

Consistent Global Value: Innovation and Collaboration

Even as Samsung maintains a worldwide presence with production and distribution facilities spread across the globe, the company strives to maintain a uniform, original character. Innovation and excellence are the company's keywords in pushing forward its product development agenda. The company wants to be known as an innovation leader in digital solutions and new-age technologies, including artificial intelligence, Big Data, 5G, and high-performance semiconductors. This is what pushes the innovation capabilities of Samsung to the forefront of the smartphone manufacturing world.

The company conducts business by what it calls core values, namely, people, excellence, co-prosperity, change, and integrity. The company believes in creating value across the value chain through innovation. It religiously follows the global vision of "Inspire the World and Create the Future" and looks forward to exploring new territories, including health, medicine, and biotechnology. The company is also committed to creating a brighter future by developing new values for its core networks: industry, partners, and employees. Through these innovations, Samsung aims to contribute to a better world and a richer experience for all.

There are three pillars that have shaped the history of Samsung Electronics' innovations (Samsung Electronics, 2015):

- **Product**. Samsung can be credited, to a great deal, with how their smartphones have transformed people's lives. The company was the first one to produce big screen mobile phones when they were not popular, a clear example of trend setting. Even in the television industry, the company broke the stereotype image of a TV set by bringing LED TVs to the market. Its premium refrigerator range re-modeled the workings of a refrigerator, offering consumers more convenience and facility. Recently, the company has launched innovative products, such as the FamilyHub smart refrigerator with voice support, AddWash washing machine, and Wind-Free air conditioner without direct airflow.

- **Process**. Samsung pays utmost attention to standardization and unified processes, which are integral to operating a multinational and global company. For instance, through a standardized operating system, the company efficiently manages the flow of parts and products and stays close to its partners across the value chain.

- **People**. "People" forms one of Samsung's core values: "a company is its people" (Samsung Electronics, 2017b). The company has a "People First" management philosophy, which is inculcated to encourage its employees to reach their potential. The company's Annual Expertise Development Process (EDP) helps employees identify their competencies and set up development plans. Samsung offers internal and external Samsung Talent Review (STaR sessions) to help employees take up training in leadership and expertise, as well as apply for a wide range of human resource development programs — MBAs, career training, and job skills training.

The second keyword that is fast becoming a major contributor to the company's success is collaboration. Samsung collaborates with several global key partners; one such strategic collaboration is with Google that offers its operating system (OS) Android for most Samsung smartphones. This was a smart move by Samsung, who had initially developed its own OS called Tizen in 2015. However, in order to deal with its main competitor Apple — which also has its own OS, with more than 1 million apps — Samsung continues to bank upon its collaboration with Google (Scolaro, 2015) to provide customers with several advanced sophisticated features and tens of thousands of applications to choose from.

Regional Strategy and Local Tactics: Product Leadership and Omni-Channels

Product Leadership in the Asian and ASEAN Market

Samsung has its eyes firmly set on the rapidly growing markets of Asia, and one crucial strategy in its endeavor to expand market share is to continuously develop new advanced products and be the first to market them. This not only caters to the market demand but also whets the appetite of the increasingly tech-savvy Asian netizens. One such example is the 85S9 television, which was launched as the first ultra-high definition TV in Asia in 2013. Being the first company to launch such a product not only gave Samsung a first-mover advantage but also helped the brand to maintain its image for releasing new, high-end products.

Furthermore, Samsung also believes in the localization of its products and services to suit specific local market needs. The company works actively in each market to develop local content and services. The "Made for Asia" term signifies Samsung's strong focus in catering to the local needs of its Asian consumers. For example, Samsung RT38 refrigerator comes with customized compartments for the integrated ice and water dispenser, as well as a basket for storing medicine and cosmetics.

Samsung is also highly focused on a specific region that shows great potential: Southeast Asia. While developing the highly customized AddWash washing machine, Samsung listened to the concerns of its Southeast Asian consumers who often felt the need to add laundry after starting a cycle. AddWash not only was a hit with consumers but also won the "Design of the Year Award" at the President's Design Award in Singapore and "Ergonomic Design Award" at the Asian Conference on Ergonomics and Design. Samsung's refrigerators are integrated with the Twin Cooling System that takes care of its Southeast Asian consumers' needs for storing food items with strong spices and pungent flavors, by controlling the cooling of the refrigerator and freezer separately.

Air conditioners are used all year round in Southeast Asian countries and, hence, Samsung came up with the wind-free air conditioner. This creates a cooler indoor atmosphere and also ensures energy efficiency without the discomfort of direct cold airflow (Samsung NewsRoom, November 2017b). It is evident that the company came up with the term "Made for Asia" products that focus on the unique needs of its Asian consumers. Designed with Asian customers in mind, these products take into consideration the different preferences and habits that consumers may have (Kotler, Kartajaya and Hooi, 2014).

Samsung is one of the most preferred home appliance brands in Southeast Asia, which shows just how much customers love the brand (Samsung Electronics, 2017b).

Samsung's Localized Channel Tactics

Apart from product innovation, Samsung also carefully selects its distribution channels, especially to target the lower end of the market. The company is resourceful in terms of creating campaigns and targeting customers with its low-range smartphones in order to save costs and counter its Chinese rivals. Samsung uses leading online commerce channels in India, Vietnam, and China to sell its handsets directly to consumers. If the company sells more of its smartphones via its online channels, then it can save a huge amount in costs, and consumers can get its products at more affordable prices (Yoo-chul, 2015).

Samsung also aims to use the online channels tactically, mainly to counter Xiaomi — the fast-emerging Chinese smartphone manufacturer of low-cost high-end smartphones. One interesting point about Xiaomi is that it mainly sells its handsets via its official websites. Samsung management believes that this strategy helped the Chinese smartphone producer improve its bottom line in such a short time.

That said, Samsung must pay closer attention to the selection of channels, which needs to be in line with the demands of the local market, as online channels will not always be the most appropriate, especially while targeting rural markets, such as those in Vietnam, where Samsung relies more on traditional distribution channels and promotions. In December 2017, the company's Vietnamese unit forged a strategic partnership with Vietnamobile and FPT Retail — a subsidiary of local information technology company FPT — to make its smartphone line-up more competitive with Chinese brands in the countryside. The partners plan to bring in combined offers to consumers and high-speed connections on Samsung mobile phones at affordable prices, specially tailored to the rural markets that are currently swarmed with Chinese smartphone brands, including Oppo, Xiaomi, and Huawei. The company views this as an opportunity to push sales by bringing its gadgets to the masses.

Samsung plans to launch tailored sales promotions aimed at rural markets. The idea is to boost the sales of entry-level smartphones priced between USD130 and USD220. In Vietnam, 95% of nearly 130 million cell phone subscribers use prepaid plans — contrary to countries like Singapore where most people use long-term smartphone plans with low upfront costs.

The use of offline channels remains effective for some markets — especially in rural areas — as Samsung is aiming to do, through FPT stores. However, in this New Wave era, technology utilization is still useful if they are in line with market conditions and customers. In order to manage the risks associated with the low payment track records of Vietnamese rural customers, Samsung's technology has helped FPT, its retail partner, employ solutions to deal with users who are unable to honor their contract terms.

References

Grobart, S (March 2013). How Samsung became the world's no. smartphone maker—and its plans to stay on top. *Bloomberg.* http://www.bloomberg.com/news/articles/2013-03-28/how-samsung-became-the-worlds-no-dot-1-smartphone-maker#p2 [8 March 82018].

IDC (February 2018). Apple Passes Samsung to Capture the Top Position in the Worldwide Smartphone Market While Overall Shipments Decline 6.3% in the Fourth Quarter, According to IDC, https://www.idc.com/getdoc.jsp?containerId=prUS43548018 [8 March 2018].

Ihlwan, M (December 2007). Motorola's pain is Samsung's gain. *Bloomberg* https://www.bloomberg.com/news/articles/2007-12-26/motorolas-pain-is-samsungs-gainbusinessweek-business-news-stock-market-and-financial-advice [8 March 2018].

Kotler, P, H Kartajaya and DH Hooi (2014). *Think New ASEAN*, Singapore: McGraw Hills.

Lunden, I (April 2012). Samsung may have just become the king of mobile handsets, while S&P downgrades Nokia to junk. *Techcrunch.* https://beta.techcrunch.com/2012/04/27/samsung-may-have-just-become-the-king-of-mobile-handsets-while-sp-downgrades-nokia-to-junk/ [8 March 2018].

Michell, T (2010). *Samsung Electronics: And the Struggle for Leadership of the Electronics Industry*. New York: John Wiley & Sons.

Nikkei Asian Review (December 2017). Samsung Woos rural Vietnamese with affordable smartphone plans. https://asia.nikkei.com/Business/AC/Samsung-woos-rural-Vietnamese-with-affordable-smartphone-plans?page=1 [8 March 2018].

Samsung Electronics (2015). Samsung electronics CEO BK Yoon shares innovation strategy. *Samsung Newsroom*. https://news.samsung.com/global/samsung-electronics-ceo-bk-yoon-shares-innovation-strategy [8 March 2018].

Samsung Electronics (2017a). *Samsung Electronics Sustainability Report 2017*. http://images.samsung.com/is/content/samsung/p5/global/ir/docs/Samsung_Electronics_Sustainability_Report_2017.pdf [8 March 2018].

Samsung Electronics (2017b). How meeting local needs has made Samsung a leader in the Southeast Asian home appliances market. *Samsung Newsroom*. https://news.samsung.com/global/how-meeting-local-needs-has-made-samsung-a-leader-in-the-se-asian-home-appliances-market [8 March 2018].

Scolaro, CM (January 2015). Samsung makes a big beton its own operating system. *CNBC*. https://www.cnbc.com/2015/01/14/samsung-makes-a-big-bet-on-its-own-operating-system.html [March 2018].

Ullah, Z (February 2017). How Samsung dominates South Korea's economy. http://money.cnn.com/2017/02/17/technology/samsung-south-korea-daily-life/index.html [8 March 2018].

Yoo-chul, K (March 2015). Samsung to focus on online marketing. *Korea Times*. http://www.koreatimes.co.kr/www/news/tech/2015/03/133_175675.html [8 March 2018].

Infosys Limited

Starting as a little-known humble company from India back in the 1980s, Infosys Limited today is a world leader in terms of Information Technology (IT) and Business Process Management (BPM) services. The company not only has put India on the global map as a software service destination, but it has also undergone global expansion, creating a brand of international appeal, and securing several Fortune 500 giants among its clients. This global appeal is well complemented by a strategic regional delivery approach, making Infosys Limited the second largest IT service firm in India and the first Indian IT company to be listed on NASDAQ. It is also the first Indian software company to attain the CMM Level 5 certification for its onshore and offshore operations.

The Indian IT Industry — An Introduction

The Indian information technology (IT) industry is a leading contributor to the country's GDP. According to NASSCOM — India's apex non profit information technology-business process management (IT-BPM) body — India's IT-BPM industry is estimated to be worth nearly USD154 billion in 2017 and its contribution to India's GDP grew from 1.2% in 1998 to 7.7% in 2016 (see Fig. 10.2).

The Indian IT industry mainly consists of four primary sectors: information technology (IT) services, business process management (BPM), software products, and engineering service and hardware (IBEF, 2018). The Indian IT market is mainly controlled by home-grown giants (NASSCOM). Among India's top five IT firms — Tata Consultancy Services (TCS), Infosys, Cognizant, Wipro, and HCL Technologies — only Cognizant is a foreign company from the United States, whereas the remaining are domestic players. TCS, having earned the first-mover advantage, is the largest IT firm in India.

IT services in India were primarily started with the establishment of the Tata Group in the 1960s, which has now been restructured into TCS. TCS is the top IT service firm in India and the second largest IT service

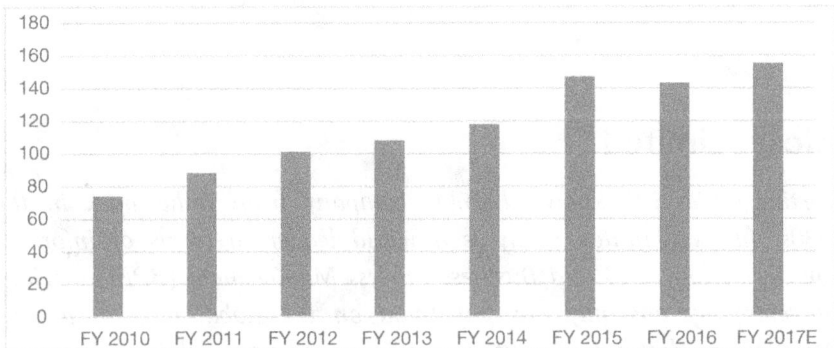

Figure 10.2:   Market size of Indian IT Industry (in USD billion).
Source: NASSCOM.

company in the world by market capitalisation and profit. The company generated consolidated revenues of USD16.5 billion in the year ended 31 March 2016 and is listed on the National Stock Exchange and Bombay Stock Exchange in India (Tata Group, 2018).

The Indian IT industry's stellar growth over the past two decades has stemmed from soaring demand from the global sourcing market — India is the world's top sourcing destination, with a 55% share of the global market (IBEF, 2018). The growth is also a result of cost-competitiveness as the services are deemed three to four times cheaper than in the United States. Recently, India's intellectual IT capital is also gaining prominence, as several global technology firms have set up their innovation centers in India.

Considering its significant importance in pushing India's economic growth, the country is keenly focused on further developing its IT industry, to help realize its goals of increasing GDP growth, creating employment and digitalizing the economy. In recent years, the IT industry in India has fast progressed to encompass services in the digital space, with TCS — India's biggest IT industry employer — claiming to earn one-third of its overall revenues from digital technologies, such as artificial intelligence, cloud, Big Data, IoT, and cybersecurity (LiveMint Report, 2017). The growth is also driven by a fast-growing Internet penetration in the country. India is projected to have 730 million Internet users by 2020 from around 420 million, according to the June 2017 estimates by the Internet and Mobile Association of India (IAMAI, 2017) and the market research firm IMRB.

Infosys: The Beginning

In the 1960s, the Indian IT industry grew on the back of software exports due to limited demand in the underdeveloped domestic market. The movement gained further impetus with the availability of technically qualified professionals in the country. Following the liberalization of the Indian economy in 1991, investments in the IT industry jumped significantly. This was also due to cutting bureaucratic red tapes, which made it easier to open new IT-related businesses. Many of these businesses were, in fact, opened and assisted by technically qualified Indians based out of Silicon Valley in the United States, who were early movers in gauging the untapped opportunity back home.

India's second largest IT company — Infosys Limited — is also an example of such a company that began its fledgling journey in India with the help of its six co-founders who worked on assignments in the United States for the company, while the main founder N. R. Narayana Murthy held the fort back in India.

Infosys was born out of a vision to create a world-class professional IT service organization. It was founded in 1981 with a capital of USD250 by N. R. Narayana Murthy and six engineers: K. Dinesh, Nandan Nilekani, S. D. Shibulal, S. Gopalakrishnan, N. S. Raghavan, and Ashok Arora in Pune, India. Narayana Murthy worked with a computer company at that time and eventually convinced six of his friends to set up their own company.

In an interview with Indian news channel NDTV in 2005, Nandan Nilekani, one of the founders reminisced about how, for Infosys, India was never the target market in the beginning. Infosys was always envisioned to be a global organization, utilizing its base in India and the country's vast talent pool. This was largely because, in the early 1980s, India was simply not primed to be a target market; it was still a closed economy where businesses faced friction, in Murthy's own words, and telephones and computers were considered luxuries. Recounting Infosys' early days, Murthy remembered how it took 2 years for the company to import one computer and a similarly long waiting period to get a telephone line. In those days, most Infosys co-founders worked on assignments from the United States, the earnings from which were put back in running Infosys in the early years. Narayana Murthy, meanwhile, was the one-man army back in India, handling the affairs single handedly and spearheading Infosys into its golden period, which began with the liberalization of the Indian economy in the 1990s. Some of the milestones of Infosys are listed in Table 10.1.

Creating a Global Appeal

The vision to create a professional organization of world-class standards has been a guiding principle behind Infosys' global outreach and success.

Table 10.1:   Infosys' major milestones.

Year	Events
2015	A USD250-million fund named "Innovate in India Fund" was announced to support Indian startups.
2012	Infosys was listed on the NYSE Market and was ranked by Forbes among the world's most innovative companies.
2010	Infosys earned revenues of more than USD5 billion.
2009	Employee strength surpassed 100,000.
2006	It celebrated 25 years since its founding, and annual revenues doubled to USD2 billion. N. R. Narayana Murthy retired.
2004	Its annual revenues touched USD1 billion.
2003	It set up ventures in China and Australia.
2002	It touched revenues of USD500 million and launched a business process outsourcing service Progeon.
2000	It established Banks 2000, the universal banking solution, when Finacle™ was launched.
1999	It earned revenues of USD100 million and got listed on NASDAQ; expanded its international presence with offices in Germany, Sweden, Belgium, and Australia and development centers in the United States.
1998	It began offering packaged application solutions for enterprises.
1997	It was assessed at CMM Level 4.
1996	The Infosys Foundation was set up.
1995	The first European office was opened in the United Kingdom and e-Business practice was initiated.
1993	It went public and acquired the ISO 9001 certification.
1987	Its first international office was opened in Boston.
1983	It relocated its corporate headquarters to Bangalore.
1981	Infosys, set up by N. R. Narayana Murthy with a capital of USD250, bagged its first client, Data Basics Corporation, in New York.

Source: Infosys Limited (2018).

It would not be incorrect to say that, together with TCS, Infosys and a handful of other home-grown IT firms have helped put India on the map as a global destination for software services. The company's global expansion was fueled early on as it opened its first international office within 7 years of its operation. The rapid expansion across major world markets through organic growth, as well as inorganic growth through several acquisitions, has helped Infosys become a recognized global brand. The company maintains what is called the Infosys Innovation Fund, which helps it acquire the latest technologies through worldwide investments in startups.

Infosys divides its services into three divisions: consulting, business, and technology. The consulting arm offers seven core types of services in 14 industries, as listed in Figure 10.3. Various software development, maintenance, and re-engineering services form part of the business and technology services (Infosys Limited, 2018). Despite an array of services, Infosys offers what is called the GDM (Global Delivery Model), which allows the company to combine intellectual capital from various divisions to offer its clients an "intelligent work breakdown" (Asia's Star Brands, 2006). This GDM allows Infosys to deliver low-cost high-quality solutions with the help of teams based in different geographical locations. These teams work seamlessly at the "lowest work breakdown level" and within

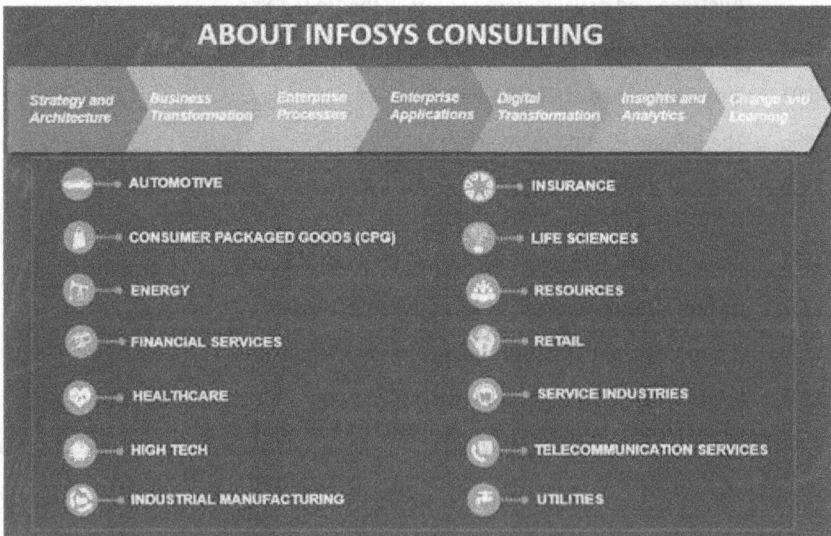

ABOUT INFOSYS CONSULTING

Strategy and Architecture | Business Transformation | Enterprise Processes | Enterprise Applications | Digital Transformation | Insights and Analytics | Change and Learning

- AUTOMOTIVE
- CONSUMER PACKAGED GOODS (CPG)
- ENERGY
- FINANCIAL SERVICES
- HEALTHCARE
- HIGH TECH
- INDUSTRIAL MANUFACTURING
- INSURANCE
- LIFE SCIENCES
- RESOURCES
- RETAIL
- SERVICE INDUSTRIES
- TELECOMMUNICATION SERVICES
- UTILITIES

Figure 10.3: Infosys Services (2018).
Source: Infosys Limited (2018).

multiple time zones, with the help of worldwide offshore development teams (Cases on Strategic Information Systems, 2006).

Notwithstanding its global appeal, Infosys' sales teams maintain a regional focus based on particular territories. Infosys' delivery teams are divided into strategic business units (SBUs), which usually consist of a geographical area or domain specialization.

The company's move to get listed on NASDAQ, an American stock exchange, has been a milestone in its efforts to nurture its global appeal. In the late 1990s, Infosys leaders realized that, in order to go global, it was important to become a globally listed company since several of its clients were Global2000 companies (Leadership @Infosys, 2010). In anticipating its customers' preference on working with a company with international standards of public governance, the listing on NASDAQ gave Infosys an international standing. The effect multiplied with its own sales offices set up in the United States to bring it closer to its global customers. Recalling the move, founder Narayana Murthy said, "it was a small step for NASDAQ, but a giant leap for Infosys and the Indian software industry".

A global alliance with Microsoft further sealed Infosys's position as a world-class player. In 2000, Microsoft and Infosys came together for a USD8 million IT Transformation Initiative, which included 1,200 professionals trained on Microsoft's latest technologies and deployed globally to more effectively serve its clientele.

In time, Infosys has succeeded in creating a global brand, building a global workforce, and a company that is motivated by a similar set of values.

C-Life Values at Infosys

The company's transformation from one that provided technologies to one that provides sophisticated business solutions is noteworthy (Leadership @Infosys, 2010). The company's ability to stay nimble and meet the quickly changing demands of the IT marketplace has helped it to stay relevant. In making this happen, the company's leadership has led by example, by being living role-models to propagate a culture of learning, development, and integrity.

These values gave birth to a mnemonic that was to be remembered by all at Infosys: the C-Life Values.

Table 10.2: The C-Life Values

Customer Delight	A commitment to surpass customer expectations
Leadership by Example	A commitment to set standards and be an example for industry and people
Integrity and Transparency	A commitment to be ethical, sincere, and open in dealings
Fairness	To be objective and transaction-oriented, thus earning trust and respect
Pursuit of Excellence	Strive continuously to improve to become the best

Source: Barney (2010).

As India's as well as the world's leading IT service company, Infosys has played a significant role in stimulating the development of India's IT industry. It was part of a vision that the founders shared early on, to create a large number of jobs with high disposable incomes. The vision, as it slowly materialized into reality, not only aided the development of the industry but also made IT a much-coveted profession among Indian graduates and thereby, expanding the talent pool.

Infosys, on its part, realized early on, the advantage of honing leadership within its organization. As most of the company's founders approached retirement age, Infosys helped develop a strong leadership pipeline and prepare a cadre of leaders who could eventually take up senior-most positions at the company. A giant step in this direction was the setting up of the Infosys Leadership Institute. This institute in Mysore, South India, has turned out to be the world's largest corporate university — spreading across 37 acres and housing 400 instructors. It has a capacity to train over 14,000 employees at any given time (Infosys Limited, 2018).

Focus on Digital Technologies

In the past half a decade, Infosys has acted fast in anticipating the developments unfolding in the information technology space. Over the years, the company has acquired several companies engaged in digital technologies, from artificial intelligence to SaaS, Big Data, Cloud solutions, 3D assets, and so on (Infosys Limited, 2018).

Infosys has set up Infosys Digital, a specialized team offering real-time solutions in design, digital transformation, cloud solutions, omnichannel commerce, data and analytics, and so on.

IT firms all over the world are in a race to display their advanced and sophisticated capabilities to win clients in the digital age. Instead of just focusing on creating and selling technology products, these companies are now focusing more on consulting and designing. That has also changed the way clients are handled. For example, the clients of IT companies today have direct access to the companies' research and development hubs, giving a sneak-peek into the solutions first-hand. For example, in the case of Infosys, customer visits now encompass a tour of the company's design thinking labs, where clients get up close and personal, with the benefits Infosys can deliver, using a user-centric approach of design thinking. A constellation of digital technologies that these IT companies can amass usually helps this approach of showcasing their capabilities to the clients. That's how companies such as Infosys are co-innovating along with their clients to help solve real-world business problems in the digital era.

References

Barney, M (2010). *Leadership @Infosys*. Published by Penguin Group. ISBN 9780670084951.

Indian Brand Equity Foundation (June 2018). *IT & ITeS*. https://www.ibef.org/download/IT-ITeS-Report-June-2018.pdf [3 November 2018]

Infosys Limited (2018). *Platforms*. https://www.infosys.com/products-and-platforms/ [10 March 2018]

Infosys Limited (2017). *Infosys Digital*. http://www.infosys.digital/be-more/digital-studio [10 March 2018]

Internet and Mobile Association of India (28 April 2017). Mobile Internet in India 2016 Report. http://www.iamai.in/research/reports_details/4860

Miller, RR (2001). Leapfrogging? India's Information Technology Industry and the Internet. http://documents.worldbank.org/curated/en/59684146 8750845416/Leapfrogging-Indias-information-technology-industry-and-the-Internet

Temporal, P (January 2006). *Asia's Star Brands*. Wiley. ISBN: 978-0-470-82156-5.

Huawei Technologies Co., Ltd

Starting as a local distributor of telephone switches, Chinese company Huawei has cemented its position as a global ICT player today. Since its inception in 1987 — within just three decades — some of its products and services are ranked in the top 3 in their categories worldwide. Huawei's success can be attributed to its ability to maintain the consistency of its global value proposition, co-ordinated regional strategy, and customized local initiatives.

Huawei: A Brief Company History

Huawei was set up in Shenzhen in 1987 as a sales agent for a producer of private branch exchange (PBX) switches. The company, which launched its wirelesses GSM-based solutions in 1997, has emerged as a global information and communications technology (ICT) solutions provider, offering end-to-end telecom and enterprise network solutions, devices, and cloud technology-based services. The ICT solutions, products, and services of the company are now used in more than 170 countries and regions, serving over one-third of the world's population. As of 2016, it employs about 180,000 people, including more than 40,000 non-Chinese (75% of employees outside China are local hires) (Huawei Technologies, 2017; De Cremer & Tao, 2015).

Huawei's vision is to "bring digital to every person, home and organization for a fully connected, intelligent world". Within two decades of its establishment, the company was regarded as the world's third-largest manufacturer of mobile telecommunications gear (Reuters, 2009). Some of its products and services — such as mobile broadband service and radio access equipment — are even ranked No. 1 and 2 in the world (Huawei Technologies, 2018). Huawei's projects, partners, data centers, and research and development (R&D) facilities are now spread worldwide. The company's global appeal is evident from the fact that it is the only Chinese company that receives more revenue from markets outside China (67%) than that from within (De Cremer & Tao, 2015). Huawei has established its name as a multinational company that harnesses the power of innovation in connecting the world. This has helped the company gain recognition from various reputed industry observers, including the

Boston Consulting Group. It was ranked 50th in the Boston Consulting Group's Top 50 "Most Innovative Companies 2014" report. Huawei was also named one of the Top 100 Global Innovators by Thomson Reuters in 2014. With this, it became the first and the only mainland Chinese company to make the list (Huawei Technologies, 2018b). Table 10.3 summarizes Huawei's journey from a local player to a multinational company.

Table 10.3: Huawei's Milestones

Year	Selected Events
1987	Was set up in Shenzhen as a sales agent for a Hong Kong-based producer of private branch exchange (PBX) switches
1992	Initiated R&D and launched rural digital switching solution
1997	Launched wireless GSM-based solutions
1999	Established a R&D center in Bangalore, India
2000	• Established a R&D center in Stockholm, Sweden • Generated USD100 million from international markets
2001	• Established four R&D centers in the United States • Joined International Telecommunications Union (ITU)
2004	Established a joint venture with Siemens to develop TD-SCDMA solutions
2005	• International contract orders exceeded domestic sales for the first time • Selected as a preferred telecom equipment supplier and signed a Global Framework Agreement with Vodafone • Selected as a preferred 21st Century Network (21CN) supplier by British Telecom (BT)
2006	Established a Shanghai-based joint R&D center with Motorola to develop UMTS technologies
2007	• Established a joint venture with Symantec to develop storage and security appliances • Became a partner for all the top operators in Europe • Won a 2007 Global Supplier Award by Vodafone
2008	• Recognized by BusinessWeek as one of the world's most influential companies • Ranked No. 3 by Informa in terms of worldwide market share in mobile network equipment • Chosen No. 1 by ABI in mobile broadband devices

(Continued)

Table 10.3: *(Continued)*

Year	Selected Events
2009	• Ranked No. 2 in the global market share of radio access equipment • Launched the world's first end-to-end 100G solutions from routers to transmission systems
2010	• Established a Cyber Security Evaluation Centre in the United Kingdom • Received the "2010 Corporate Use of Innovation Award" by The Economist
2011	• Built 20 cloud computing data centers • Launched the HUAWEI SmartCare service solution
2012	• Stepped up investments in Europe • Partnered with customers in 33 countries in cloud computing, which is used by approximately 70,000 employees for work every day • Launched middle-range and high-end flagship smartphones, such as the Ascend P1, Ascend D1 Quad, and Honor
2013	• Remained the leader in commercial LTE deployment worldwide • Global brand awareness of Huawei mobile phones saw an annual increase of 110%
2014	• Established 5G technology R&D centers in nine countries • Built more than 480 data centers
2015	• Expanded the coverage of its LTE networks to more than 140 capital cities • Launched the world's first SDN-based agile IoT solution • Ranked No. 3 in the global smartphone market and No. 1 in terms of market share in China, according to GFK
2016	• Supported the operations of over 1,500 networks in more than 170 countries and regions, serving over one-third of the world's population • Deployed over 60 4.5G networks worldwide • Huawei Smart City solutions have been in use in more than 100 cities in over 40 countries • Huawei's global smartphone market share rose to 11.9%, cementing its rank as one of the top three players globally

Source: Huawei Technologies (2018).

Global Value Proposition: Building a Better-connected World

The ICT industry is undergoing a rapid transformation and advancement with a slew of digital technologies, such as big data and cloud computing. Hence, there is a convergence happening between information technology (IT) and communications technology (CT). This shapes the way for ICT advances and consumers to utilize their devices to connect with each other and other devices. In response to these revolutionary changes, Huawei continued to innovate around customer needs and focusing on the development of leading technologies that meet those needs.

Huawei's commitment to innovate by sticking to the principle of customer centricity is demonstrated in its efforts to develop R&D centers in various countries. In 2017, Huawei launched a Global OpenLab program that entails the creation of 15 new cloud-based OpenLabs, which would allow Huawei to work with vendors based anywhere in the world and undertake joint innovation. Under this program, Huawei has so far certified over 70 vendors, supporting carriers' network evolution and operations transformation. For example, the company's virtual reality (VR) OpenLab aims to facilitate industry cooperation and technological innovation in the cloud VR industry and help build a cloud VR industry ecosystem.

Going forward, the company has plans to allocate nearly 1,000 talents around the world and invest a total of USD200 million in the program (Huawei Technologies, 2017b).

With a diverse set of teams in different countries, Huawei ensures that all of them are united by one common value: a spirit to build a better-connected world. Every Huawei employee uses this global value proposition as a guideline while developing new products and services. This value is then translated into the adoption of three main pillars: ubiquitous broadband, agile innovation, and inspired experience (Huawei Technologies, 2017):

- **Ubiquitous Broadband**
  The widespread penetration of ICT makes it easy for consumers to share and gather information, whenever and wherever. They could go online with a few clicks and stay connected to anyone from anywhere and consume high-quality content through sophisticated applications on their hand-held devices. They could even work remotely using their mobile phones. This increasing demand for connectivity and increasing information consumption, however, calls for a greater reliability of the network, tighter security, and stronger bandwidth, where there is still a long way to go. In response, Huawei provided carriers with solutions that best reflect their needs at different stages of development to bring the benefits of greater connectivity to more and more people.

Put simply, the company is working to connect more people, more homes, and more organizations.

- **Agile Innovation**
  Enterprises in all industries — as Huawei's clients — need to rapidly identify business opportunities and leverage the collaborative potential of IT to launch new products and services faster and more effectively. The IT sector is fast evolving into a full-fledged operation system, from a support system, and thus acts as the main lever of competitive advantage. Huawei is working towards the creation of more innovative one-stop ICT infrastructure and to proactively help clients leverage new opportunities and attain more agility in pursuing business innovations. It does so by enabling greater synergy among devices, networks, and the cloud.

- **Inspired Experience**
  Smart, intelligent devices will become more and more ubiquitous in the future, and Huawei aims to be at the forefront of this movement. The company wants to meet every need and expectation of consumers with regard to what these smart devices will do for them in their everyday lives. The company is focused on product innovation, mobile services, and channel transformation to improve customer experience and deliver an intelligent, immersive experience across all user platforms, including smart homes, health and fitness devices, tablets, and PCs. In delivering this experience, the company is especially focused on video, which it believes is the most crucial means of sharing data and the key to growing and monetizing telecom networks. The company is working to help its clients connect their video systems to networks and provide analytical solutions supported by the cloud. It thus helps them in transforming their business processes, data sharing and leveraging new business channels (Huawei Annual Report, 2017). Huawei also strives to take user experience to the next level by providing consumers around the world with a convenient online-to-offline (O_2O) purchase experience and services.

Coordinated Regional Strategy and Customized Local Tactics

At a regional level, Huawei aims to focus on the potential that exists in each of the regions, and it has a well-coordinated strategy. For example, in 2017, Huawei announced its enterprise service strategy that is designed to support companies undergoing cloud transformation in Asia-Pacific. The enterprise cloud strategy focuses on four key areas — cloud innovation, creating a digital platform, supporting smart operations, and enabling businesses. The aim is to offer service solutions to its clients and to provide them with end-to-end cloud transformation that allows them to create, utilize, and manage their cloud platforms efficiently and effectively (Telecom Asia, 2017).

Europe, Middle East, and Africa (EMEA) contribute the largest share to Huawei's total revenue from outside China (Huawei Annual Report, 2017). Europe clearly has a strategic importance for the Chinese player due to the fast digital transformation of enterprises there and growing smartphone penetration. Moving forward, the company is pursuing a joint innovation strategy in Europe, partnering with leading companies and governments. For instance, the company is working with Groupe PSA, the second largest automaker in Europe, on connected cars — the partners will build a Connected Vehicle Modular Platform (CVMP) based on Huawei's OceanConnect IoT platform. Several retailers in Europe also use Huawei's smart connectivity and data analytics solutions.

Its success in the western markets also comes, in part, from how well it intersperses Chinese cultural principles — constant improvement, sharing benefits and burdens, working from periphery to center — with the customer-centric principles of the West. This has consequently made Huawei one of the fastest growing ICT multinationals in the region. The company won the Best IoT Platform award at IoT World Europe 2017 (Hensman, 2017).

Meanwhile, more localized tactics are executed in each country, considering the unique character and circumstances of clients in each country, which requires different approaches. As an example, Huawei Taiwan decided to focus its resources only on the larger-sized P10 Plus Android Smartphone in 2017, while variants with smaller screens were not launched in the market. The tactic was inspired by the fact that the 5.5-in. P9 Plus — the previous generation of the series — accounted for over 70% of smartphone shipments in 2016, indicating the market preference for larger screen sizes (Li, 2017).

Moreover, in early 2018, in India, Huawei — in line with the country's commitment toward the "Make in India" initiative — announced the manufacturing of its mid-priced segment device Honor 7X at a facility in Tamil Nadu (The Economic Times, February 2018). The company is yet to achieve a big success in the Indian market despite striding ahead in several global markets, where it is rapidly closing the gap with Samsung and Apple. The company has its eyes firmly set on the Indian market, which is the world's largest smartphone market today. The company has launched the Honor brand to target the low and mid-price segments in India, while the newly launched Huawei P20 range will target the mid and premium range customers (MoneyControl, April 2018). It is now gearing up for a renewed push in India, the world's second-largest smartphone market (The Economic Times, January 2018). Huawei's initiative in India — focusing on the mid-price segment — is different from that in Taiwan where the focus is on the higher segment.

Through tactics and initiatives tailored to local market conditions, Huawei is well positioned to respond to customer needs quickly and correctly. Innovation is also set to be in accordance with the philosophy of customer centricity, which serves as a global value to the company. This is Huawei's formula to cement its position as an innovative multinational company.

References

De Cremer, D and T Tao (September 2015). Huawei: a case study when profit sharing works. *Harvard Business Review*. https://hbr.org/2015/09/huawei-a-case-study-of-when-profit-sharing-works [9 March 2018].

Hensman, M (August 2017). Conquering Europe through a joint innovation strategy: how Huawei blends cultural revolution and customer-centric principles. *European Financial Review*. http://www.europeanfinancialreview.com/?p=17425 [9 March 2018].

Huawei Technologies (2017a). *2016 Annual Report*. http://www-file.huawei.com/-/media/CORPORATE/PDF/annual-report/AnnualReport2016_en.pdf?la=en [9 March 2018].

Huawei Technologies (2017b). *Huawei Launches Global OpenLab Program to Create an Open Ecosystem*. http://www.huawei.com/en/press-events/news/2017/3/Huawei-Launches-Global-OpenLab-Program [9 March 2018].

Huawei Technologies (2018a). *Milestones*. http://www.huawei.com/en/about-huawei/corporate-information/milestone [9 March 2018].

Huawei Technologies (2018b). *Who We Are*. https://consumer.huawei.com/en/about-us/ [9 March 2018].

Li, L (April 2017). Huawei launches P10 plus smartphone in Taiwan. *Taipei Times*. http://www.taipeitimes.com/News/biz/archives/2017/04/12/2003668526 [9 March 2018].

Reuters (July 2009). Timeline: the meteoric rise of China's Huawei. https://www.reuters.com/article/huawei-china/timeline-the-meteoric-rise-of- chinas-huawei-idUSPEK24147220090701 [9 March 2018].

Telecom Asia, (2017). Huawei unveils APAC enterprise cloud strategy. *Telecom Asia* https://www.telecomasia.net/content/huawei-unveils-apac-enterprise-cloud-strategy [9 March 2018].

The Economic Times (January 2018a). Huawei to take India first approach to become world's third largest smartphone. https://economictimes.indiatimes.com/tech/hardware/huawei-to-take-india-first-approach-to-become-worlds-third-largest-smartphone-brand/articleshow/62548365.cms [10 March 2018].

The Economic Times (February 2018b). Huawei begins manufacturing Honor 7X in India. https://telecom.economictimes.indiatimes.com/news/huawei-begins-manufacturing-honor-7x-in-india/62734143 [10 March 2018].

Kao Corporation

Kao Corporation is one of the Japanese business entities that has succeeded in transforming itself into a multinational company. The company, which was founded in 1887 and incorporated in 1940, is known as a major Japanese player of consumer products in areas such as beauty, health, and hygiene. This case aims to throw some light on Kao's success in achieving market expansion through a consistent global value, supported by a regional strategy and localized tactics.

Kao: Company at a Glance

Kao Corporation is a leading cosmetics and chemical company headquartered in Tokyo, Japan. The company was founded by Tomiro Nagase on 19 June 1887. The company's corporate name "Kao" originated from the name of its first product, *Kao Sekken* quality facial soap. The company eventually expanded its portfolio to include other products, such as shampoos, detergents, and sanitary napkins, as well as skincare products. The company, whose mission is to strive for the satisfaction and enrichment of the lives of people, is said to have created products that "changed the way Japanese lived". For instance, the company introduced Kao Shampoo back in the 1920s, making shampooing easier than before when women used to wash their hair using washing soda and white clay. The company eventually expanded its offerings by including skincare, female hygiene, and household cleaning products.

Kao segregates its business divisions into three fields: Beauty Care, Human Health Care, and Fabric and Home Care. The Beauty Care segment includes cosmetics and skincare and haircare products. The Human Health Care segment consists of food, beverage, sanitary, and personal health products. The Fabric and Home Care segment is responsible for detergents, cleaning, and homecare products (Forbes, 2018). Moreover, Kao has a chemical product business, which focuses on the manufacturing of environmentally friendly chemical products while also improving functionality and utilization in several industries. The Chemicals segment consists of oleo chemicals, performance chemicals, and specialty chemicals. Figure 10.4 demonstrates the sales contribution of every segment in 2017.

Global Expansion with Consistent Global Value

Starting as a simple soap manufacturer, Kao today is a multinational corporation that offers a wide range of products used by people from all walks of life. Currently, Kao products are used by customers in about 100 countries and regions (Kao Corporation, 2018b).

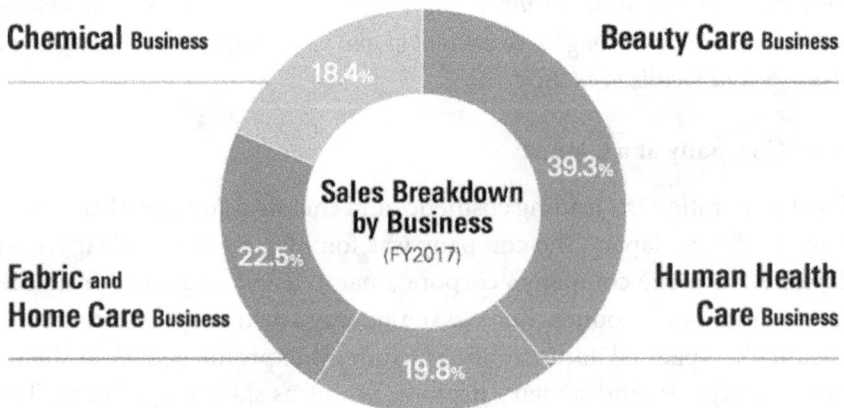

Figure 10.4: Kao Group's Business Segments
Source: Kao Corporation (2018a).

The company's expansion into foreign soil began with the export of Feather Shampoo to Thailand, back in 1957. Its involvement in overseas markets was restricted to Southeast Asia until it established Kao Corporation of America in North America in 1986 (Sim & Othman, 1995). Table 10.4 details how Kao expanded its wings by establishing new companies and entering into joint ventures and acquisitions.

Table 10.4: Kao's Milestones and Market Expansion

Year	Events
1887	Mr Tomiro Nagase, Kao Founder, established a dealership "Nagase Shoten", which dealt with Western goods and eventually transformed into Kao.
1923	The Azuma Factory in Tokyo (currently Sumida Complex) started operations in a bid to expand the company's soap production.
1934	The company set up the Housework Science Laboratory as a research facility to introduce scientific research to household products. The facility was later renamed Nagase Housework Science Laboratory in 1937 and eventually came to be known as Kao Housework Science Laboratory in 1954.
1957	Kao first exported Feather Shampoo to Thailand.
1964	• Kao Industrial (Thailand) Co., Ltd., was established as Kao's first company outside Japan. • Taiwan-Kao Company, Ltd., was established. The company was renamed Kao (Taiwan) Corporation in 1991.
1965	Malaysia Kao Company (Private), Ltd., was established in Singapore. The company was renamed Kao (Singapore) Private Ltd. in 1973.
1970	• Kao (Hong Kong), Ltd., was established. • Sinor-Kao S.A. (Spain) was established.
1971	• Nivea-Kao Co., Ltd., was established as a joint venture with Beiersdorf AG (West Germany). • Kao Life Science Laboratory was founded to carry on and expand the functions of Kao Housework Science Laboratory.
1973	Kao (Malaysia) Sdn. Bhd. was established.
1974	Kao-Quaker Co., Ltd., was established as a joint venture with Quaker Oats Company (UA) to manufacture and sell furan resin for use with casting sand. (The new company became a wholly owned Kao subsidiary in 1997.)
1975	• Quimi-Kao, S.A. de C.V. (Mexico) was established. • Kitt Siam (Thailand) Co., Ltd., was established. (The company was renamed Kao Commercial (Thailand) Co., Ltd., in 1991.)

(Continued)

Table 10.4: (Continued)

Year	Events
1977	• Pilipinas Kao, Incorporated (Philippines), was established. • P.T. Pole Kao Indonesia Chemicals was established. (The company was renamed PT. Kao Indonesia Chemicals in 1996.)
1985	Kao Soap Co., Ltd., was renamed Kao Corporation to reflect the increasingly broad scope of its businesses.
1987	• Kao acquired High Point Chemical Corporation (UA). The company was reorganized as Kao Chemicals Americas Corporation, High Point Textile Auxiliaries LLC, and Kao Specialties Americas LLC in 1999. • Sinor-Kao S.A. and Molins-Kao S.A. merged to form Kao Corporation S.A. (Spain).
1988	Kao acquired the Andrew Jergens Company (UA). (The company was renamed Kao Brands Company in 2004.)
1992–1999	• Kao (Australia) Marketing Pty., Ltd., was established. • Kao Corporation Shanghai was established. • Kao adopted the Kao Management Principles as its corporate philosophy. • Kao Vietnam Co., Ltd., was established.
2000	• Kao Consumer Products (Southeast Asia) Co., Ltd., was established in Thailand.
2004	The Kao Management Principles were revised and adopted as the Kao Way, a statement of the Kao Group's corporate philosophy.
2005–2009	• Kao acquired Molton Brown Ltd. (UA). • The Kao Group acquired Kanebo Cosmetics Inc. • Kao announced the Kao Environmental Statement and unveiled a new corporate identity.
2013	Corporate acquisition to strengthen Scandinavian beauty care, renamed as Kao Sweden AB.
2014	Construction of the second consumer products plant at Kao Indonesia was completed.
2015	Construction of a new plant was completed at Kao (Shanghai) Chemical Industries Co., Ltd.
2016	Kao acquired Collins Inkjet Corporation (UA) and renamed it Kao Collins Inc.

Source: Kao Corporation (2018c); Sim & Othman (1995).

Expanding its business into various diverse regions for a company the size of Kao had been a task fraught with challenges. As a company that is over 130 years old and currently employing around 33,560 people worldwide and managing over two dozen brands, it is imperative for Kao to be able to maintain a single identity. This unified identity is indispensable for the company to be able to instill in its employees — coming from various backgrounds and regions — the same unique spirit and purpose. Otherwise, the various companies and businesses spread across Asia, Europe, and America would not be able to converge and connect as "one big family".

To this end, Kao's management has developed internal guidelines, known as the "Kao Way", to ensure the creation of a consistent global value in all regions. This "Kao Way" is an embodiment of the company's corporate philosophy that serves as the founding principles of all the business activities undertaken by the Kao Group. The "Kao Way" is what lends consistency to the activities of the Kao Group, including all tasks, be it the formulation of mid- or long-term business plans or any important management decision that has to be taken by the Board of Management on a daily basis.

This Kao Way, which is centered on the satisfaction and enrichment of people lives, is therefore a guiding principle for everyone working at Kao. This helps bring the employees together and facilitate a sense of common ownership among employees, resulting in a drive to achieve growth for the company as well as for each individual working at Kao. This makes their job more rewarding and instills a sense of purpose in them.

Kao Group companies and members share the "Kao Way" not merely as a manual or set of rules but as a foundation from which they can determine both the value of their work and the concerns that they face (Kao Corporation, 2018d).

One of the key principles listed in the "Kao Way" is "Yoki-Monozukuri". In Japanese, "Yoki" means "good or excellent", while "Monozukuri" means "development or manufacturing of products". Kao defines "Yoki-Monozukuri" as "a strong commitment by all members of the company to provide products and brands of excellent value for consumer satisfaction".

This spirit of "Yoki-Monozukuri" is realized by harnessing a collective synergy among various teams working at Kao, to focus on innovation and develop products and brands to provide the utmost customer satisfaction. The profits realized from the Yoki-Monozukuri-enabled process is then funneled back into the development of more products and brands of excellent value. This continuous cycle of excellence, supported by innovation, earns the respect and trust of all stakeholders, including consumers, employees, business partners, local communities, and shareholders and thereby enables profitable growth.

Through religiously imbibing the corporate philosophy of the "Kao Way" into its very core, the company is able to create a more consistent brand globally, even though some of its products and brands are not developed internally, but obtained through acquisitions. The new companies and brands work together with Kao to slowly inculcate the same Kao way of living and earn the same identity under the umbrella "Kao Way". Such a consistency of this measure and magnitude is rare among multinationals and, thus, serves as one of the keys to success for a company that has managed to create a foothold in various countries across the world.

Regional Strategy and Local Tactics

For a multinational corporation like Kao, a consistent global value should also be supported with a coordinated regional strategy and customized local tactics. The values that have been formulated globally should be translated into actions that are attuned to be more local. Due to the uniqueness of customers' characters and inferences in every region and country, the company needs a variety of approaches for its products to click with the diverse sets of consumers.

In view of this, Kao has vigorously pursued research and development activities in Asia, the United States, and Europe. In consumer products, Kao meticulously studies the evolving tastes and preferences of consumers in various regions. They may, for example, belong to various ethnicities and with requirements dissimilar to each other. This intimate understanding of consumers' evolving lifestyles and needs, is combined with product development know-how and research findings, to create products that are in sync with market demand in all the diverse regions that Kao serves.

In Asia, Kao's coordinated strategy especially targets Greater China and ASEAN. With the increasing flow of people, goods and information between Japan and the Chinese-speaking world (China, Hong Kong, and Taiwan), as well as the heightened trust in and the need for Japanese products, Kao is following a aggressive strategy by promoting development in the massive Greater China market (Kao Corporation, 2017). Moreover, the company is eyeing growth in ASEAN by adding more products to its line-up, which are especially catered to the middle-class consumers, in markets such as Indonesia and Vietnam (Kao Corporation, 2018e).

That said, the company is also cognizant of the underlying need of every market to be targeted with more customized tactics. To that end, the company translates a general regional strategy into more specific local initiatives. This is achieved by developing products that suit the specific needs of the local market. An example of such a product is Kao's laundry detergent Attack Jaz1, which was launched in Indonesia, its prime market in Asia besides China. Kao's R&D team discovered that hard water, which is aplenty in Indonesia, makes the removal of stains difficult. Therefore, Attack Jaz1 incorporates a technology that breaks up stains. Attack Jaz1 simplifies the laundry process through superior cleaning power, even in hard water. It thus has earned strong approval from the local consumers.

In this New Wave era, an omnichannel approach — which combines online as well as offline — is also an effective tactical choice for Kao. To expand market participation in new countries, Kao makes use of local distributors and e-commerce and promotes collaborative efforts with its existing global and Japanese retailers (Kao Corporation, 2017).

In particular, Kao focuses on expanding online sales in China, because the ratio of online sales to overall sales at Kao is higher than the market average. Due to younger Chinese, who are buying more and more online, e-commerce companies are in a frenzy to build large-scale distribution networks to cater to the growing demand. Although exact figures are hard to come by, most estimates state that about 10%–15% of consumer goods in China are now bought online. That's why Kao plans to deepen its ties with major domestic e-commerce companies — including the Alibaba Group Holding — to sell its products and increase its e-commerce share. Kao is also already partnering with five to six e-commerce companies. Different companies have different strengths in different areas, such as sanitary products or cosmetics. Kao chooses different platforms for different product categories. With such initiatives, Kao is working to strengthen its position in every local market it exists, by continuing to appeal to customers with constant innovation and an unwavering focus on customer satisfaction.

References

Forbes (2018). *Kao Corp.* https://www.forbes.com/companies/kao-corp/ [8 March 2018].

Kao Corporation (2017). *Kao Integrated Report.* http://www.kao.com/content/dam/sites/kao/www-kao-com/global/en/investor-relations/pdf/reports_fy2017e_all.pdf [8 March 2018].

Kao Corporation (2018a). *Business Fields.* http://www.kao.com/global/en/who-we-are/business-fields/ [8 March 2018].

Kao Corporation (2018b). *Kao by the Numbers.* http://www.kao.com/global/en/who-we-are/data/ [8 March 2018].

Kao Corporation (2018c). *Corporate History.* http://www.kao.com/global/en/about/outline/history/company-history/ [8 March 2018].

Kao Corporation (2018d). *The Kao Way.* http://www.kao.com/global/en/about/policies/kaoway/ [8 March 2018].

Kao Corporation (2018e). *Global Network: Contributing to People and Diverse Industries around the World.* http://www.kao.com/global/en/research-development/basic-concepts/network/ [8 March 2018].

Nikkei Asian Review (July 2017). Kao focuses on expanding online sales in China. https://asia.nikkei.com/Business/Companies/Kao-focuses-on-expanding-online-sales-in-China [8 March 2018].

Sim, OF and MD Othman (1995). Innovation: the way to competitiveness. *Journal Ekonomi Malaysia, 29*, 37–77.

INDEX

XL, 250, 255
   3R strategy, 255
   subscribers, 251, 252
XL Tunai, 255
Xmart Village, 255

Y

Young Global Leaders (YGLs), 134
YouTube, 271, 272

Z

Zafar Iqbal, Muhammed, 227–229, 231
Zalora, 121

www.ingramcontent.com/pod-product-compliance
Lightning Source LLC
Chambersburg PA
CBHW061235220326
41599CB00028B/5428